Travelers, Immigrants, Inmates

TRAVELERS, IMMIGRANTS, INMATES

Essays in Estrangement

FRANCES BARTKOWSKI

UNIVERSITY OF MINNESOTA PRESS

Minneapolis / London

Published by the University of Minnesota Press
111 Third Avenue South, Suite 290, Minneapolis, MN 55401-2520
Printed in the United States of America on acid-free paper

Bartkowski, Frances, 1948-
    Travelers, immigrants, inmates : essays in estrangement / Frances
Bartkowski
        p.   cm.
    Includes bibliographical references (p.   ) and index.
    ISBN 0-8166-2361-9 (acid-free paper) — ISBN 0-8166-2362-7
(pbk. : acid-free paper
    1. Alienation (social psychology) in literature.   I. Title.
PN56.A45B37   1995
809'.93353—dc20   94-32674

The University of Minnesota is an equal-opportunity educator and employer.

for my father and to my son

Another offering to the soul of civilization
whose other name is travel.
Zora Neale Hurston

The history of shame is also a history of civilizations.
Silvan S. Tomkins

They did not know that you could take a train to Hell . . .
Charlotte Delbo

Contents

~

Acknowledgments

This book germinated for a decade. So there are many friends, coworkers, and institutions to thank. The intertwining of people, places, and knowledge may start with meetings between strangers, but more engaging is what occurs where recognition begins.

In the fall of 1984 I was scheduled to teach a course on travel writing, Voyages of Repetition and Discovery, for the Center for the Humanities at Wesleyan University. I thank my students there and colleagues like Richard Ohmann, Richard Stammelman, Richard Vann, and Khachig Tololyan. The support of the Andrew W. Mellon Post-Doctoral Fellowships in the Humanities made possible the gift of such a productive working time and place. Neil Lazarus and Miriam Silverberg, friends from that time and place, have been generous and critical readers of parts of this book.

By 1986 I was teaching at Carnegie Mellon University; Discourses of Displacement, a course on immigrant autobiographies, led me to realize the generic and rhetorical connections between two sites of my teaching and research, by way of dislocation. The Dean's Office generously encouraged further research through a Faculty Development Grant. I owe much thanks to the group of undergraduate and graduate students who attended my classes there and helped bring these issues into ever sharper focus.

In the winter of 1991 I had my first research leave from Rutgers University-Newark, and it is then that this book took its current shape. A Rutgers

Graduate School Research Grant and a Faculty Research Grant helped to bring this work to its conclusion. Numerous friends and colleagues there have supported this work. I am especially appreciative to Jean Anyon, Barbara Foley, and Gary Roth who read parts of this manuscript at crucial stages.

Biodun Iginla was essential in seeing this manuscript into a book from 1992 on. I thank him and colleagues of his at the University of Minnesota Press, as well as Sidonie Smith and the two other readers who asked for more.

I cannot measure the thanks I owe to those who sometimes read, but more importantly, listened, and, when asked, would administer the required nudge back over the threshold to work: Jessica Benjamin, Renae Bredin, Susan Ghirardelli, Deb Gilbert, Charna Meyers, Lee Quinby, Leslie Ross, Phyllis Ziman-Tobin.

Judy Butler and Jim Creech are due very special thanks for their expertise at friendship that led them to read every word there was to be read at different stages and to respond with extravagant doses of enthusiasm and critique.

I trust that Jules will one day know how much I owe to his endless capacity for wonder.

~

Who Speaks?

Consider this an exercise in translation—reconstituting in another medium that which is elsewhere. That is, a working with and through what is already absent, long gone. If origins and the search for them haunt the epistemological efforts of earlier centuries, we in our late-twentieth-century wisdom, with our indefatigable interrogation of identities in embodied times and spaces, are busy mapping their irremediable loss, their dispersion in place and history.

In my work here a question that drives me circles out of and away from Europe, scattering my knowledge and concerns, but also shaping them in some of the following ways. A euro-centrifugal tale, read by a once girlchild who first learned to speak the language—German—of those who had just been the enemy while living in a camp for displaced persons, awaiting refuge and refugee status, elsewhere. That elsewhere called America. A postcard sent by my parents to friends already safely harbored on the western side of the Atlantic in New Jersey, where I was to grow up, recounts that I, at two, had already learned to say, "I love you," "Thank you very much," and "I go home." Mind you, this was learned from a mother to whom this English was also a foreign tongue. "We dream only of going to New York," she would also say, about the anxiety accompanying their awaiting a transport bound for the U.S. The lived realities of cultural dislocation characterize the everyday lives of so many people in so many places, and color the problems that I want to address in this book; I tell this fragment of my story in order that my readers may glimpse some of the idiosyncratic inflections in how this project came to assume its current shape.

Travel as/is . . .

Insofar as we retain the capacity for attachment—the energy of desire
that draws us toward the world and makes us want to live
within it—we're always returning.
Eva Hoffman, *Lost in Translation*

"But he has got nothing on," said a little child. . . .
The Emperor writhed, for he knew it was true.
Hans Christian Andersen

Opening a book is like opening a door. We don't know what awaits us across
the threshold, unless we've been there before. What I'll do in this book is
read some stories of encounters at crossroads: people in places and the
knowledge they acquire as they interact there. They do not know each other.
They are strangers, and at least one of them is not at home. The telling of
these tales is captured best for my purposes in the Andersen classic, "The
Emperor's New Clothes," and the scenario involving the reigning adult and
the finger-pointing child; imagine the figure of this child showing and
telling the way through some narratives of mistaken identities. What we will
see on parade through all these stories are versions of dislocation and displacement that construct relations to the new and unknown, even when already thoroughly imaginatively colonized. I want to array for my readers

some repeated questions that arise when we try as we might to know—some one, some place, some scene.

Identities are always mistaken. The mistakenness of identities must be taken very seriously; I mean by this assertion to bring into some relational dynamic both the psychoanalytic, specifically Lacanian, resonances of this statement, while simultaneously asking my reader to think also of how mistaken identities are at the center of our global politics at this very moment. To choose just one euro-centered example, the man set aflame by neo-Nazi youths who "believed" he was a Jew, this in 1992. That year, which has just ended as I write this, may go down as one that forced a recognition of the clash between the ever more refined quests for virtual reality in our postmodern scene and their coevalness in time and space with the resurgence of hatreds we wished to believe had been outgrown with the internationalizing of an enlightenment (sometimes seasoned with socialist) ideology.[1]

Once we see the fiction of the emperor's clothes, what makes him still an emperor? There, in the speech of the child who proclaims the fraud of the emperor and, in doing so, takes up the space of potential wisdom opened by this tale—that is where I locate this project. In other words, identities may be the garb of necessity clothing and cloaking dissimulation. Our station is so radically marked by our costuming of the self. And those selves are fashioned not only by their draperies, but by their verbal emanations as well, our speech; by their manifestation in flesh that we insist upon covering to avoid exposure by a child pointing its finger; by our gestures that already draw and cross boundaries simultaneously. Consider, for example, that when hands are shaken it ensures that other body parts do not touch.[2]

What is it about identities that makes the claim or disclaimer of them such a contested site in contemporary life? Across the political spectrum, left to right; across the globe, along borderlines of language and territory; across disciplinary lines established institutionally—the academies, the churches, the schools—identities are being staked out, defined, and simultaneously rejected even by those they are meant to include. The debates about in- and exclusion are among the most charged sites of contestation.[3]

There is a tension I want to maintain here that is like the moment when we briefly behold in the effect of the figure-ground representation both the profile *and* the vase. At that moment we can, for fractions of a second, name both elements of the representation, realizing that our eyes will soon insist on simplifying and choosing one element in this ambiguous visual field. If identity is a prism, and identities are prismatic effects, then I want to attempt to maintain the ambiguities our eyes no less than our cultures want to unify. No sooner is the naming done than someone finds the name does not suit her/his circumstances and situation. For naming tends to reduce complexity. Collective histories need to be accounted for even as many within those collectivities refuse the general in favor of their own specificities. Can we follow the shift to the mixed blood of cultures while also taking into account those who have been mixed? Isn't the critique of identity politics meant to warn us against forms of purism as well as against endless proliferation of pluralisms? My contention is that we have much to learn from the collision of identities, as fragmentarily framed as they may be, in order to understand why we must construct them even if only to discover their misrecognized morphologies. My opening premise that identities are mistaken is both necessary and contingent. It arises out of a late-twentieth-century epistemology underwritten by homelessness and belatedness.[4]

Among the desires motivating my search here is a wish to move between ways of knowing and modes of inquiry that all too often operate as if in deliberate ignorance of each other: the psychoanalytic and the political. The histories and methods of both these discourses have much to tell us about relations to authority, a term with its counterpart in identity, as much as invocations of the other call the self into question. I am reading here for how a position(ality) is constructed in order to found an identity, even if only a fleeting one, as all identities must be. Psychoanalytic scenarios, like the mirror stage, are also political ones; in seeing ourselves in the face of the other we mistake both ourself and our presumed reflection. But this is not merely an unfortunate mishap in terms of our late-twentieth-century troping of subjectivity; it is a historical base for forms of presumptive hierarchy, political structures of domination, which have shaped identities larger than individual ones and which are always already cultural, national, gendered, racial, sexual, classed, geographical, regional, religious, generational—the problem of the exhausted etcetera, as Judith Butler has called it.

My aim is to read the merge of psychoanalysis and politics in the question of domination and its instantiation in dislocated subjectivities. And the site of their merging can be read only in textuality, and in narratives, whether poetic, journalistic, or theoretical. I will be taking a route that encompasses three genres of writing in order to keep in play several theoretical questions. The three forms of narrative might be categorized most easily as (1) travel writing, conventionally conceived, and only more recently theorized;[5] (2) U.S. immigrant or ethnic autobiographies as they are coming to be theorized;[6] and (3) concentration camp memoirs, or postmodern captivity narratives, as I will suggest we might come to comprehend them. The theoretical questions include the following: (1) How can we begin to think the necessity and mistakenness of identities through the ways that they surface in situations of dislocation and displacement? (2) What comes into view about the structuring of relations of identity and authority if we assume that a scene of dislocation restages a profoundly psychoanalytic and political moment? (3) What can we learn about the workings of power—the meeting ground of ideology and unconscious, and the site of subjectivity at work? At stake is a wish to study the particular dialectic of people in places and the dispersive effects of power in such scenes.

Let us assume that certain unconscious structures obtain in meetings between strangers, while ideological filters give specific form to what comes into speech and language. Some of those structures are not only about processes of differentiation but also about the relations between and among speakers, the necessity to master pronouns, for example, or what counts as such in languages that don't include them. Beyond the familial site of traditional psychoanalytic thinking, we need to read the transferentially displaced structures that shape our relations to those we invest with authority, or the selves we take to be so invested—the emperor, falsely named and no longer protected once his garments have been rent. For such structures seem to operate in the foreground of moments of cultural dislocation. Who knows? Who will tell? Whom to ask? Who speaks? And when? What is the order of things, we might say, when it comes to encounters between and among strangers? When, as in the Andersen tale, it is a child who is empowered to pose such provocative questions, some crucial features of the distribution of authority become significantly destabilized.

The familial, then, and its outlying networks of kinship form the frame through which we are first constructed and located, even if the structures that constitute this site are not specifically those of bloodties/lines; for the child coming into life and language in an institutional setting, for example, those relations and structures in force will become the "familial" or a first introduction to the social. In this space what we find are movable identifications and dis- and misidentifications as they are grafted onto specific intersubjective moments. Not only a psychoanalytic site, this is also a political site by virtue of the distribution of power relations in such spaces. Subjectivity is thus constructed with all its constitutive ties to authority.

Another of my guiding presumptions in reading narratives of dislocation is that the journey narrated and taken is a representation of earlier journeys into language and subjectivity, as we come to understand through the magical theatrics of the unconscious as we have known it and as we continue to invent it. Some of the dramaturges of the unconscious who matter most in developing this project are the Freud of "The Uncanny," with his over-whelming interrogation of the question of home; the Lacan of "The Mirror Stage" and the Law of the Father, followed by his feminist readers; the Melanie Klein who puts a maternal spin on the female body-in-parts; the Winnicott who puts the mother into play in a fuller way than had been done; the Fanon who increases the complexity of the cast of characters when once and for all he brings the question of race onto the psychoanalytic stage.

Why travel?

The journey, a strong motif in all storytelling, is already a rewriting of the journey into culture that all of us must make when we begin to speak. That first journey, like the later ones, places us in a position of dependence and vulnerability even as it opens the way to forms of mastery. As we come to terms with the demands of language and the capacities it confers, we simul-taneously come to terms with relations of authority and identity. Think of such a model operating in the instance of the traveler who must find the way, and its resonance with the instance of the child who also must make its way. Countless journeys and their narrations begin with a harking back to a moment that recalls the helplessness of infancy; when learning a language even in the confines of a classroom and certainly in the context of a new cul-ture we rely on the truism that we must become like a child again in order to achieve any success in the venture. However, as children, we encounter but do not consider the forms of power at stake in such becoming; as travelers we are apt to think precisely in these terms, for we are not at home, and our helplessness is very often cast in a mode of needing nevertheless to reassert our right to be, to have, to make ourselves understood, and to have our way. Consider the case that this becoming-a-child-again holds the potential for jubilation as much as it does for humiliation at any given moment; this vac-illation tells readers much about the relation of writers to their own sense of authority and identity. I will be tracking this ambivalence between wonder and shame.

The demands placed upon the subject in situations of unfamiliarity and dislocation produce a scene in which the struggle for identity comes more clearly into view as both necessary and also mistaken. Among the problems with pronouns, for example, is the knowledge that what lets us say I, you, she, he, they, and we is that we know that in the saying we are fixing, if only for a moment, that which is constantly shifting. The subject, no matter how decentered, cannot *not* be a subject or it lapses into aphasia. We must speak, and once we do so we enact an enabling fiction of identity that makes social life possible. Even as we do so we soon learn how disabling, because mistaken, that offer to an other may become.[7] It is the trust and hope in understanding and recognition that makes the moment of misunderstanding a site of violence: psychic, political, emotional.

Each of the parts of this book is meant to contribute to an exploration of relations to an elsewhere. The first two parts of the book deal with conventionally defined narratives of travel and their ethnographic textual kin, the writings of voyagers thrilled to be leaving home for some farther shores. Here, then, the elsewhere is framed by a model of seduction.[8] Motivation to travel emerges from specific relations to privilege, choice, and time. The third part of the book turns to immigrant genres, where the elsewhere encountered will be both the imagined and the experienced site of America. The fourth part of the book is located in a European nowhere that has nevertheless been mapped in detail by records of all sorts; these are the memoirs of the camps and the concentrationary universe they produced.

Where travel suggests an affirmative sense of groundlessness, a delight in the necessary fictions of language and pleasures of motion, displacement suggests an other/underside of the dialectic—that moment when the headiness of motion turns into fear, into disavowal, and into the abyss in the ground. This dialectic—the traveler's sublime, as it were—will be at play in all three parts of the book, but the movement along the continuum from wonder to shame, from delight to fear, will shift measurably as we move from narratives of leisure to narratives of confinement and captivity.

The issue of the construction of identity requires us to think broadly and narrowly at one and the same time: global questions and microscopic efforts toward responses; theoretical problems with partial textual solutions. A Euro-American confrontation will be just one of the more familiar axes of the crossroads where the crucial questions converge; other axes will be Afro-European, Euro-Caribbean, Euro-African.

Another of the territories of this groundlessness will be the "new world" and its site, the already misnamed America, although the mapping of this territory may also read as a trope of colonial and postcolonial writing more generally. For privileged Europeans who come in search of some essence with which to infuse their sense of dissipated and dissipating culture, America is a potential or empty space; for those less fortunate who come seeking fortune, America is a site of abundance that must be negotiated through a struggle to reweave separate strands of cultures all too easily lost in translation—hence, the merging of two types of writing (travel and immigrant autobiography) in order to study the forms that cultural dislocation will take in this geography both of promise (Baudrillard's America as "utopia achieved") and betrayal.

The discourses we now might collectively name as orientalizing, thanks to the work of Edward Said, constructed the continents as entities to be encircled, then penetrated—America, Africa, Asia. I want to rewrite some of Said's insights for the questions that arise here, because the politics of the search to name and a search for names must be more atomized, more localized, in terms of specific signatures and the "needs" on the part of those writing to name.

We must also learn to read through those entanglements of subject, self, and text that emerge when we, users of languages, encounter the other's tongue. The most operative metaphors that guide the twentieth-century focus on subjectivity are found in the discourses of signs and mirrors, as we can see most clearly perhaps in the literature on spectatorship that emerged in feminist film theory in the 1980s as it trained its gaze on the knowledge and power relations of seeing. These metaphors ask to be placed in relation to the rhetorical gesture of naming and its ever more corporate imaginary. Whose voice will this be? One that sounds in situations of cultural dislocation, both chosen and constrained or compelled. That is to say, blurred genres will serve as templates for unraveling the opening knot about the mistakenness of identity.

Who travels?

From the anonymous chronicler of Marco Polo's *Travels* to the characters of Don DeLillo's *The Names*, the traveler typically wears the suit of the international business*man* of his day, whether offering cowries or credit cards for trade.[9] Thus I will be looking at symbolic exchange and interaction in texts that tell of encounters at the crossroads of selves and others. Concurrent with the stories of the navigators are the stories of their cargo—those convicts, refugees, slaves, emigrants, pilgrims whose narratives emerge by implication long before more intrepid scholarly explorers unearth them.

In the face of the new, whether the landscape or its inhabitants, a name is offered, found, or given. In this simple act of domination and exploitation we can read the motions and markings of the specification of difference and its concomitant, identity. The gestures we choose to read may be reported speech, importation of goods, or translation in its widest sense. The epistemological and disciplinary frameworks of a politics and a psychoanalytics of authority, domination, selfhood ask that we consider the speaker, whether traveler or migrant, to be an amalgamated subject. S/he will be mixed, an alloy, a combination of elements already whole and integral unto themselves. S/he will be trying to decipher the phenomenological ups and downs of being or feeling both more and less oneself.

My work here is to assemble some stories of how we seem driven to tell stories about those we cannot understand and by whom we are not understood. And yet, through those stories, we come to discern something of who we may be, if only in the mirror of the other's gaze. The poststructuralist, postmodern climate in which I write keeps me mistrustful of questions of identity. Yet my own unremitting concerns with subjectivity keep returning me to qualities that emerge in writing that speaks of the pleasure and pain of the recovery and loss of the sense of self. What guide my tasks here are the ways and means of provisionally losing and finding selves. In such searches, as they become textualized, there is a complex movement toward definition of a subject in time and place. The times and places are "foreign" in some fashion yet to be explored; the selves will also become foreign or have been made so by the scene of the encounter at some crossroads of cultures. The questions of place and relations to place are of crucial importance. Place evokes position, for we come to understand ourselves in place/space through particular vantage points, none of them privileged.

Seeing as a Child

> "But he has got nothing on," said a little child. . . . The Emperor writhed,
> for he knew it was true. But he thought, "The procession must
> go on now." So he held himself stiffer than ever, and the
> chamberlains held up the invisible train.
> Hans Christian Andersen

Indeed, if identity is always a posture, a challenge to the mirror of distortion, then I want to gather moments of such posturing and ask how their valence shifts depending on the position of the one who defies the mirror—that "little child" in the Andersen tale, for example. What are the multiple attitudes from which a speaker or writer assumes any posture in order to bring into language an encounter with difference that seems to require that something be said in order momentarily to grasp a self? The models for working out questions of identity construction can only be read in linguistic or rhetorical practices. We must say "I," whether in words or some other semiotic system, in order to enter into dialogue with others, and in so doing we necessarily falsify both our fragmented place in the universe of discourse and the place of our interlocutors. The paradox of moving through an experience of cultural dislocation is that we must do violence to ourselves and others to maintain a shred of corporeal standing so that something verging on exchange may occur. The tenuousness of this exchange will operate in all the textual analyses offered here. But it will be matched by the tenacity of the desire to exchange while everywhere encountering inadequacy and failure, but also momentary, evanescent passages of mutuality.

This will also be, by necessity, a study in the rhetoric of cultural difference and how it is marked in language. What becomes immediately evident are the ways in which language itself forces us to assert differences. This study is aligned with current critiques of culture and critiques of postcolonial conditions by the complications and networks that tie together difference and hierarchy: the self that says "I" is purchased at the cost of obliterating or minimally distorting another. This matters for our current situation because an "I" is not all that is at stake; that I is located in a history and culture that also prize themselves at the cost of another history. Writers involved in this dilemma negotiate this exchange with varying and multiple stakes in putting domination and exploitation into question. The pronouns that "we" cannot seem to forgo will get us into trouble, as even this sentence demonstrates.[10]

In Motion

What are the ceremonies for such departures—departures that are neither entirely chosen nor entirely forced, and that are chosen and forced at the same time?
Eva Hoffman, "Paradise"

Travel is movement, movement through territorialized spaces, movement by those who choose to move and those who are moved by forces not under their control. Travel then could suggest crossing cultural boundaries, trespassing, visiting, capture. It could open up the possibility of removing the term from its class-bound associations with exploitation and pleasure-seeking, and remind us that those exploited are often forced into movement as an integral part of their exploitation. Travel and displacement, in fact, stage encounters with class and caste divisions, as well as with other significant and signifying barriers. The three terms of my title—travelers, immigrants, and inmates—are meant to suggest different and descending relations to privilege, and the dialectic of in- and exclusion. Think of these privileges as including also those of skin, gender, sexuality, religion, nation, to name some of the paradigms that currently define our understanding of the hierarchies and hegemonic structures of everyday life. The most salient division will occur in language, native languages as we say, and the matter of whether the writer shares a language with the culture into which s/he moves.

What is seen then gets written—another kind of visible language, or language made visible. While linguistic policies may be hegemonic in situations of cultural transformation, linguistic practices remain rooted in the uses made of language by its speakers. It is always both acquired and imposed—the two-way street of mastery as pleasure and domination. Languages, rhetorical structures—those of protest or welcome, for example—are the site where the psyche and the polis come to need *and* misrecognize each other, for these are the forms that resistance will take, whether the language of the book or the language of the crowd. Language will emerge in its hegemonic aspects from numerous perspectives; cultural costs will become evident in the loss and gain of languages, the mastery of new tongues, the adaptation to forms of domination most easy to read in what has, in a variety of fields, come under the question of the voice in feminist and in poststructural and postcolonial debates.

The geopolitical aspects of voice are mapped in the debates themselves, which are subject to topographical metaphors: centers and margins, crossing boundaries, borderlands. The multidisciplinary cross-cultural calls that have come to proliferate in the academic context, as well as in ongoing struggles over borders and boundaries, demand an agenda that any of us who try to write by way of response to such calls necessarily experience as overwhelming. Our efforts seem lilliputian. The task I am setting myself here is to struggle with these demands, broad as they are, by narrowing my horizon to those microtextual moments that I hope will create a mosaic of discoveries where we can see mirrored certain structural repetitions in the construction of identities. These identities remain with us, however mistaken we may presume them to be, however ironically we wear them at any given moment.

Shaking Hands

Showing our faces, telling our names—these are everyday occurrences we may not and often cannot stop to consider. But when we do, it is my con-

tention that we must see in these minute exchanges the rudiments of our relation to subjectivity, our positions in that realm, positions we are given or
assigned by others. We know so well that naming is power and that power
both confers and limits identity, shape, and place. To come into language is
to enter into community, family, and kinship relations that make for us a
web, a network. It is to encounter authority and learn our own relation to it,
to own it, too, if only for ourselves. It is a self-authorship that, historically,
has been withheld from or granted to some by others. This is the case if we
think of agency in its relationship to (self) possession, property, or citizen-
ship. All speech acts occur between and among differing networks, idiolects;
all encounters with the self take place in the face of some form(s) of alterity.
Placing the issue of language in relief by reading texts that tell of dislocation
in time and place allows us to highlight differences and confrontation; every
day such cultural confrontations go on in shared language communities, as
well, although these are not the materials of my work here. I hope to be able
to keep the positions of speakers and writers movable so that my task becomes both more complex and ambiguous (a risky business always), so as to
retain the emphasis on the mistakenness of identities, and more politically
grounded (let the sense of urgency and danger be clear), with an emphasis
on the identities themselves.

All of the texts chosen are ones in which the "graphing" of a self knows itself to be shot through with differences even in the moments of specifying.
Rather than predetermining the questions to be asked, I want these texts to
allow appropriate questions to emerge. This strategy will lead to an unfolding of the pertinent theoretical questions and the interconnections between
and among these problematic areas of debate. The project demands that we
as readers be on the watch for what Denise Riley calls a "skat[ing] across several identities."[11] While Riley's focus is on the troublesome category of
women in feminism, mine will be trained on a process at work in texts in
which a self comes to cohere momentarily—an anatomy of identity and its
vicissitudes, if you will.

There is a kind of privilege I am granting the geographical. My interests
in cultural dislocation are framed primarily through place marked cartog-
raphically, which is also already marked geopolitically. How are we made
through maps? Maps represent boundaries we know we are crossing at some
times, while at other times there may or may not be border guards to remind
us. We will see the differences as lived out by some who have been compelled
to redraw the borders. I want to push further with the transgressive urge as a
hunt for alternative modes of signification. A new place is always an oppor-

tunity for sanctioned cross-thinking, inter-speaking (we could say, borrowing from Irigaray), cross-"dressing"—out of which something may emerge
that transforms, transvalues, translates.

This book works at the crossroads of contemporary thought in cultural
studies and ethnicity, race and gender, nationalisms, and the politics and poetics of identity. The construction of identity depends on a relation to
agency and the empowerment conferred by a sense of agency. Many histories have been written in which agency comes at the expense of the often un-
recognized or sometimes even self-justified domination over others. In this
book I am setting up an array of speakers and writers with differing and developing relations to agency and empowerment. Among the reasons for
looking at these three kinds of narratives is that they open a horizon for seeing subjectivity at work along a continuum from wonder to shame.

The relation between wonder and shame that I will explicate reinflects
questions of agency and authority. This relation is what I will refer to as the
traveler's sublime, an existential, phenomenological category. As we move
from the text of travel to the text of immigration and on to the text of
confinement, we will become able to discern the shifting valences of wonder
and shame. And as we read a model of dislocation that turns from seduction
to survival, we will find that our travelers are as surprised to discover shame
in the midst of seduction as they are to find wonder still alive in the middle
of nowhere. Now wonder and shame are rudimentary, if not to say primitive, in their invocation of the subject in question. They are affects in which
the subject is suddenly reduced, rendered small in the face of the new or unknown. However, whereas wonder carries with it a positive charge to this
sense of diminishment—jubilation—shame carries a charge that is negative
—humiliation. And, of course, the traveler who sets forth boldly is searching
out the former, while the traveler who never meant to go elsewhere is more
subject to the latter affect. This continuum determines both my choice of
texts and the moments in those texts where I will stop to read more closely.
For I think that it is in negotiating this destabilizing register of the new and
the elsewhere that we can sift out some of the ways we process knowledge of
ourselves and others, ourselves in others, and others in ourselves.

The question of position is inevitably tied to the question of place in
communities. Texts of travel, immigration, and confinement are intended to
make most bold the contrast in possible positions of subjects and writers
who look, hear, speak, touch, taste, and smell their way by, through, and into
an already existing community to be deciphered. The consolidation of identity, even if mistaken, exhibits a logic of displacement in which we can read

the work of empowerment at its most innocent and at its most presumptuous.

To resume then: identities, while mistaken, are as necessary as air to sustain life in and among communities. If the questions of identity are posed too simply we find ourselves awash in false or presumptuous sameness; if posed too differentially we may find no one with whom to make common cause. If posed only psychoanalytically we risk losing social and historical context; if only politically, we risk forgetting the micro-cauldrons from which we each emerge to do our work in the world. However, not to ask the question of identity is to miss the political and the psychoanalytic altogether. And to do that is to miss the infinite testimonies to what can and does occur when identities collide.

We will navigate by way of some landmark texts of identities colliding, emerging, and seeing the light of day under foreign suns. The guides, as I have said, will be narratives of travel, ethnicity, and captivity. Some of these voyages out have been undertaken for pleasure, remembrance, escape, profit; some for the purposes of exploitation, enlightenment, information gathering; some have been the result of political force and forces; and some have motives that remain unknown even after the writing is done. The voices are those of men and women of many colors and several nations, of diverse sexualities, ages, and classes. They all find themselves having left "home" and ventured out, and having some new faces and places in the world tell them something about where they have come to *and from*. Travel writing, ethnic discourses of displacement, and the postmodern captivity narratives of concentration camp memoirs offer unique opportunities to examine the rhetoric of submission and domination, that is, the analytics of power. Through this rhetoric, we can read the consolidation of identities as inevitably and simultaneously a strategy of appropriation and accommodation, claim and resistance, provisionality and necessity.

Identities are both/either claimed and/or resisted because of their representational status. Travel narratives that turn to the moment of the self as represented *for* others and even *by* them offer ways of reading this representation as both seduction and reduction of the self in question. It is through a logic of dislocated subjectivity that a self may emerge along with a sense of its relation to a collectivity. With this emergence there may also be an active assumption of responsibility that begins to shape a politics of willed displacement. Many of the writers treated in this book have chosen to voyage out or have created fictions of those who have done so. This is their willfulness even as they actively aim to divest themselves of identity; nevertheless they will stumble on moments of its imprints whether through language, dress, demeanor, beliefs, or a variety of cultural practices that will need to be specified.

It is in the attitude or bearing of the traveler or migrant that we most often see a form of submission to the new that can recall the powerlessness and receptivity of infancy. However, this same submission may be easily withdrawn and reformulated as judgment and domination if the moment or experience calls it forth—the infant become petty tyrant. How much can a self suspend of its own shaping forces in order to confront an other's culture? In trying to answer this and other related questions I expect to come to a clearer understanding of how and why we need those identities that we wear and those we may be able to exchange, try on, inhabit, or become. If, in our current wisdom, we know all our identities to be only partial, from what degrees of partiality, fragmentation, and even shattering can and do we gain pleasure and knowledge? What becomes of power in realms of such knowingly fragmented selves?

~

Seduction by Elsewhere

Concluding her introduction to *Imperial Eyes: Travel Writing and Transculturation,* Mary Louise Pratt states that she has "aimed not to circumscribe travel writing as a genre but to suggest its heterogeneity and its interactions with other kinds of expression" (11). Other forms of such expression are the immigrant autobioethnography and the concentration camp memoir. All three of these genres engage in representations of selves shaped in relation to an elsewhere. In the first two of the book's four parts I am looking at those texts that are most conventionally described as travel writing.

One of Pratt's rhetorical figures is the seeing-man, the one with the imperial eyes. I want to see what happens when we stop to observe some of the seeing-men. We will move from Victor Segalen in China to André Gide in the Congo, Roland Barthes in Japan, and Michel Butor in the United States; then we will observe what happens when seeing-women are the bearers of the imperial gaze, as is the case with Mary Kingsley in West Africa and Zora Neale Hurston in the Caribbean.

Elsewheres are with us still, whether or not they have been contaminated or colonized rhetorically and politically. Pratt calls the writing about elsewhere narratives of and from the contact zones: "social spaces where disparate cultures meet, clash, and grapple with each other, often in highly asymmetrical relations of domination and subordination" (4). And these zones still exert their force upon those who meet there, a force that I will probe, in the course of this book, in a dynamic that moves from seduction to survival.

A dynamic of seduction is productive for exploring the kinds of texts grouped in the first two parts of this book, for it suggests explicitly a set of interactions and exchanges that establish relations of power/fully moved subjects-in-process. Seduction puts into motion the search for pleasures both transgressive and sanctioned. Such a search puts its subject into positions that vacillate between power and powerlessness; such ambivalence generates and propels the text of dislocation and its narration with a mix of anxiety and anticipation. Pratt's seeing-man, when he manages to see an other in a manner that may suspend imperial posturing, might be able to doff his emperor's borrowed authority and find himself rendered childlike.

~

Time and the Traveler

Victor Segalen's *Exoticism*

. . . un jeune homme, très simple et très beau. . . . Pas de jour ou il ne vienne
me regarder peindre ou sculpter.
Et le voir, quand je me reposais de ma journée, nous causions; il me faisait
des questions de jeune sauvage curieux des choses européennes, surtout des
choses de l'amour et souvent ses questions m'embarrassaient. Mais ses
réponses étaient plus naives encore que ses questions. Il me dit . . . que, moi,
je n'étais pas comme les autres, que je pouvais des choses dont les autres
étaient incapables. Je crois que Jotépha est le premier homme au monde qui
m'ait tenu ce langage, ce langage d'enfant. Car il faut l'être, n'est-ce pas pour
s'imaginer qu'un artiste soit quelque chose d'utile.

[. . . a young man, very simple and very handsome. . . . Not a day went by
without his coming to watch me paint or sculpt. I'd see him, when I rested
from my day, and we would chat; he made up questions for me, those of a
young native curious about things European, especially things about love,
and often his questions embarrassed me. But his answers were even more
naive than his questions. He told me . . . that *I* was not like the others, that I
could do things the others couldn't. I think that Jotepha is the only man who
has ever spoken to me like this, like a child. For isn't that what one must be in
order to imagine that an artist is something useful?]
Gauguin, *Album Noa-Noa*

Nous sommes avec Segalen déjà dans l'ère du soupçon.

[With Segalen we are already in the age of suspicion.]
Jean-Pol Madou, "Segalen: Un exotisme nietzschéen"

5

Victor Segalen missed meeting Paul Gauguin in Tahiti by three months. The painter's death, in fact, cast a certain shadow over Segalen's sense of exploring recently left traces, walking in Gauguin's steps, as it were.[1] For Victor Segalen, theorist of the exotic, the above passage from the notebooks of Paul Gauguin, one of the exotic's exemplary practitioners, merits close attention for its rather distilled rhetorical contextualizing of that discourse of exoticism that Segalen, and even we, have inherited. It is a legacy of which Segalen is already suspicious, but that he inhabits thoroughly. Our historical distance and the skepticism we might bring to such a passage need to be temporarily held in suspension as we try to don an earlier century's comfort in its efforts to bridge vast spaces of what we have come to understand as cultural differences.

The scene above takes place between Gauguin and Jotepha, the artist's regular visitor and younger friend. What occurs between these two announces the kind of scene that will become climactic for Segalen in the texts to be read below. The "curious native" whom we meet in this passage is also Gauguin himself as we read the vicissitudes and ambiguities of the above excerpt from his notebooks. Look at the vacillation between the so-called subject and object of this reported and repeated encounter between Gauguin and Jotepha. Three moments stand out: Gauguin tells us first that the "young native's" questions about "love" (we surely understand by this some connection to sex) "embarrassed," burdened, or perplexed him. However, some significant switches are thrown when Gauguin continues about Jotepha: "But his answers were even more naive than his questions." Answers? To whose questions? Whose perhaps equally naive questions? This is an exchange in which the positions of knowledge and power keep shifting back and forth. For this statement is followed by Jotepha reportedly telling Gauguin that he, Gauguin, is "not like the others"—other Europeans, no doubt. That he can do (*pouvais*) things the others can't. Or don't? Jotepha shores up Gauguin's self, Gauguin whose naiveté has just been exposed by *his* questions in this reported dialogue with Jotepha. But even more to the point is the final phrase: Gauguin tells us that Jotepha was the first man ever to speak to him in such a fashion ("qui m'ait tenu ce langage, ce langage d'enfant"), like a child. Here is the ambiguity opened by this exchange: Isn't Jotepha speaking to Gauguin like the child Gauguin takes him to be—with his embarrassing questions? Isn't he also speaking to him like a child in awe of the one who "can do things the others can't"—the older, wiser man instructing the younger? But when we read the final sentence, which explains that one must be(come) a child to believe that the artist is useful, we realize that it is Gauguin who is spoken to as if he were a child—he, too, has made himself naive. He, too, has granted Jotepha the power to confirm him in his confident childlike self, the one who paints and sculpts and wonders about his own usefulness, as he and Jotepha chat away the evenings. This slippage between men into and out of the position of the "curious native" ("sauvage curieux") leaves open the question of who is in possession of knowledge and power, and thus represents yet another framing of the moment between the child and the "emperor" when fraudulence falls away and ambivalence is allowed.

Segalen in China will play out such a scene—the "mirage" of an encounter with a younger other he takes to be his double. Pratt's seeing-man sees himself, and the power and dominance usually ascribed to the visual in the discourse on the exotic are thrown into question at such a moment. Some of the questions thus thrown open are the objects of my regard. Gauguin's scene makes clear the extent to which the presence of others colors our coming to self, whether as artist or as traveler.

Recent years have seen the republication of some of Victor Segalen's primary works, as well as a growing number of critical books, articles, and dissertations about his writings. Segalen, a French navy doctor who lived from 1878 to 1919, is being reread, I would suggest, because of the degree to which his few and idiosyncratic published works speak clearly against the grain of the late-nineteenth-century French discourse on difference. Thus, Segalen seduces late-twentieth-century interpreters of relations to place and self because the range to be found in his profoundly self-doubting voice resonates with our own vexing questions concerning differences. Another postmodern reader of Segalen, Chris Bongie, couples Segalen with Conrad as exemplars of an exhausted discursive universe.[2] I will work between two of Segalen's texts: his theoretical *Essay on Exoticism* and his travel narrative about China, *Equipée*. What we will see theorized *and* represented here are repeated scenes of loss and gain of identities in the face of differences and misrecognitions. Some of the dynamics of self-fashioning that characterize the scenario of seduction in an alien place will here become plain.

Segalen is a pivotal figure because of his suspicion of his own wish to create himself by way of alienation in time and space. The critical essay on the exotic, "a moral treatise on looking and listening,"[3] was worked and reworked, although never finished, over some fourteen years of note-gathering. The fragmentary and sometimes aphoristic travel narrative of *Equipée*, subtitled *Voyage au Pays du Réel*, recounts a trip to China taken in 1914–15, but was not published until 1929, ten years after his death.[4] It is particularly worth tracking in Segalen's narratives the vicissitudes of his critical distance during the course of his voyages. *Equipée,* the "escape" to China, shows us how departure and return are figured in Segalen's ideas of time and space as they shape his sense of the exotic. The *Essay* goes to great lengths to phenomenologize, as it were, his sense of time and space, our place *in* them, their marks on *our* minds and bodies.

> L'Exotisme ne vous prend pas à la gorge. Il faut savoir lentement le provoquer pour se laisser ensuite étreindre par lui. (64)

> [Exoticism doesn't take you by the throat. You must know how to arouse it slowly and then let yourself be grabbed by it.]

As with Gauguin and Jotepha, the dynamism of the exotic and its seductions are shot through with play and struggle, sweet talk and surrender.

Published posthumously, as were many of Segalen's works, *Essay on Exoticism* puts into relief some of the specific questions of language in and out of its place. Segalen's essay begs to be read as an inscription, a mapping of the cul-de-sac that had become the discourse on the exotic by the late nineteenth and early twentieth centuries. It also belongs among the historical texts that have come out of French intellectual life on the problematics of otherness, or differences, a discursive space that represents for Segalen, according to Bongie, an exhausted ideology.[5]

Both Dennis Porter and Chris Bongie read travel writings for access they provide to the understanding of temporality, particularly the past and present. Where Bongie's emphasis is clearly on loss, Porter's is on desire and transgression. Porter would allow us to read Segalen (whom he does not treat) as an "iconoclast rather than the rhapsodist" (12) of the exotic. For Bongie, Segalen is an already fallen nonhero. Bongie sets up a lineage among travel writers that leads to the "decadentist" moment that is with us still, and he devotes his last chapter to the neoexoticist writings of Pasolini. Porter gives a very different valence to the problem of the belatedness and melancholia that haunt travel writing and the discourse of otherness. Porter's project is animated by a strong reliance on the insights of the Freud of *Beyond the Pleasure Principle*; Bongie tries to outrun the entropic impulse he finds in the exotic. There is a certain resignation to Bongie's "postmodern poetics, and politics of 'survival,'" for the postmodern has not only divested itself of a sense of a future, but also regrets a past it cannot hold.

What is it that goes into action when the subject is interpellated as traveler, as displaced person? What kind of scenario *is* the restaging of a mirrored and mirroring moment? A story of desire and dread, of memory and entropy, of plenitude and loss. Powerful narratives against which the writing self is defined. Time and space, the subject in place, the subject in the face of another—some of the refracted bits of identification and dis- and misidentifications. Perhaps the apt template for this experience is neither mirror nor screen—early and modern versions of illusion in the midst of reality—but the postmodern hologram's shimmering. I want to connect to the vocabularies of Bongie and Porter, with their affective resonances, Pratt's offering, which is also intrapsychically suggestive but which rests as thoroughly in the geo- and topographical—the contact zones.

This renaming of the process of travel with its clear notation of people in places invites a reframing of Segalen's relation to an elsewhere. Even a writer as self-critical as Segalen still reveals the ways in which earlier notions of cultural gaps seem, in spite of themselves, designed to locate in differences reassuring ideas of hierarchy. We might imagine the iconoclastic xenophile, Segalen, as first wearing and then casting off the emperor's clothes—going native—in the ethnographic mode of self-refashioning, cross-dressing.

The structure of the *Essay* itself is fragmentary, consisting of notes gathered both before, during, and after the trip to China that is remembered and recorded in *Equipée*. Segalen attested in letters and other writings that he was destined to vagabondage, and, as a vagabond, was the proper subject to take up the question of the exotic and a critique of its travestied versions in popular forms by the likes of Pierre Loti.[6] As an *exote*, an adept at encounters with diversity and difference, Segalen considered himself uniquely able to disentangle the confusions of subject/object commingling that characterize the discourse on difference of the late nineteenth century. These commonplaces bore the imprints of an ideological set of discourses inherited from and constructed during the era of colonial expansion and settlement in the New World.

> Avant tout, déblayer le terrain. Jeter par-dessus bord tout ce que contient de mésusé et de rance ce mot d'exotisme. (36)

> [First of all, a clean sweep. Throw overboard all that is misused and rancid in this word, exoticism.]

What renders Segalen a salient figure for late-twentieth-century investigations into differences is the degree of his suspicion, self-consciousness, and doubt about his own ways of coming to know his own subjects/objects. He acknowledges that his project is to speak about what has only been mystified by earlier writers. Segalen knows quite clearly that in reading the

East he is implicitly, and even overtly, explicating the West; that in fixing China he is etching Europe; in pushing his way into the Orient, he fails to discard pieces of the Occident that cling to him nevertheless. How does such a degree of self-knowledge and self-consciousness inflect the inevitable appropriation and incorporation of the alien scene? For after all, he asks us not to jettison the word, only its used and abused histories.

From China in 1911 Segalen writes to a friend, reminiscing about Polynesia:

> Toute l'île venait à moi comme une femme . . . la jeune fille est distante de nous à l'extrême, donc précieuse incomparablement à tous les fervents du divers. (*Essai*, 61)

> [The whole island came to/approached me like a woman. . . . the young girl is most distant from us, therefore, incomparably precious to all the disciples of the diverse.]

Equating the enticing female, both *femme* and *fille*, with the other, and the seeker after the exotic with men (*nous*), Segalen performs for us that topos of the seduction story—the inevitable seizure of desire by power—the desire for the other and the desire of the other, all at once. Segalen knows well that the exotic has been (hetero)sexed and gendered; that it has comprised a sensorium. Not only fictively embodied, the exotic also inhabits the register of the emotions, the most significant one for Segalen being surprise. The exotic takes one unawares, even those, like himself, who seek it out, if only to dismember and dissect it. Trained as a physician, Segalen brings an anatomical and physiological attention to his perceptions of the diverse with its material as well as aesthetic components. Then, in the late nineteenth century, somewhat like now, medicine and its allied fields—psychiatry, biology, neurology—were promising to unlock the connections between feeling, knowledge, and bodily states. And analogies from the physical, individual body to the social body were everywhere; the medicolegal underpinnings of naturalistic discourses legitimized them in literature and elsewhere.

As Gauguin named his last home in the islands the Maison du Jouir, Segalen hoped to live and write as a *Maître-du-Jouir*. What exactly were the elements of Segalen's sensorium of surprise? His first sketchy notes from 1904 insisted predictably on sight and sound, mixed, indeed somewhat surprisingly, with a special emphasis on smell ("[l]'odorat surtout"). Given Segalen's spectrum, broader than that granted by the conventionally visual, what comes as even more of a surprise, however, is the absence of touch or taste in his taxonomy of surprise ("[l]e gout et le toucher nuls"). No tasting, and yet the language of intoxication is everywhere apparent, suggesting nevertheless a rather consuming encounter with the exotic, the diverse. One of Segalen's recent French readers, in fact, characterizes him, kin to Rimbaud, as the "poète ivre."[7] Segalen begins in full contradiction with himself when he writes:

> Commencer par la sensation d'Exotisme. . . . Passer à la belle saveur. Ne pas essayer de la décrire, mais l'indiquer à ceux qui sont aptes à la déguster avec ivresse. (33)

> [Begin with the *sensation* of Exoticism. . . . Move on to its wonderful savor. Try not to describe it, but point it out to those apt to consume it with drunkenness.]

This plain a contradiction—sensations not to be described, but digested, ingested, even as we come by them in the medium of words—becomes one of the structuring principles of the essay. Segalen comes back to his ideas here peripatetically, with devotion, even fervor, but from a distance, that distance concomitant with his theoretizing of exoticism itself. That movement, toward and away from definitions and the urges that prompt them, establish some of the distinct features that lead Segalen to presume to undertake this task critically. Like so many of the writers who give themselves over to an examination of the diverse, he is captivated, seduced by difference even as he is determined to elude its grasp, precisely by grasping its "essence." We, postmoderns, are as properly skeptical of the discourse of essences as were Segalen's contemporaries when it came to the discourse of the sentiments. Therefore, intoxication must be rewritten upon reflection, removed in time and space from the experience itself. For Segalen the only way to approach the experience is through imbibing, and then extracting himself in order to leave his readers with the "saveur objective" of the exotic. Even as he says this, he regrets that he must trip over the same words as always with their same force and enforced significations. What he will try to do in the narrative of China, *Equipée*, is always to remind us that his words are everywhere doubled by doubt. But given all these caveats, what then is the essence of exoticism for Segalen? "Celui de l'Objet pour le sujet!" (49)—the pleasure of the object and its objectness for the seeing, hearing, sniffing subject as they meet in time and space. Implicated in the very critique he is attempting to sustain, Segalen's voice comes to us inflected in the accents of the century's turn, or end; these linguistic resonances—talk of subjects and objects—are undoubtedly why his words come through so clearly and poignantly when our own millennial moment beckons and looms.

In *Equipée* Segalen will take his theoretical questions on the road, as it were, and work out further aspects of his doubly doubting discourse on the diverse. The moves between the physical and the metaphysical are immediately apparent in the opening of the narrative of the China escapade:

> J'ai toujours tenu pour suspects ou illusoires des récits de ce genre . . . ce problème,—doute fervent et pénétrant qui doit remplir les moindres mots ici comme le sang les plus petits vaisseaux et jusqu'à la pulpe sous l'ongle,— et qui s'impose ainsi: l'imaginaire déchoit-il ou se renforce quand il se confronte au réel? (11)

> [I have always considered tales of this sort dubious or illusory. . . . This problem—the fervent and penetrating doubt that fills the least of my words here as blood fills the tiniest arteries, even those beneath the fingernails—which imposes itself in the following fashion: is the imaginary diminished or bolstered when confronted with/by the real?]

This is the question that will drive Segalen on in his narrative as in his journey: the power of the imaginary when confronted with the real. We must remember that for Segalen these words belong to the realm of the senses. With doubt for his compass, true north is where this encounter is lived concretely—the imaginary face to face with the real. And we must keep in mind that Segalen reverses the tropological discourse of Orientalism that would have made "China" the polar force of the imaginary; *Equipée* is the narrative of a *voyage au pays du réel.*

Segalen claims that the map inhabits "the future"—that anterior future before the journey was taken: "J'interroge un à un les éléments précis sur quoi s'établit l'avenir. Ce sont des relations de voyage, (des mots encore), des cartes géographiques—purs symboles, et provisoires [I demand to know one by one the precise elements on which the future is established. These are relations established en route, (still words), geographical maps—pure symbols, and provisional]" (19). In the present of the journey as retold, the map is mobilized. Its rivers, roads, and mountains, as well as its blank spaces, are filled in by the weight of one's own body, the fatigue of the excursion, the presence of means of transport—other men, bearers, wagons, beasts of burden, walking sticks, sandals, boats, rafts, and so on. Here, too, we read the further gendering of the journey and its inevitably missed rendezvous between the imaginary and the real. They are in opposition, a necessary duality, polarities:

> L'Inventé, c'est le Blanc-mâle, le souffle aux milliers de couleurs. Le Réel sera le Noir-féminin, masse de nuit. Le Réel m'a paru toujours très femme. La femme m'a paru toujours très "Réel." La matière est femme et toute com-

paraison est possible et sans restreinte, vague. C'est pourquoi je n'en veux pas. (50–51)

[The Invented is the White-male, the many-colored breath. The Real will be the Black-feminine, the mass of night. The Real has always appeared very womanly to me. Woman has always appeared very "Real" to me. Matter is woman and any comparison is possible and without constraint, vague. That is why I don't want anything to do with it.]

The invented, that is to say, the imaginary renamed, is light or white and male or masculine; only it can take on form, color, shape. The real is dark or black feminine, a mass undifferentiated except by colored, allegorized attributes. Its very lack, or nondifferentiated status, looms as if it were quicksand this traveler must avoid. The map this calls up suggests those monstrous margins that for many centuries told as much about what was imagined to constitute the globe as what was known to constitute it; where borders had not been laid, traced, and patrolled one might founder. The fear and challenge of uncharted space can be read in the margins of those early maps; its hold on our imaginations may be said to constitute narrative traditions in imperial cultures. The demarcation of space that is geopolitics reaches from mapmaking to the making of what Althusser called lived relations.[8]

Let me take this meeting in time with the exotic, "the feeling we have of the diverse," in Segalen's term, and search out a philosophical framework for posing these questions of differentiation and identification. Between Segalen's fin de siècle and our own there is the epistemological and historical fault line of the second "world" war.[9] It is Emmanuel Lévinas who will meditate on "Time and the Other" as they have their encounter in the space Lévinas calls "this always of non-coincidence, but also this always of relation . . . distance that is also proximity" (10).[10] Lévinas's *Le Temps et l'autre* is a text in which difference becomes irrevocably linked with death, rather than *jouissance* and renewal. The projects of Segalen and Lévinas meet dialogically and productively, however, in their effort to maintain the tension of difference. In Segalen's case this is maintained through the very movement of travel that *L'Equipée* will demonstrate and critique; Lévinas understands such movement as always already departure and return *à soi*. Lévinas grounds in ontological terms how identities are always mistaken, and yet must *be* taken as we shiftingly occupy the place of the one who speaks, names, takes responsibility, witnesses, records, explores, imbibes—all functions that form bits of the general economy of being in everyday life.

Where Segalen's thoughts soar when he is most distant in space, Lévinas draws his energy from a moment in time that puts him in direct yet distanced contact with the others who have just lived the break of the German occupation and Vichy France. Lévinas avows the liberation and its force that make him speak and think these questions of difference and diversity, which are "ni extase où le Même s'absorbe dans l'Autre ni savoir où l'Autre appartient au Même [neither ecstasy where the Same is absorbed in(to) the Other nor knowledge where the Other belongs to the Same]" (13). Time, for Lévinas, is a "social supplement," and as such implies an anthropology, and more particularly for his interest, an ontology. Responding to what he takes as an invitation from the work of Heidegger, Lévinas wishes first to read solitude ontologically, in a manner that would not participate in what he calls the "pathétique brillant" of the social, the relation, the *miteinandersein* (being-with-another) that is of necessity allied with happiness and, therefore, in opposition to solitude. Not only a phenomenology of solitude and/with otherness, he wants to attempt a transcendence of those very categories. Lévinas wants to investigate "the place of solitude in the general economy of being" (18).

One further juxtaposition: the phenomenological and epistemological inquiries about time and the other with a more recent moment—the ethics of touch and sexual difference in Luce Irigaray's work, where she reads a certain obstinacy in the philosophical sensorium she has inherited, from Lévinas, among others. This effort will take us back to Segalen's drive to know the exotic and its surprises. We need to recall that in the privileging of the sensory ways of knowing, Segalen will set aside taste and touch in his theory. So to prod Segalen with Irigaray is to make his text give up some of its silences: "L'avenir, c'est l'autre [The future is the other]" (Lévinas, 64). "Et tous les sens sont du registre de la caresse [All the senses are in the register of touch]" (Irigaray, "Fécondité de la caresse, lecture de Lévinas," 180).

Lévinas asks, "How can the I *(moi)* become other to its self *(soi)*?" (85). There is only one way, he replies to his own question—in paternity. Paradoxically and anti-oedipally speaking, this is the only sphere outside of sex and death that excludes the operations of power, according to Lévinas. How can he miss the corporeal alterity of incipient maternity, he who asserts in an earlier moment in this series of lectures that femininity is the difference cutting across *(tranchant)* differences? And in so doing, femininity is absolute alterity, a flight into darkness, which Lévinas allies with (feminine) modesty. What Lévinas seeks is a difference in/of duality rather than fusion, the problem with the maternal body for Lévinas, as it was for Segalen. It must be noted that fusion in Lévinas's lexicon is associated with power, possession, and seizure. It will require a reader like Irigaray to take the bold next step of asking, Why the problem over fusion, and what is its ethical stake? Her answers produce a metaphysics of touch the outlines of which suggest a formidable contestant in the heliotropisms we know so well since the early modern epistemological shift to sight/light as the origin, the way out of the Platonic cave. These problems with the maternal, with fusion, which is also the material and the real, are certainly not only Segalen's or Lévinas's; they can indeed be read as among the strongest undercurrents in that formulation of Pratt's that she names "transculturation."

To turn our glance from Irigaray back to Segalen, it is almost as if his physiology, anatomy, and aesthetics of the diverse had been awaiting their feminist hermeneut. Irigaray wants her readers to make way for the *entrouvert*, the ajar, the threshold; Lévinas demands duality that knows itself to be held in suspense; Segalen insists upon tension as a motion of throbbing, an afterhum we can't stop hearing. *Equipée*, written between Saigon and Brest, is where we can see how Segalen himself managed this instability of identity and difference in the instance of his dislocation in space and time (China, 1914–15).

For all the problematizing of matter as gendered, what are we to make of the many ways that Segalen is a materialist of the exotic in its manifestations through the bodily? He claims we know the diverse through encounters with climate, temperature, nourishment, as well as through our limbs, fatigue, heaviness. A phenomenologist of the highway (like Butor and Baudrillard later and elsewhere), he spends a good deal of his account of the journey he took telling us of his means of transport, both what carries him and what he carries. This yoking of the metaphysical and the physical underwrites his retheorizing of the exotic as much as the journey itself:

> Ce livre ne veut donc être ni le poème d'un voyage, ne le journal de route d'un rêve vagabond. Cette fois, portant le conflit au moment de l'acte, refusant de séparer, au pied du mont, le poète de l'alpiniste, et, sur le fleuve, l'écrivain du marinier, et, sur la plaine, le peintre et l'arpenteur ou le pèlerin du topographe, se proposant de saisir au même instant la joie dans les muscles, dans les yeux, dans la pensée, dans le rêve . . . (13)

> [This book aims to be neither the poem of a voyage nor the notebooks of a vagabond dream. This time, bringing the conflict to the moment of the act, refusing to separate the poet at the foot of the mountain from the mountain climber, and on the river, the writer from the sailor, and on the plain, the painter and the surveyor or the pilgrim from the topographer, proposing to

grasp in the same instant the joy in the muscles and the eyes, in thoughts and in dreams . . .]

Segalen becomes the pilgrim speaking his body, making the pose palpable through the musculature. Françoise Han notes the "physical *and* intellectual joy" (emphasis mine) reported by Segalen when he arrives at the mountain-top—the site and panorama for which all the efforts made have been engaged. This is one of the ways that China (like Barthes's "Japan" later) is made the perfect testing ground for the answer to Segalen's opening question, "Is the imaginary diminished (*déchoit-il*) or is it bolstered when confronted with/by the real?" The real is that materiality of the body, his body. But matter is "woman" and therefore, all comparisons are possible, and are also vague—"c'est pourquoi je n'en veux pas" (51). Doubt is equated with a curiously clear-eyed skepticism, Segalen's epistemological article of faith. Vagueness, however, is not fit company on this manly journey. Matter is the real: all those tired muscles, well or ill-shod feet, burdened shoulders. And for Segalen, it turns out that some aspects of the part "China" is asked to play require, even allow, him this ejaculation: "J'ai brutalement étranglé ma peur du réel [I have brutally strangled my fear of the real]" (53).

In this strangulation of the feminine/real we can read a set of diacritical marks within the histories of difference, where Segalen is more than merely a petulant schoolboy forced to obey the principles of matter/mother. He perpetuates a long and venerated tradition, strangling his own femininity, simultaneously displaying the scarring effects of gender inscriptions through an act of self-inflicted violence. "Mother Nature and Company" are a drag; they drag the pilgrim down from the summit, into descent, back to the real of the concrete. And Segalen will say, "Descendre est voisin de déchoir [Descent is neighbor to diminishment]" (34–35). Intoxication has been transformed/lost; in its place the best that can be found is satisfaction, obedience, and the flattening effect of the real. The imaginary, in answer to his own earlier question, clearly falls apart in confrontation with the real.

In the vis-à-vis with his own contradictions Segalen is the first to remind us of the "fervent and penetrating" doubt that underwrites this text that is "not a book" (22). Whatever it may be, he cannot help but write it because of the "puissance du Divers" (12). In looking for a motto to govern his trip through China, which has traditionally stood in for the European subject as the ultimate land of the imaginary, Segalen has called his native culture to task. However, his simple inversion is no less imaginarily deluded. We know a simple reversal is only barely a first step to our own impossible disentanglement from metaphysics or ideology. More to the point for us as readers is Segalen's passing insight that the map is "of the future"; and the future, we recall from Lévinas, is the other. Our access to the future and the other and the future of the other is only possible through the mediation of representation—the map: the fictive space where in time we may go, plan to go, wish to go.

To close by leaving ajar these questions of identification and identity in the vis-à-vis of these texts juxta- and superimposed, I will return to Irigaray, who reads the making of differences as corporeal encounters. In order to come to terms with nagging questions and doubts about subjects-objects, she specifies these terms into an economy, an exchange. The agents in the exchange, the lover and the beloved, find themselves bound willfully *and* with abandon. The beloved grants to the lover availability and thereby gains time. Time as . . . the future of the other? the future with an other? the yet to be explored site in space?

> Peint sur la soie mobile du retour, tout ce qui suit du voyage m'apparaît desormais tout déroulé d'avance. (123)

> [Painted on the moving silk of the return, all that follows of the voyage seems to me henceforth all unfurled beforehand.]

For Segalen this gift of time in space is imaged as a painted silk scroll that can be read in both directions; for in looking forward he sees the beloved of his past: it is his younger self waiting for him at the crossroads of the imaginary and the real. Departure already embraces return. Reorientation in space and time—the *déja su, vu, et vécu*—recognized as the other he has already lived. Vis-à-vis not with an other, only a self once real, now imagined and reevoked.

Like Gauguin in his chats with Jotepha about love, in which Jotepha was asked projectivley to reembody a younger self who had come along with the artist to Micronesia, Segalen, too, will resolve his vagabondish urges in an encounter with another younger self. These are solipsistic solitary travelers painting in images and words an elsewhere peopled by "white" men and "dark" women; they are finally seduced by the access through very real others to heed the call of an other self left somewhere en route.

Seeing Is Believing

André Gide's *Voyage to the Congo,* Roland Barthes's *Empire of Signs,* and Michel Butor's *Mobile*

> The travel narrative is then one in which the transgression of losing or leaving the home is mediated by a movement that attempts to fill the gap of that loss through a spatialization of time. This articulation of space with time smooths that initial discontinuity into the continuity of a line that can be drawn on the map.
> Georges Van Den Abbeele, "The Economy of Travel"

We are to read discourses of alterity and identity differentially, through lenses that are at least bifocal. From the prism to the hologram, the metaphors are inevitably optic ones, refractions of light caught in motion, held still long enough to catch a glimpse of what occurs in the mirrors of subjectivity. Theorists in the field of film studies, another template for modern and postmodern subjective optics, have done a great deal of work on questions of spectatorship, and film theory has done much to reengage narrative as an activity impelled by productive forces far beyond those controlled by a single author. The site of reception, the spectator, has also been understood as traversed by potentially multiple and mobile identifications and disidentifications. Cinema's status as scene, screen, and scenario seems not out of the way as a place from which to export questions in relation to travel narratives that clearly desire to take their readers somewhere else. Travel writing places in relief some of the problematics of spectatorship and its relation to identification, a moment necessary in the constitution both of subjectivity and narrative. In the dialectic of representation of others and of selves we can begin to specify the politics of "flexible positionality" that Said called for in *Orientalism*.

Can we go further than simply to invert our fear and idealize the exotic—that which comes from afar? To apprehend more honestly the erotics of otherness would inevitably lay bare more of what is at stake for the subject narrating a new landscape and its inhabitants and practices. What would it mean to encounter and engage with the alien within? What would it mean to learn some of the operations of the desire I would like to name as the opposite of nostalgia—forelonging—to see what we've never seen, go where we have never been before? How might such an understanding shift the terms of power, knowledge, and pleasure such as we've known them?

"Better be imprudent moveable than prudent fixtures": a phrase from the letters of John Keats, this motto serves as an epigraph to André Gide's *Voyage au Congo*. It also forces some questions of mobility, its imprudence and impudence, as may be the case with certain kinds of travelers, such as those in this chapter—those who are in motion, movable, at whim and by privilege.

The three texts recount journeys taken by twentieth-century French travelers: André Gide, who spent nearly a year in French Equatorial Africa in 1925–26; Roland Barthes, who went to Japan in the late 1960s and wrote *L'Empire des signes* about what he called that "fictive nation"; and Michel Butor, a writer generally grouped among the French "new novelists," whose fiction, *Mobile*, published in 1962, has the typographical appearance and narrative structure of a postmodern epic poem. If Segalen may be said to have closed the nineteenth-century discourse on exoticism with his insistence on skepticism and doubt, these three writers speak clearly with voices that announce a tone of belatedness. In various ways they each name their desire as the opposite of nostalgia, its nonidentical twin, perhaps—a yearning aimed not at the past but toward the future: forelonging. To be late, to know the exotic as exhausted, mapped, and packaged, is to reinscribe desire in space, for time has been sealed off. Elsewheres continue to exert their force; it is crucial to understand the allure and the dynamics of the contact zones.

For each of these writers in their estranged landscapes there is a discourse produced by virtue of being *elsewhere* that makes it possible to explore the narrative of a voyage as a kind of writing both highly conventionalized and yet not strictly codified. It is in this sense that travel writing itself is imprudently mobile and has produced forms that are desultory, episodic, or autobiographic—forms largely relegated to a domain considered popular and historically marginal to the concerns of literary canon formation. But an emerging body of critical work on this kind of rhetoric and its discursive strategies has shown how travel writing implicitly poses questions of historical specificity: for example, what is "the Congo" in 1925–26, and how will the colonial structures in place there intersect with the troublesome politics of a writer like Gide? Such a question stops us at the crossroads of disciplines including literature, anthropology, and history.

The traveler may assume a flexibility of positions, and about his imprudence and his mobility we might pose the question of the scene of writing in an alien place and ask, In the sort of subject-object vacillation we saw with Gauguin and Segalen, are there sometimes nonimperial eyes? ears? touch? What happens to the relations of power when the glance or voice reports to us about the taste and smell of elsewhere? Or is writing "elsewhere" or writing *from* elsewhere or *about* elsewhere already saturated with a need to reassert the power of the one who turns the alien (space) into language? Preeminently permeable to a genealogical suspension of space and boundaries, the travel writer is not only on holiday from writing while writing, she or he is also away from home, *ex patria*, the father land, and sometimes the mother tongue. In this displacement and the enticement it offers, what asks to be read is (hypostatized) political writing. Its political nature would consist in representing a moment in the relationship between "imperialism and culture," to which Said gave voice with the publication of *Orientalism* and, more recently, *Culture and Imperialism*. In the 1990s the academic debates about the politics of culture have flowed into public discourse.

What politics of the unconscious could be gleaned here in the traveler's romance if we read this form as a restaging of the gaze? The writers arrayed here search out a kind of play in the space of difference that is mostly blissful. These are scenes of wonder—the traveler's sublime. (In later chapters I will take up that other aspect of the sublime we inherit from eighteenth-century aesthetic discourses, that aspect connected with awe and its affective kin, terror. For those elements are more clearly displayed when displacement is more forced, less chosen.) The specularity of travel narrative—what I saw there—is one of its foremost tropisms. In the mirror scene we know what happens: the budding subject finds its "place" as an already gendered I of and in language. In the case of the traveler, we can further theorize the emergence of subjects not only sexed and gendered, but also already located in relation to place, nation, race, and class. The mirror reflects more than one aspect of subject positioning; that is to say, a psychoanalytics of Lacan with

Freud, of course, but also Homi Bhabha with Fanon, for example. I raise this question in order to pose one in closer focus: What can we read in the glance, voice, or touch that would be/would wish to be noncolonizing? These three travelers imagine they see something of themselves in what they take to be mirrored in the eyes of others. What can we garner from the innocence and presumptuousness of their imaginings?

Travel writing and the reading of travel narratives seem to involve us in an intersubjective position of voyeurism. Perhaps all narrative does. In its means and moments of production the writing is occurring perhaps at the window of a train, high in the seat of a *tipoye*, or in the solitary space of a hotel room. We readers are often watching someone watching. The eye is securely lodged as the most trustworthy of the senses, but the intrusions on that sense are many, and seductive in unexpected ways. Surprise, we recall with Segalen, is so much of what constitutes seduction, and to leave "home" is to ensure a rather constant supply of surprises, at least for a while.[1] At a second level of isolation comes the condition of writing and the remoteness of the traveler from the visited scene. For the reader then, there is an even greater distance, as well as the protected and vicarious nature of voyeurism recognized and named in the locution "armchair traveler," the one who has asked the storyteller to speak.

On Gide's journey this situation of voyeurism is doubled, since his traveling companion, Marc Allegret, is a filmmaker who is both creating and capturing photographically many of the scenes recorded graphically by Gide, particularly the dances.[2] Barthes in Japan, where unreadability masks and erases differences, becomes a seer unseen, a voyeur who nevertheless feels "starred" by Japan as if it were photographing him. In *Mobile*, Butor drives through the landscape so quickly that it creates the effect of heterotopia, a squinting that produces perpetual motion in the landscape in view. (Baudrillard, two decades later, flying over America, will add further dimension to this phenomenology of speed as simulacrum.) In this form of watchfulness the motion is too quick to allow us to see the seer, who may also be more hidden through narrative devices.

Some of those devices derive from the situation of travel writing itself. A field of intertextual plenitude, it reveals the history of its own conditions of possibility. Often travel writers tell us which texts about the region visited are part of their baggage, and we are reminded just how travelers differ from explorers, for books have taken them "there" before. The place has already been named and preconceived. There is the referentiality of places and their texts that each new voyager relies on and denies simultaneously. The dynamics of pleasure and danger, if you will, which are part of the seduction of travel, occur both in the never-seen or never-been-there-ness and in the assurance that you *can* get there from here, as it were. The assumption that the distance is manageable, that dislocation will produce pleasure in the unknown, is particular to those who are compelled to push off for elsewhere; they then bring it into language and compel us readers to go along for the now scripted ride.

The Would-Not-Be Imperial Traveler

> I assure you that there is something tragic in my Soviet adventure. I arrived
> as an enthusiast and a believer to admire a new world, and I was offered *with
> the purpose of seducing me* all the privileges that I abominated in the old.
> André Gide, *Afterthoughts to My Back from the USSR*

The "haunted journey" of Gide's that I want to follow is his trip to French Equatorial Africa, where he did not fail to be seduced. In Africa, as in the Soviet Union, Gide travels as political witness, a long-standing tradition Dennis Porter relies upon and also reexamines in *Haunted Journeys: Desire and Transgression in European Travel Writing.* What I share with Porter as a focus is the interest in how "the discourse of political observations on place shares a vocabulary with the fantasies of our psychic life—'dream,' 'homeland,' 'hope,' 'utopia' " (240). However, where Porter would examine a relation to the desire and/for transgression that is fueled by a relation to the paternal authority, I am watching more closely how the maternal is also part of the baggage Gide is carrying along. His long-standing wish to go to "the Congo" constitutes a thoroughly textualized encounter with the discourses of nativism and exoticism; the travels are dedicated to Joseph Conrad, and Gide's "holiday" reading will include earlier writers on Africa and travel itself.

Settling into the lyricism of travel writing (the first sections are called "Voyage Out—Brazzaville," "Up River," "By Car"), Gide opens the text with the following sentence: "My state is one of inexpressible languor; the hours slip by empty and indistinguishable."[3] This is not merely a bow to the romantic tradition (of French travelers), but also to the lyric and nostalgic mode of travel writing, as we readers are moved out of time, thus setting the stage for the voyage as an imaginary, liminal moment of being. The first page of his travel story literally restages the infant's cradled state, as Gide takes us inward to a curious meditation on the customary aspects of child-rearing:

What a mistake it is not to rock children's cradles from their earliest baby-hood! I even think it would be a good plan to calm them and send them to sleep by means of a special pitching-and-tossing apparatus. As for me, I was brought up according to rational methods and by my mother's orders never slept in beds that were not fixed; thanks to which, I am particularly liable to seasickness. (3)

Gide is thankful here for orders that he first structures as "errors" in caretaking; we must begin to watch here for how early senses and scenes of authority come to illuminate moments that the search for the new has reopened—not raised properly for the rigors of life at sea, like his dedicatory surrogate father, Conrad, Gide both thanks and chides the mother.[4]

Further narrative beginnings and bows to convention are offered: the traveler seems always to need to explain or justify the reasons for going. When asked by an extratextual voice, "What are you going out for?" Gide says, "I shall see when I get there." We are reminded by Gide of the extent to which the urge to set out (and I would add, the urge to narrate) is rooted in the imaginary, that is to say, pushed by the pleasure principle to go beyond. What has brought him to the Congo, one of "the important events of my life"? This is a journey neither into nor out of the past, but one conceived by another: "I come near forgetting that it is nothing but a project made in youth and realized in maturity: I was barely 20 when I first made up my mind to make this journey to the Congo—36 years ago" (3–4). Unlike Segalen's haunting by his younger double, this younger self is taken along as a participant in this journey after all, as we can see in passages like these: "If I had been 20 my pleasure would not have been keener" (10); "My heart beats as if I were 20" (11). Gide often tells his reader what he reads along the way. About the first book mentioned he says, "I am re-reading with rapture all La Fontaine's fables" (11). Perhaps La Fontaine because he has already told us that his Goethe was found "floating lamentably in a swamp" (4), but La Fontaine is also a fitting originary kind of narrative for the beginning of Gide's own fabulation of Africa. The continent where he has never been is already cast in memory.

Recurring in Gide's narrative of the journey through the landscape with his companions is the notice paid to means of transportation. In the first thirty pages of the book, carriages, motorcars, whaleboats, oilboats, and canoes appear as conveyances. The emphasis on modes of transport and the attention Gide pays them are not surprising if we recall that early moment of cradling; it keeps the reader mindful of a sense of the physicality of travel, a welcome balance to the specular.[5] Central to this motif of conveyances is the *tipoye* or dandy placed at Gide's disposal; surely his mixed feelings about using this means of transport cannot be unrelated to the maternal rocking cradle evoked earlier, for this method, another kind of cradling, depends on the labor of four black men to hold one white man aloft from the mud below. Gide moves continually into and out of the *tipoye*, and this movement sparks thoughts on the racial divisions of labor he has entered by coming to colonial Africa; his investigations of these relations will eventually become his reason for having come here.[6] The repeated accounts of brutality of white colonists toward "their natives" arouse in Gide the clearest purpose for his visit: to do everything possible as a French citizen to right some of the worst abuses. A series of appendices (in the French text, not the English) includes letters to the colonial governor about a village massacre ordered by whites, although carried out by an African, Sergeant Yemba, who was put in place by the governor. Just as Gide has remarked that "every master gets the servant he deserves," in one letter he says, "It seems to me, however, that Yemba took his inspiration from the spirit of his master," a man who does nothing to hide his "hatred of blacks" (453). Also included in the appendices are letters and an article, printed in the *Revue de Paris* in October 1927, detailing the abusive labor practices of the colonial commercial enterprises, primarily the Foresting Company, engaged in the production of rubber. This article is titled "The Distress in *Our* Equatorial Africa" and underscores the tone of responsible reporter and loyal subject. Gide asserts, "One doesn't go to the Congo for pleasure." In the text of the *Travels* it is the desire to locate responsibility for the wretched conditions of the Boda prison that rewrites the wishes of the twenty-year-old Gide who wanted to see Africa: "I know things to which I cannot reconcile myself. What demon drove me to Africa? What did I come to find out in this country? I was at peace. I know now. I must speak" (72).

This mission, however, does not lead him to oppose the French presence in Africa; rather he imaginatively reformulates the workings of imperialism, colonialism, and racism according to his own ideas and experiences of "mutual confidence and cordiality" between himself and his servants. In a falsely modest footnote in the second chapter of the return voyage Gide tells the following tale: "I have omitted to say that after Lamy the boys, and with them the whole crew, promoted me. 'Commander' was no longer good enough. Or 'Governor' either. In their enthusiasm they called me 'Government'" (191).[7] Reified, Gide the moralist will take his high seat, from which he will do his utmost to assume the figure of benevolent paternal authority with which he has been invested by his "boys."

If the itinerary reconstructed here has been an effort to trace the means of identification available to the traveler, Gide, in the play between *tipoye* and titles, has disclosed a gaze paternal. What of the beginning moment where the maternal hand at the stationary cradle was imaged? To sketch that trajectory it would be necessary at least to mention and briefly explore Gide's relation to another of his traveling companions, Dindiki the potto, an indigenous monkey, given as a gift to Gide. Their mutual affection is exemplified by the fact that Dindiki clings to Gide's arms, torso, or legs when he is not feeding. Toward the end of the journey, when Dindiki dies, Gide says:

> My little Dindiki's death has cast a gloom over me. . . . It may appear monstrous, but I felt that I understood, as I never had before, what it may be for a mother to lose a very young child—the ruin of a whole edifice of projects and the feeling of interrupted carnal contact. (302, 303)

About his potto, as about Africa, Gide will claim the following prerogative: "I shall have plenty of time to contemplate the immutable. . . . [G]ive me leave to make haste and love what is so soon to disappear." Wonder is evanescent; "projects" and "contact" seem so much more reliable, but they, too, can become transitory. Perhaps one of the fables of travel and travel writing is the urge to distill the essence of that which is briefly disclosed only to close back in on itself. Gide knows better than to insist on making the new hold still for him; he will be won over simply in his passage through the landscape and among its inhabitants.

The traveler's identity is constructed by a remobilization of psychic shifts in the face of cultural dislocations in which, as an adult, the writer once again comes to terms with questions of language and power, authority and selfhood. What Gide's text offers are clear illustrations of the emotional and familial textures that reconstitute this process of becoming in an instant, and for an instant, simply by virtue of having landed elsewhere. To come to terms with the cultural baggage of identity and its claims, we have begun to discern in this narrative the multiple selves who have come along for this rather bumpy ride, and, in this respect, Gide offers up a rather full complement of ego-fragments for study. I am trying to hold the prism still for some very brief moments.

No Stopping Here

For "to read" a country is first of all to perceive it in terms of the body and of memory, in terms of the body's memory. . . . That is why childhood

is the royal road by which we know a country best.
Ultimately, there is no Country but childhood's.
Roland Barthes, "The Light of the Sud-Ouest"

It is in the love of what disappears that I suspect we will find the intertextual kinship of Gide and Barthes as travelers.[8] Barthes's voice in *Empire of Signs* is, as always, a critical, not a fictional, one, although certainly fictive. A pertinent early piece of his writing from *Mythologies*, called "The Writer on Vacation," begins with the following sentence: "Gide was reading Bossuet while going down the Congo." In that essay Barthes offered us, projectively, the key to reading his later book about Japan before he'd ever gone there. He is foregrounding the intertextual knot of reading, writing, and travel that Butor will also explore.

In "The Cabinet of Signs," the last prose piece of *Empire of Signs*, Barthes, the traveler, takes up the following position as spectator:

> I am never besieged by the horizon (and its whiff of dreams); no craving to swell the lungs, to puff up the chest to make sure of my ego, to constitute myself as the assimilating center of the infinite: brought to the evidence of an empty limit, I am limitless without the notion of grandeur, without a metaphysical reference. (107)

Where signification is in retreat for Barthes as reader, Barthes writes in order to valorize his own dispossession in this scene; we might reread the title as empire in the sense of domination or sway that signs have over us. The only means of staring down the emptied nature of language is to reclaim it for writing. To allow for and even thrill in this self that is absent because misrecognized in language, we must stop a moment and recall the morality at work in such finalizing moments. Closure can only be attempted by acknowledging its own metaphysical referents, at least within the structure of narrative.

The later Barthes of *A Lover's Discourse* repeats the same gesture or posture of "nothing-to grasp," of saying no to the desire to seize upon signification. Early in *Empire of Signs* Barthes proposes that representing and analyzing reality are two of the major gestures of Western discourse. In the Orient Barthes seems to be doing his all to jump out of his Orientalist's skin —to make the leap into loss of meaning that he understands as Zen satori, if only to avoid becoming the hieratic, imperial voice of the writer on holiday. No, Japan must mark *his* skin, star him, sear him with its otherness; he will not name it because he cannot name it.[9] To avoid framing Japan, the country, with his Western eyes Barthes will go so far as to claim Japan, the word, as the name of a system. This, then, is his private combinatory out of which he will make the fictive nation where a mirror scene can take place. For if indeed travel writing privileges the staging of the look seen and returned, then Japan works for Barthes as a stage or scene or nation where his own way of wishing-to-see is privileged. To shut his imperial eyes and squint "so as to obliterate all perspective, the way children do,"[10] suggests his urge to jettison the entire problematic of perspective and its predominance in privileged Occidental ways of seeing.

The conventional map as frontispiece that serves to represent visually what the travel narrative will reveal is present in its classic form in Gide's book. We can follow the dotted line going down the Congo River and returning from Lake Chad. But for all its claim to representing the real, the Congo becomes as fictive a space for Gide as Barthes makes of Japan. We might understand Barthes's imperial stance as one taken in the guise of wishing to say something not *about* Japan, but indeed provoked by its reality. Japan then becomes more clearly a catalyst than a site. By 1970, when both *S/Z* and *Empire of Signs* were published, Barthes the structuralist had already disappeared. The study of narrative in *S/Z* and the study of place in *Empire of Signs* reveal a poststructuralist Barthes, a lover of fragments, who finds pleasure "where the garment gapes." It is in the fetishizing of fragmentation, scraps, bits, parts that Japan most delights Barthes. Everywhere he sees collections of fragments—in cooking, gift wrapping, map making, dramaturgy, and home furnishings—that need his reading if not his representation to become system.

There are aspects to the system that are named maternal or feminine. This move to gender Japan becomes necessary and obvious when at the outset the father tongue is made the Occidental. Stemming from this division is the associative link between food and the body and the body in language, permitting Barthes the formulation that food in Japan is a system of writing. This is not the penetrating stylus of Occidental fountain pen to paper, or knife to meat, but the maternal gestures of chopsticks, which transfer food, rather than "pierce" it, with "the same precisely measured care taken in moving a child" (16). In keeping with the feminization of food in Japan is the "virginity of its cooking." Speech is masculine, writing feminine, even when the cook, a "young artist," is male.

Barthes's *impressions de voyage* are named fictive occasions for a *raison d'écrire*, whereas Gide sought out a *raison d'être* for his voyage. Filling with significance the longing for the faraway of a twenty-year-old, Gide finally takes on the voice of the good government or authority, vested in the symbolic of the bureaucracy and the law of the colonial father. The motion for

Barthes is in rather the opposite direction—his is a journey toward mean-inglessness, a movement taken on in willful alienation and disorientation. Barthes's daring play with dangling signifiers I have elsewhere discussed as his final turn toward the body as traversed by language and as the site of language's source and failure.[11] Barthes also reminds us that the look and its re-turn framed in the mirror are lodged historically in the preoedipal—the ma-ternal space—although the dramatic structure of that moment is replete with consequences for future oedipalization. That Barthes can flout the de-pendence on speech and the father's name is a kind of "homotextual" prac-tice of the playful mother's son in which the young artist, a man, enacts the (maternal) script of cooking or writing, as the case may be.

After the traveler flees signification and loses it in the foreign scene, meaning somehow reasserts itself but with the traveler now passively receiv-ing its flash or slash of light, no sooner perceived than erased. This instant Barthes locates, but does not wish to capture, in the fragment called simply "So," in which he examines the "haiku's task," a form both condensed and evaporated. It should come as no surprise that it is in a literary form that Barthes situates what is emblematic for him about Japan. The haiku is de-signed to frustrate the critic in its refusal of commentary except as restate-ment, lost in prose. In the haiku both pleasure and bliss seem available, but both are sent packing by the haiku's form that does not permit the Occiden-tally related gestures of description and definition. What is blissful about the haiku is set by Barthes in the discourse of scopophilia; he says:

> The haiku's flash illuminates, reveals nothing; it is the flash of a photograph one takes very carefully (in the Japanese manner) but having neglected to load the camera with film. Or again, haiku reproduces the designating ges-ture of the child pointing at whatever it is . . . merely saying: *that!* (83)

I would pose the question here of whether Barthes's gaze works otherwise than by way of the fetishistic response to the revelation of femininity, the maternal difference to which he seems to say, "Yes, I know" without the need to add, "but all the same." Have Gide and Barthes, both mothers' sons, each in his own way internalized—we could say introjected—the female body-in-parts? Is this what allows them both to occupy the imperial pose and to drop it at whim? at will? Porter, implicitly reading Said, states what we need to keep in the foreground all the way through these varying scenarios of se-duction, that "it is far from clear that in the hierarchical opposition between Western civilization and Eastern barbarism—the fundamental Orientalist trope—the good is on the European side" (234). Porter goes on to mention the unexpressibility of the homoerotics of Orientalism "as defined by Said." It takes the *jouissant* libidinal economy of a writer like Barthes to arrive at the question of "who is bowing to whom" in the everyday ritual of Japanese life. The emperor of the European fairy tale has absented himself from this empire.

Gide wished to spell out the landscape. Barthes wished to read it—in the semiotics of food, games, urban organization of space, manners, and finally in the Japanese face. In the piece called "The Eyelid," once again Barthes's gaze is clearly and distinctly other-directed: "The eye is flat . . . the pupil, intense, fragile, mobile, intelligent . . . not dramatized by its orbit." He will go on to say "the Japanese face is without moral hierarchy . . . its morphology cannot be read in depth." This is an open critique of the Occidental privileging of the eye as revelatory of depth and as primary source of differentiation and alienation; it reveals a fissure in the French language that calls the Asian eye *bridé* (bridled, constrained). Like the autobiography *Roland Barthes by Roland Barthes*, which he wrote in 1975, *Empire of Signs* is also an illustrated book. Among the effects of Japan reproduced is the newspaper photo where Barthes, the visiting foreign author, is japanned by the conventions of local typography—it is precisely his eyes that are transformed.

What is imprudent and, yes, impudent in Barthes's narrative is his desire not to grasp hold and fix, or photograph, Japan, yet the cabinet of signs as he furnishes it becomes a storehouse of hints, murmurs, treasures of moments where meaning has recurred, returned as the repressed, in order to make sense of this fictive nation. Signs will have their way with Barthes. The house is paradigmatic maternal space, the space of the dreamer, according to Bachelard, and Barthes's last stop is the Japanese house, which is "often deconstructed" because its furnishings are mobile. To bring Barthes's meditation on mobility then back to Gide's thoughts from a rickety *tipoye*: rejecting fixity, staying on the move, Barthes thinks of the European home, the place for a property that is "anything but mobile." Barthes is playing here with *meuble*, the French word designating furniture, usually plural and rarely portable, although by definition subject to being moved. In motion, in Japan, Barthes can rearrange the furniture in his maternal psychic house, undoing maternal bonds—"no site which designates the slightest propriety." It is a cultural house rearranged to suit his whim, the desire of a Westerner to see through the eyes of others, losing the center—the "domiciliary obliteration" that comes with the fact of "No Address"—the way of street plans in Japanese cities.

Travelers Only . . .

I need to digest my previous travels which I haven't yet quite finished . . . so,
in order to travel better, I actually travel less.
Michel Butor, "Travel and Writing"

Gide is involved in the production of documentary film footage of the African scene for the French government. Barthes imagines the camera with no film. To continue the cinematic-photographic-specular dynamic I am exploring, one might describe Michel Butor's fiction titled *Mobile* and subtitled *Study for a Representation of the United States* as a moving picture of America. Published in 1962, it graphically records an imaginary drive across the highways of this nation—with litanies of place names, passages from guidebooks and museum brochures, snatches of conversation, road signs. One can almost hear, like an aeolian harp, what Butor calls the "choir of races" to whom he gives voice in the text. Having dedicated the book "to the memory of Jackson Pollack," Butor places himself in an iconoclastic mode, in both the French scene and the American, and presents a scattering or dissemination of the debris of movement across the continent. How does Butor move? By means of no conveyance we can see, but automobiles are everywhere. Roadside attractions flash before us in a rush to get to "where I have never been," says Butor in an essay called "Travel and Writing." It is he who names this desire "the opposite of nostalgia, for which French has no name." In this essay, which postdates *Mobile* by ten years, Butor says about himself and writers more generally: "I travel in order to write. . . . All our writers set out on the road. . . . They travel in order to write, they travel while writing, because, for them, travel *is* writing."[12] A brief glance at the titles of some of his works reveal someone moved by questions of place, setting, geography: *The Genius of Place, The Suburbs from Dawn to Dusk, Letters from the Antipodes, Passage to Milan, Niagara, Traveler at the Wheel.* And, to continue the intertextual braid here, an early travel essay on Cordova by Butor is dedicated to Roland Barthes. In an early critical essay of Barthes's called "Literature and Discontinuity," he came to Butor's defense in what he called the "querelle de *Mobile.*" What was this literary quarrel about? Butor's text could not readily be placed, fixed in the hall of genres; it could not be seized or grasped. We are not surprised to find Barthes at Butor's side.

Mobile is multiply situated as a fictional text, with as many narratives as the changes in typography will allow. It is a voyage through and by repetition—an onomasticon, Barthes calls it—of the vast topography of America, where to traverse the country is to name it. Unlike Japan, here is a landscape full of signs, "a continent that received but alarmed us," says one of Butor's voices (95). An abundance of places but a scarcity of names—repetition will domesticate its wild(er)ness, and names that ring with the history of the European-Americans will soothe the alienation of the coastal plains and mountains: New France, New England, New Scotland, New Brunswick, New York, the list goes on.

Butor's narrative asks, "Am I not still, or rather am I not already in Europe, since I am in Milford?" This is *the* question of his text—Butor's European eye surveying the American scene read as an America settled by Europeans. Where are we to stand in order to feel both connected with and disconnected from the United States as ultimately a representation of nation that will conflate difference by trying to erase it, all the while advertising its diversity?

In a two-page chapter called "Welcome to Connecticut" ("Bienvenue au Connecticut") we find the stated motive and device of this narrative:

> In the village of Shelburne, Vermont, a number of old, condemned houses
> have been rebuilt, thus comprising a curious museum. Perhaps their most re-
> markable feature is a collection of patchwork quilts. This "Mobile" is com-
> posed somewhat like a quilt. (28)

How is it like a quilt, and what elements motivate the patchwork? Butor goes to the arbitrariness of the alphabetical to structure his narrative, but if we are readers of the English-language text we can't even see that, because only in French does North Dakota come before Delaware.

If the alphabet and the repetition of place names are among the structuring principles of this narrative patchwork, then, as in any traditional quilt, color is another. And it is in the narrative uses made of color that we will be able to place Butor in relation to the question of the look and what he sees in the United States. The patchwork of colors will draw from the repertory of American flowers, birds, and minerals, as well as American automobiles (in 1962 there were still many two-tone vehicles on the road), the 28 flavors of Howard Johnson's ice creams (when orange roofs did not compete for visual attention with golden arches and more), the notation of daylight or darkness, but more fundamentally and insistently, the racial color lines Butor confronts on his journey. This is, after all, a study for a representation of a far-from-desegregated United States. The English-language text is appropriately marked by this history, as the French word *noir* is almost everywhere translated as *Negro*, not *black*, and certainly not *African-American*, although

Butor's naming of white Americans as European Americans evokes an equally neologistic renaming.

A narrative we can piece together as it appears in the patchwork reads like a chorus commenting on the romance of a "Negro man" and a woman first described as "blue"—"to see her you wouldn't think she was black. . . . But she is black." A black woman's body will be inscribed across the text: from her "torrent of black hair" to the "blackness inside her womb" that delivers "another new black baby." As if to leave narrative time for the process of gestation, between the womb and the baby, Butor moves from the seductive text of the singular and essentialized woman of color to the social text of plural and differentiated but still anonymous black men: waiters, porters, taxi drivers, drunks, preachers; punctuating this parade are the signs in the South that read "for whites only"—repeated until Butor signals it " . . . only."

The racial tension is dialectically anchored in the whites' voices that say, "[We] preferred to import false natives, even more out of place than we whites . . . to protect us from Indian eyes we stretched this black screen" (103). The driving demand for racial distinction, that is to say, separation, is underscored for Butor in the American capital, with "its monuments of a dazzling whiteness." The cultural repression of blackness is played out in the European-American collective nightmare where blackness has taken hold of white imaginations. The images are the predictable ones of rape; both white women and men dream this dream. Later in this narrative the eye that beheld the black man and woman is caught seeing. This voice says, "I tell you those Negroes are laughing at us! . . . Black, they undress all our daughters with a nostalgic glance." Whose nostalgia insists on looking backward when to look forward risks having to rewrite the nightmare or even break from it?

To represent the official ideology of racism in the United States, Butor offers us patches in the quilt from Benjamin Franklin, Andrew Carnegie, and Thomas Jefferson. Interspersed with Jefferson's writings on slavery are statements about the architectural features and details of Monticello, such as the fact that "Thomas Jefferson at Monticello situated the slaves' quarters under the southern terrace, so that their comings and goings would not spoil the view" (301).

If the African-Americans in the United States of *Mobile* are meant to screen out Native American eyes, then we want to know what Butor sees when he tries to look behind this screen—only a history of massacres, a "path of tears." Butor includes an interpolated narrative of texts and testimonies from the Native Church of America, to which the peyote ritual is sacred and which is indulged across tribal lines both as part of a system of belief and as an effort toward unity in response to displacement and brutality. The only other voice of the text that aims to process the history of confrontation between European and Native Americans comes in the form of citations from the prospectus and press releases for Freedomland, a long defunct amusement park once meant to occupy the East Coast family entertainment space of Disneyland; for example:

> The duplicated Kansas farm area has a full-size corn field. . . . Chicago will be recreated as it was in 1871, the year of the great fire. The city will burn down every 20 minutes. . . . You may be one of those who help fight the fire to a standstill. (191)

> Roadways, walkways, shade areas, rain shelters and rest rooms are designed to accommodate 32,000 persons at any given time. . . . In Freedomland's Northwest, dummy Indians, concealed in the bushes fire harmless bullets and shoot teleguided arrows. (194)

If this is effectively a roadside rest area that can accommodate thirty-two thousand, then surely the wilderness has been tamed and the history of genocide and racism has been revised by captains of culture and reproduced and represented as entertainment.

What Butor's narrative seems to offer is the cinematic effect of matching eyeline glances—Indians seeing whites through the mystified haze of peyote dream; blacks seeing whites seeing them as bearers of projected fears; and whites returning their gaze, but with a blinkered glance, shutting out the periphery. The patchwork makes a pattern of randomness where eyes are trying to shut out the reciprocal gaze of those effaced. We can clearly see whites seeing blacks and blinding themselves to Indians; our only view of how the disenfranchised see the whites in return comes through the narrative eyes and voice of a foreigner to whom the contrasts are blindingly clear. This is a racial history rewritten for mass consumption. Butor in the United States seems to have been seduced in spite of himself.

Each of these travelers has entered into a rewriting of interracial scripts encountered at the crossroads. Yet we can distinguish, I think, the modes of desire that have operated in each case. The delight taken in the permeability of boundaries is what vacillates, shimmering before the gaze of our three travelers: Gide, in Africa, yearns to forge a connection to his hosts that would recognize his alienness, his whiteness, his Europeanness, and nevertheless allow him passage, even welcome him over the threshhold of difference in a kind of oblivion, a willful forgetting of difference, such as that which occurs between Gide and his baby/potto where the boundaries between animal and human affectively disappear. The longing is for the others to be seduced by him as he was already seduced by them years before when he first dreamed "the Congo." This would effectively beckon him onto a ground where the lines of authority might be more likely to blur than when he rides above. For Barthes, the signposts of Japan and their writerliness, their unreadability lead him to long for just the effect produced in the Japanese newspaper where he becomes an other. For him, becoming the other and losing the self seem the ultimate kind of seizure by elsewhere, not seizing it, but rather submitting to a jubilating annihilation by difference. In this mode of seduction, maps are understood as safety nets that will not function in the empire of signs that is Japan, and Barthes delights in playing without a net here. From Gide to Barthes there is a movement toward surrender to the new, the unknown. For Butor, as I read him, there is a mingling into and with the alien nation that is the United States, but there are the landmarks of familiarity borrowed through those he calls the European Americans. These landmarks make it possible and even necessary that his wanderings all signal his distance, his inability to lose himself, as Barthes may do, or even to be taken in, as Gide wishes. One never has the sense, reading Butor's journeying narrative, that there are people in the places he passes through; there are only figures in the native ground, all of whom leave him squinting, trying to blur the edges of a distance, whether near, middle, or far. Butor, like Baudrillard after him, appears seduced by images and tableaux seen through windows— a protected voyeurism—while Barthes and Gide risk moving to less mediated seductions through forms of practice. Elsewhere by choice, privilege, luxury, they try to make palpable by touching, by drawing on a broader sensory palate than Butor's predominantly visual reception and narration.

Voodoo and Fetish

Zora Neale Hurston's *Tell My Horse* and Mary Kingsley's *Travels in West Africa*

SHE: I may not even get married again. I might become an adventuress.
HE: I can just see you starting for China on a 26-foot sailboat.
SHE: You're thinking of an adventurer, dear. An adventuress never
goes on anything under 300 feet with a crew of 80.
Preston Sturges, *The Palm Beach Story*

What are the gendered optics of imperial seeing? We have presumed that the one in the royal garb was male, and the child ungendered—that is, by default male. But what takes place when the imperial subject is feminine, a woman? In a colonial or postcolonial context we might begin to see how a model of seduction, rather than conquest, allows for a more gender-inflected specification of power relations in an alien scene. As Mary Louise Pratt so pointedly puts it in *Imperial Eyes*, "As a woman she is not to see but be seen, or at least she is not to be seen seeing" (104). With Zora Neale Hurston and Mary Kingsley we see differentially refracted the scenario of identity and authority. What I have earlier referred to as the traveler's sublime—that balance between wonder and its affectively polarized relation to shame—is further sketched out in these two women's texts. It will become apparent how some aspects of this balancing act turn out when the reporting imperial subject is an agent who is minoritized back home among the colonizers. I think that to pose the gender questions around these two women who are "seen seeing" will begin to bring this particular dynamic between wonder and shame into

35

clearer focus. Shifting the emphasis onto female exemplars of the traveler will cast some rather different shadows and light onto this affective realm. Pratt reads the "capitalist vanguardists" who "often relied on the goal-directed, linear emplotment of conquest narrative" as opposed to what she describes in two early women's travel narratives "emplotted in a centripetal fashion around places of residence" (157). While my two women travelers spend a great deal of their time in the outdoors, that is, not at home, what I am suggesting by seduction as against conquest relies on a dynamic that is never quite resolved into secured forms of domination, even though it may be grounded in a discourse of mastery. With our earlier guides, I asked readers to keep in mind the complex familial, but undeclared, baggage of the seeing-men in question. Now we want to watch the daughters as they declare themselves in terms of kinship and affiliation. If women are not to be seen seeing, then we can also suppose that the experiences of wonder and shame are encoded through the script of gendered identities. This is made obvious when we remark that one of Kingsley's opening gestures is to "become" a boy; Hurston, en route, passes very self-consciously from girl to woman.

Hurston's *Tell My Horse* and Kingsley's *Travels in West Africa* are two exemplary texts of the contact zones: they narrate travel and research and they constitute anthropological, ethnographic, and personal documents. My interest in juxtaposing them is a tendentious framing of their differences. Kingsley is British and white, the self-educated daughter of George Henry Kingsley, a prominent naturalist and travel writer of the early nineteenth century; by the time she is thirty years old, both her parents have died. Kingsley has left England only once for a brief trip to Paris. Now, no longer the domesticated good daughter, she sets out for a territory her father had not already explored, West Africa. Hurston is an early student of Franz Boas at Columbia, and the first African-American woman trained as an anthropologist; having already made the journey from Florida to New York City (which I read as an immigrant journey in part 3), she later takes her training to the Caribbean to study folktales. The cultural confrontations that emerge expose the self as explorer and traveler, on the one hand, and the self as researcher who takes up scientific discourse to investigate local religious practices, on the other. In Kingsley's and Hurston's work with fetish and voodoo, respectively, their own accumulating knowledge of spiritual practices will force them to confront the paradigms of their scientific white "fathers." They will come face to face with what it means to be women who are charting in-

tellectual ground among African and African-Caribbean peoples and mapping new forms of wisdom.

Some other questions present themselves here: (1) To what extent does
gender enter into their own representations of self? (2) How does the question of race become foregrounded? (3) How can we read the tension between
the writer as traveler and as researcher? And finally, (4) how do they each
manage the uneasy mix of scientific discourse and religious practice, especially practices that their readers may very well be unprepared to take seriously? In both Hurston's and Kingsley's texts the discovery of information
about these religious practices is as if held in reserve, even while it is clearly
what compels them the most in their movement through these new worlds.

Kingsley and Hurston both set out resolutely eager to confront differences that will, in each of their cases, bring them into closer contact with
that inquiring self who set out. While there is already a tradition of intrepid
women travelers by the time Kingsley heads for Africa in 1893, still the response she finds among her acquaintances as she prepares to go is full of
caution and warning about disease and discomfort. These are the still imperial and imperious British caught in that racialized dynamic of patronizing
and fearing their colonial subjects. The political and social climate for
Hurston's voyage out, by contrast, fixes her as a somewhat displaced repre-
sentative of American imperialism in 1936 in Jamaica and Haiti. We might
measure that contrast discursively and strategically by listening to each of
these writers as they work their way into their written travels; listen here also
for the voice of the woman authorizing herself to go out among those unlike
herself and bring news to the world left behind. Kingsley, no feminist, is, in
fact, quick to repudiate the label of "new woman" that the British press at-
taches to her immediately upon her first return from West Africa. Here is
how she stages her venture there:

> It was in 1893 that, for the first time in my life, I found myself in possession
> of five or six months which were not heavily forestalled, and feeling like a boy
> with a new half-crown, I lay about in my mind . . . as to what to do with
> them. "Go and learn your tropics," said Science. (1)

While claiming ignorance about the tropics, Kingsley nevertheless had a
wide circle of informants to whom she went for advice, even ill-considered
advice, in this period when travel to Africa was far from uncommon, although misinformation was widespread. We come to understand some of
the paradoxes at the heart of colonialism as we make our way through the
Travels, for Kingsley herself might be said to embody the most receptive kind

of white traveler and ethnographer, even as she speaks the comfortable racism, nativism, and exoticism of the late nineteenth century. While she may grant complexity to the African systems of belief she encounters, still she speaks of her companions as children, ignorant of other worlds. She never willingly becomes a child in their world, although her own ignorance will come to the fore in many instances. Pratt remarks that

> It is not only Kingsley's gender that enables her to forfeit [certainty and control] in her writing. Besides being a woman, she is a child in Africa as well, at play in the ego-centered non-Oedipean world. . . . Africa is her mother, and down those shimmering, dark and slimy pathways, Kingsley is getting herself born. (216)

Kingsley's efforts at self-authorization are always ambivalent. The balancing act is very demanding; Pratt notes that Kingsley, an "imperialist but passionate anti-colonialist . . . argued for the possibility of economic expansion without domination and exploitation" (215). Her politics of gender were as conflictual as her position on imperialism. Where Pratt images Kingsley as queenly, noting her alliance with the "project of empire," Sara Mills documents the clashing of genders in Kingsley's discursive practices.[1] Mills notes that the *Travels*, "rather than being a 'feminine' text or a 'colonial' text or for that matter a 'feminist' text, seems to be caught up in the contradictory clashes of these discourses one with another" (174). My aim is to examine how the clashing is inflected by Kingsley's thoroughly ambivalent but comfortable vacillation between her self-representation as female at some moments and male at others; Mills does much to demonstrate this very clear vacillation. The boy Kingsley had taken herself to be upon setting out for Africa is repeatedly evoked also as a man and is addressed as "sir" by many Africans she encounters. Yet she reminds us insistently of her femininity, especially in matters of dress and decorum.

Notice how different Hurston's voice is, and note also her lack of ambivalence in judging her hosts even early on in her travels. Also notable is Hurston's feminist consciousness; the following comes in a chapter called "Women in the Caribbean":

> It is a curious thing to be a woman in the Caribbean after you have been a woman in these United States. . . . The majority of men in all the states are pretty much agreed that just for being born a girl-baby you ought to have laws and privileges and pay and perquisites. And so far as being allowed to voice opinions is concerned, why they consider that you are born with the law in your mouth , and that is not a bad arrangement either. . . . But now Miss America, World's champion woman, you take your promenading self

down into the cobalt waters of the Caribbean and see what happens. . . . It is
not that they try to put you in your place, no. They consider that you never
had any. (75–76)

Hurston goes on to say, in her chapter on the place of sexuality, romance,
and marriage in women's lives in the Caribbean, that "this sex superiority is
further complicated by class and color ratings."

While Kingsley writes just as the suffragette struggle is about to become
militant and yet refuses any ties to the battles of women, Hurston writes in
the rather afeminist 1930s and yet allies her perspective to one that has informed her sense of herself in her world, the United States; this cultural baggage will serve her well in her travels in Jamaica and Haiti.

Kingsley and Hurston are clear about the metaphysical aspects of their re-
spective searches; it is not treasure, objects, or evidence that they seek,
rather, they mean to understand ways of life. Kingsley in an early chapter of
her book explains that "by fetish I always mean the governing but underly-
ing ideas of a man's life" (68); Hurston in the opening of the third section of
Tell My Horse clarifies thus: "[Voodoo] is the old, old mysticism of the world
in African terms. Voodoo is a religion of creation and life. It is the worship of
the sun, the water and other natural forces, but the symbolism is no better
understood than that of other religions and consequently is taken too literally" (137). As the narratives progress the travelers recreate for us, their readers, what must have come upon them slowly: that these forms of understanding and worship resonate deeply for them. With Hurston we are more
likely to be able to imagine the force of a discovery of continuity with
African-American religions; with Kingsley we may be more apt to doubt and
wonder how she could find herself represented in these belief systems so
other to her.

What occurs for both women is bound up with one of the conventions of
travel narrative and the experience it recounts and recasts; the intermingling
of the natural and the social, and in this case, the natural with the spiritual,
is best captured in another of Pratt's hyphenated figures, the-monarch-of-
all-I-survey scene. When moving about in nature Kingsley is eloquent and
even rapt in her descriptions; however, she becomes both less articulate and
more reserved when she tries to make the shift to the sociospiritual, as in the
following tale:

> To my taste there is nothing so fascinating as spending a night out in an
> African forest. . . . [I]t takes the conceit out of you pretty thoroughly during

the days you spend stupidly stumbling about among your new sur-roundings. . . . As it is with the forest, so it is with the minds of the natives. Unless you live alone among the natives, you never get to know them; if you do this you gradually get a light into the true state of their mind-forest. At first you see nothing but a confused stupidity and crime; but when you get to see—well! as in the other forest,—you see things worth seeing. But it is beyond me to describe the process. (102–3)

The privileging of darkness as a path toward knowledge, and the forest rather than the promontory as the location of insight, firmly places Kingsley in a discourse that is other than the hegemonic "monarch-of-all-I-survey" pose of men's imperial eyes. Kingsley is adamant in her love of darkness, swamps, and forests as that which seduces her in West Africa; her fearlessness retrospectively feminizes the Conradian fears of the heart of darkness. No wonder she takes herself to be manly over and over again; yet it is as a woman that she need not fear the "dark continent." Once more, Pratt cuts to the chase: "She seeks to separate mastery from domination, knowledge from control," giving a gendered spin to the way in which "Africa is [Kingsley's] mother" (216). Some of what constitutes Kingsley's "masterful comic irreverence" is her play with the already well established tropes of gendering this continent.

Hurston encounters silences, hesitations, and secrecy from her hosts when she explains her interest in studying voodoo, especially among those upper-class Haitians who go to great lengths to separate themselves from the practices of the peasants, even though they leave gifts of food for some of the voodoo gods. But Hurston makes the effort to bring her own mystification to light, as in her chapter on zombies; the woman mentioned in this passage had been institutionalized for behavior that was inexplicable by medical paradigms, but readily so by religious ones:

What is the whole truth and nothing else but the truth about Zombies? I do not know, but I know that I saw the broken remanant [sic], relic, or refuse of Felicia Felix-Mentor in a hospital yard.

Here in the shadow of the Empire State Building, death and the graveyard are final. It is such a positive end that we use it as a measure of nothingness and eternity. We have the quick and the dead. But in Haiti there is the quick, the dead, and then there are Zombies. (189)

Hurston's fearlessness is a match for Kingsley's. It is this quality that enables her inquiry into voodoo and gains her access to several layers of extremely class-stratified Haitian society. However, this same characteristic fuels her sense of mastery and pleasure in the technology of mastering light: "I had the rare opportunity to see and touch an authentic case. . . . and then, I did what no one else had ever done, I photographed *it*" (191, my emphasis). Hurston avows that it was the "strong sunlight" that convinced even her of her doubts. Both imperious in her neutering of Felicia Felix-Mentor into "it" and yet standing close enough to touch her and listening "to the broken noises in its throat," Hurston straddles the scientificity of the documentary photoethnographer and the eager-beaver foreign researcher who tries to probe secrets and also let them be—she seems to remind herself and her readers: "These secret societies are secret" (206). This woman whom Hurston is permitted to photograph is only gradually given to us in greater detail, as if we were first to be caught by her image and only then allowed to enter into her story of twenty-nine years of life unaccounted for that seem to have left her in a death-in-life state of being.

Where Kingsley will learn trade English in order to be able to communicate with many different groups in West Africa, Hurston works conscientiously on her creole. For all their difference from the indigenous peoples they have come to learn from and about, Hurston, a black woman alone in a patriarchal culture, and Kingsley, a white woman alone in what she calls a tribal culture, are both free from the local forms of stratification, whether among classes or races or peoples. They each gain rather easy access to and movement within the cultures they encounter. Their potential associations with the colonial cultures in place are displaced; in Kingsley's case she is white, but she is neither a missionary nor a missionary's wife, nor is she French; in Hurston's case she is neither British nor French, but a black American woman, making her an object of interest to the upper-class Haitians and Jamaicans who, despite their own sexism, as noted by Hurston above, take her seriously as an intellectual, and a black intellectual woman at that. As an intellectual, Hurston's observations are not limited to her field of training in anthropology; much of the second section of the three that constitute this book takes up the political history of Haiti, "the black republic." And we find her incisive and even prescient when she says, "In the past, as now, Haiti's curse has been her politicians" (95). The struggle to rule had been complicated by Haitian class and color consciousness between mulattoes and blacks. Corruption and wealth, with European ways as the model to be emulated, had left the country further impoverished. Repeatedly, generations of young men had been killed off, men who represented the lost hope of stabilizing the government, which Hurston described as an "elected monarchy"

(96). Hurston had particularly sharp words for those she called the "talking patriots." In the chapter titled "The Next Hundred Years," she makes some pointed comparisons to the politics of race in the United States and warns the Haitians against the mistakes of African-Americans who have listened to "the empty wind bags who have done so much to nullify opportunity among the American Negroes" (97). Empty boasts of progress for the race have haunted black politicians since the Reconstruction period (the "tongue-and-lung era"), she avows, without increasing economic opportunity for blacks. Cautioning Haitians to search for realism in politics, she offers this lesson: "But America has produced a generation of Negroes who are impatient of the orators. They want to hear about more jobs and houses and meat on the table. . . . Our heroes are no longer talkers but doers" (97).

Robert Hemenway, Hurston's first biographer, notes that the chapter of Hurston's *Dust Tracks on a Road: An Autobiography* called "My People, My People" was written during Hurston's travels in the Caribbean in the mid-1930s. In this chapter Hurston works on the contradiction that all blacks must live—that they represent themselves as the privileged among God's creatures and simultaneously the most downtrodden. This contradiction is rehearsed whenever internal differences among African-Americans cannot be reconciled or are rendered shameful: "If it was so honorable and glorious to be black, why was it the yellow-skinned among us had so much prestige?" (226). Now *Dust Tracks* is not generally read for its attention to the facts of Hurston's life, but we might take these observations as particularly illuminating when we consider that the even greater stratification among blacks in Haiti gave Hurston the room to think about her situation in the United States from a new vantage point, one framed as in the closing of this chapter in the autobiography:

> I maintain that I have been a Negro three times—a Negro baby, a Negro girl and a Negro woman. . . . There is no *The Negro* here. Our lives are so diversified, internal attitudes so varied, appearances and capabilities so different, that there is no possible classification so catholic that it will cover us all, except My people! My people! (237)

This call resonates with a phrase that closes many chapters of *Tell My Horse*, "Ah, Bo Bo." In this phatic sigh we can hear resignation and sympathy for a situation in which Hurston recognizes in the most profound sense an identity with the Haitians and their own continued submission to various forms of ignorance and oppression from without and within. We read Hurston's critiques of internalized racism with a degree of acceptance because she speaks so clearly as an African-American herself. Many if not most contemporary readers of Hurston stop and note how idiosyncratically Hurston frames her own blackness at times in her published work, particularly her journalism of the 1940s, in which she claims a problematic transcendence of cultural and racial difference in favor of an individualism that resonates in the 1990s with black neoconservative discourse of the 1980s.

What a different effect is produced by Kingsley's imperial distance from the "minds of the natives." Yet Kingsley, too, finds in West Africa, where she is reborn, and South Africa, where she dies, a form of recognition and self-recognition that we may find hard to imagine or to accept as easily, simply because she is a white woman traveling in a colonial scene with all the implicit protection and privilege that can afford her. However, after thirty years in England, captive to tales of her father's exploits and her mother's hypochondria, Kingsley goes actively seeking danger in the bush and on the rivers of West Africa. We can read this most clearly in her changing notions about one particular group, the Fans, who live nomadically in the French Congo. Downplaying her motivations and reminding us of her self-set tasks, "to search for fish and fetish," she explains:

> My reasons for going to this wildest and most dangerous part of the West
> African regions were perfectly simple and reasonable. I had not found many
> fish in the Oil Rivers. . . . [T]his river [the Ogowe] harbours and protects a
> set of notoriously savage tribes, chief among which are the Fans . . . a bright,
> active energetic sort of African, who by their pugnacious and predatory con-
> duct do much to make one cease to regret and deplore the sloth and lethargy
> of the West Coast tribes; but of Fans I will speak by and by. (104–5)

That "by and by" only comes some two hundred pages later when she speaks of "my friends, the Fans," and about her "partiality for this tribe" (328). After a physical description of members of the group, Kingsley comes to their "mental characteristics":

> The Fan is full of fire, temper, intelligence and go; very teachable, rather
> difficult to manage, quick to take offense, and utterly indifferent to human
> life. I ought to say that other people, who should know him better than I, say
> he is a treacherous, thievish, murderous cannibal. I never found him treach-
> erous; but then I never trusted him. (329)

A passage such as this one exemplifies the all-too-comfortable epistemology of the ethnographic present that singularizes, essentializes, and dehistoricizes with impunity. In one of the odder juxtapositions in Kingsley's narrative, she moves from this description of her experience of the Fans to a recollection of her youthful reading of literature and her love for tales of mountaineering, especially moments of supreme danger on the edge of a precipice. The recollected safety of her easy chair at home leads her to realize with some surprise that she, in fact, feels safe among these people because her ideas of them are not shaped by what she hears but rather by what she actually finds in their midst. Her drive to encounter danger and not lose face in its sight has brought her down from the precipice into the rivers and swamps.

Mills notes that the "character of most travel narrators is their ability to handle difficult situations and not lose face" (142). This discussion in Mills's "gendered colonial discourse study" is closely tied to the tradition of the westerner in disguise "going native." Kingsley does not go native in the usual sense, for she does not ever give up conventional British feminine attire; she would sooner make a caricature of herself in muddied skirts than to adopt more appropriate clothing for walking about in swamps and rivers. Even years later during her extremely successful but brief career as a lecturer on Africa, she is described by one of her biographers as dressed "in a style at least thirty years out of date."[2] This she used to great effect on her audience at Cheltenham Ladies' College when she "launched into her talk with, 'I expect I remind you of your maiden aunt'—a pause for effect—'long since deceased' " (258). Kingsley maintains her irony along with her self-respect, "the mainspring of your power in West Africa" (330), and refuses to tell her readers any "cannibal stories" of the Fans, as other travelers have (332). Hearsay and paternalistic speculations give way to experience whenever Kingsley finds that her reality of West Africa challenges the dominant view of the colonizers. She is able to silence her Cambridge intellectual inheritance in view of practices that appear to dominate the facts of everyday life; these range from linguistic oddities to food gathering and preparation to rituals surrounding the life cycle—birth, a refusal of death, and the belief in different kinds of souls. Yet however much Kingsley may be able to grant the people she visits their own differences and integrity, such understanding is always set in a framework that the nineteenth-century European traveler cannot do without, one that constantly must reaffirm her own culture's superiority. A traveler as apt as Kingsley reminds her readers nevertheless that her position may still be far from fully informed. What strikes me as unusual about Kingsley as an observer and ethnographer is her ability to travel dialectically between presuppositions regarding African customs and beliefs and what she comes to understand is more complex than any predigested accounts: "The truth is the study of natural phenomena knocks the bottom out of any man's conceit if it is done honestly and not by selecting only those facts that fit in with his preconceived or ingrafted notions" (441). This particular piece of acquired wisdom Kingsley offers just as she begins her five chapters on fetish, which she says she has saved "owing to its unfitness to be allowed to stray about in the rest of the text" (73), almost like those souls who need to be properly attended to even after death. Kingsley recognizes that fetish touches not only on beliefs about the seen and the unseen, but also on African concepts of law, inheritance, marriage, and authority. All the while giving these beliefs their due, Kingsley can still readily efface differences, as we see in the following: "In all cases I feel sure the African's intelligence is far ahead of his language" (504). She offers two examples to illustrate this inadequacy of language, which she takes to belong to African but not European languages. There are the misnamed Bubis, inhabitants of Fernando Po, "undoubtedly a very early African race. . . . They never wear clothes unless compelled to, and their language depends so much on gesture that they cannot talk in it to each other in the dark" (439). Kingsley moves constantly from specificity into essences; while insisting that there is "nothing really 'childlike' in their [African] form of mind at all," still she will find them "deficient" as compared to Europeans "in all mechanical arts."

Another moment of speculating on Africans and their relation to language brings the discussion back again to the questions of gender—our questions—and to Kingsley's own vexed relations to the disparities between sex and gender:

> [The African's] foolishness in not having a male and female gender in his language amounts to a nuisance, and has nearly, at one fell swoop, turned my hairs gray, and brought them in sorrow to the grave. For example, I am a most ladylike old person and yet get constantly called "Sir." I hasten to assure you I never even wear masculine collar and tie, and as for encasing the more earthward extremities of my anatomy in—you know what I mean—well, I would rather perish on a public scaffold. (502)

We might recall Gide being promoted from "Sir" to "Governor" and finally to "Government" by his traveling companion–servants, just as Kingsley is rendered masculine—"Sir"—as if they each somehow surpassed the expectations the indigenous people had constructed of Europeans, whether men or women. The impatience Kingsley generally holds in check in reaction to African practices becomes unfastened here in the face of what we might call gender anxiety of a perfectly Victorian stripe—the unmentionability of body parts, legs, and the pants that cover them has Kingsley doing a fine imitation of a swooning female of her own native time and place. I daresay there is plenty of irony here, given Kingsley's wit, which rarely leaves her as she travels. Still her "hastening to assure" *us* of her properly feminine attire in situations that must make her uncomfortable, if not ridiculous, has a ring of urgency about it—the urgency of a woman who knows there are women challenging authority about proper female behavior and who wants to dissociate herself from them. We might say that Kingsley's seven years of life after the death of her parents read as a rather sharply etched challenge to authority, given her activities and subsequent fame. And to her, the appurtenances of the new woman with her bloomers, bicycles, and cigarettes strike Kingsley as foolishness on the part of English women. She has bigger things on her mind, even in her falsely modest quest for fish and fetish. Kingsley is too sharp not to realize that the figure she has become, mediated by the press, indeed, is nevertheless the daring "boy" she had set out to be when she moved from her easy chair in Cambridge into an African canoe.

When she discusses the judicial function of secret societies, which are sex segregated, Kingsley notes in passing that women—and she does not specify African women, as she might have—"are notably deficient in real reverence for authority, as is demonstrated by the way they continually treat that of their husbands" (526). The obliqueness of her critique of marriage is an ironic rhetorical strategy we have seen her use before in other contexts; by first acknowledging "deficiency" (in women), she can then go on to point out their challenge to their husbands, for which I would suggest she has evident admiration and respect. Kingsley adds her voice to the chorus of late-nineteenth-century discourse on the lack in women's relation to and respect for authority. Yet we must read her contribution to this discourse as one haunted by an all-too-apparent ambivalence toward the training of femininity.

Hurston's similarly characteristic irreverence for certain forms of authority and orthodoxy is what allows her to become the observer not only of Caribbean but also of North American politics and religion. The contradictions we hear in the voices of Hurston and Kingsley may be not only inevitable cultural contradictions, but also the price each must pay as a woman who risks her hard-won education in order to voyage out and test the assumptions on which her learning was based. By not bending so easily to authority, because they are not identified wholly with it as male subjects might need to be, they gain access to insights and wisdom that allow them both to see and to deny their own kinship with those among whom they travel and whom they must regard as other. Clearly Kingsley's investment in the otherness of the "natives" is greater than Hurston's. In fact, Hurston is searching for forms of continuity and kinship. Yet she, too, must, when she can, caution her Haitian and Jamaican brothers and sisters with lessons she feels African-Americans had already learned. Where Hurston's view might seek to minimize the historical and cultural distances between the Caribbean and the United States in terms of racial and political identities, we read Kingsley as inevitably seeking to clarify the differences between Africans and Europeans. The denial of coevalness, contemporaneity, and simultaneity that Johannes Fabian has read at the core of anthropological discourse may haunt Hurston and Kingsley equally, but I would suggest that while Hurston is the itinerant ethnographer who comes to collect and return home, her eyes fixed on the future, in a mode of "forelonging," Kingsley leaves home in search of natural phenomena and finds some part of herself that keeps taking her backward—the nostalgic undertow in setting out for the new, even as it leads her to her death in Africa.

I have suggested that there is a tension to be read in both these writers around the issue of self-authorization. And the discursive site of this tension can be found in the ambivalent rhetoric of the traveler who is also a researcher—on a scientific quest, if not a conquest. Now Hurston and Kingsley both titrate for their readers the knowledge they gather about local practices and beliefs—voodoo in the Caribbean, fetish in West Africa. The delicate balance they are each aiming for works not only to preserve their positions as experts in the field but also to slowly win over the potentially skeptical (white) American and British readers. We have read passages where it is evident that they are engaged in nondefensive assertion of the systematicity of their hosts's practices. Simultaneously they avow their own positions as convinced observers, leaving their readers to wonder about that which has been so cautiously revealed as well as that which remains unrevealed. What renders both these texts ultimately so powerful rhetorically is that we readers have indeed seen these women seeing, and have come to know their knowing; if we aim still to retain some distance from the scientificity of voodoo and fetish, Hurston and Kingsley leave us with the realization that they have gone where we have not followed.

~

Heartless Travelers

If by the early twentieth century the exotic, the elsewhere, was already exhausted, by midcentury, after 1945, the contact zones were understood to be quite thoroughly contaminated ideologically but with us irrevocably. The three travelers we are following in this section are highly aware of their intrusion into foreign spaces, and like the earlier group they trespass willfully, transgressing cultural codes, crossing geopolitical boundaries with their identities masked, coded, or in question in a variety of ways. They are all mistaken for others of their "kind," as determined by those who meet them at the intersections of language, custom, skin. The temporality they each inhabit is postimperial. Emperors have been unmasked repeatedly; leaders have been publicly shamed for alliances marked by convenience, or in the false hope of deterring the forces of fascism. Here we have seduction without sentimentality.

As with the earlier group of travelers to Africa, Asia, North America, and the Caribbean, these travelers have likewise been preceded by the books they have each read about places they have never been before. Elias Canetti will dissimulate and say he is from London in order to gloss over his continental European roots and branches. Caryl Phillips, Caribbean-born black Briton, will be continually taken "for" a black American in Europe. Tété-Michel Kpomassie, who is Togolese, will be mistaken for a Frenchman because the European language he speaks belies his Africanness among his northern hosts. It is Canetti who says that "good travellers are heartless"; let me suggest that heartlessness is the very condition of postmodern travel.

~

Among Camels and Women

Elias Canetti's *Voices of Marrakesh*

A marvelously luminous, viscid substance is left behind in me,
defying words. Is it the language I did not understand there, and
that must now gradually find its translation in me?
Canetti

The objective notion of the anatomical incompleteness of the pyramidal
system and likewise the presence of certain humoral residues of the
maternal organism confirm the view I have formulated as the
fact of a real *specific prematurity of birth* in man.
Lacan

"Good travellers are heartless," says Elias Canetti, recounting his visit to Morocco and providing an axiom for this portion of my exploration of relations to elsewhere. If, as has been suggested, knowledge, "to avoid the circularity of ideology, must read the processes of differentiation, not look for differences,"[1] then let us take the case of Canetti in Marrakesh as an instance where languages of many sorts are summoned to capture the writer's losing and finding the self in the foreign scene. Because Canetti shares no native language with the locals and shares only a foreign language, French, with those who have made some sort of identificatory accommodation with the colonizers, the languages he will resort to in order to satisfy his need for meaning are those of late-nineteenth-century discourses on race, physiognomy, and national characteristics. His comfortable reliance on these forms of received biologistic wisdom mark Canetti's formation as Eurocultural polymathic male.[2]

The first prose piece in Canetti's *Voices of Marrakesh* is called "Encounters with Camels." While many might imagine camels not to be particularly amenable to the urge to anthropomorphize, Canetti finds no problem:

> I tell you they had faces. They all looked alike and yet they were so different.
> They put one in mind of elderly English ladies taking tea together. . . . We
> were proud of having come across this caravan that no one had told us
> about, and we counted 107 camels. (11)

We need to unravel the processes of differentiation at work here between Canetti, the place, its denizens both human and animal, and the wisdom he takes from his time in Marrakesh and environs. The auditory—Marrakesh and its voices and sounds—will be the privileged sense of reception. Canetti is, after all, a traveler who dreams of the "man who unlearns the world's languages until nowhere on earth does he understand what people are saying" (23). The wish inherent in this dream is transformed into the power that language-as-cry will have for him. This sense of language, he believes, will allow his impressions to be "unmitigated by deficient and artificial knowledge on my part" (23). Canetti believes he has given up the urge toward an *Ursprache* that subtended many forms of late-nineteenth-century work on the divisions of knowledge and searches for origins and affiliations, which, at their high-liberal best, went under the sign of humanism with its presumptions of universality.

The heartlessness of the good traveler is founded precisely upon the denial of universality in the urge toward specificity. We may better understand Canetti as a traveler who knows the conceits and clichés of the genre and who even realizes his participation in a process in which neither the traveler nor the camels, as is the case here, can see or hear the other in any way that might translate. One of the effects Canetti is after in his searches, like Segalen before him and Barthes after, is a letting-go of meaning that speechlessness might be believed to confer. As for heartlessness, Canetti is the traveler who will not intervene or intrude in certain local practices out of a misguided sense of good will; this is the case when he tells his readers the tragic aspects of "camel existence" from which he can only turn away, full of guilt and shame. In his first effort to find the camel market in Marrakesh, he and his unnamed male companion come upon the following scene:

> We had gone to the market expecting to see hundreds of these gentle, curva-
> ceous beasts. But in that huge square we had found only one, on three legs,

captive, living its last hour, and as it fought for its life we had driven away. (11)

While Canetti may recognize his outsiderness regarding these animals, he is also relentless in his wish to know something of them:

> I had lost sight and sound of the camel, which had now stopped its roaring, and I wanted to see it again.
>   I soon found it. The butcher had left it where it was. It was kneeling again, still tossing its head from time to time. The blood from its nostrils had spread further. I felt something akin to gratitude for the few illusory moments for which it had been left alone. but I could not look at it for long; I knew its fate and stole away. (17)

This kind of furtive looking and listening will predominate in *Voices*. Turning away from the fate of these beasts of burden brings about what reads like a rather forced identification with a creature so unlike his human self. The identification is both made and denied in his heartless "stealing" away. Canetti's vision and hearing are experienced as illegitimate and invasive when he turns from animals to people. And, no doubt, part of the shame and furtiveness comes from the fact that he cannot and will not deny his simultaneous will to know.

"The cries of the blind" section recounts several episodes that cast in an aural mode what is more often theorized in the specular. That is, the mirror stage and its sound effects are projected through Canetti's encounters with the blind beggars. The blind beggars become "the saints of repetition," and through their cries Canetti, the traveler who "is roused to enthusiasm by the most dreadful things because they are new," comes to understand the "seduction there is in a life that reduces everything to the simplest kind of repetition." There is a shedding of the ego where the unconscious holds sway. It is not surprising that this would take place for Canetti among the blind, for they cannot see him, and here his own gaze is freed rather than constrained, as it so often seems to be in Morocco. But it is not only the moment of seeing without being seen, it is the cries themselves that seem to promise release from the rigors of life in language. It is upon returning from Morocco that Canetti "sat down with eyes closed and legs crossed . . . and tried to say 'Allah! Allah! Allah!' over and over again . . . wanting nothing else, sticking to it utterly." Is it through a tongue loosened by alien sounds, even those he can surely understand—the name of God—that his heartlessness is made "luminous," that the exotic is made his own, through a return to a realm inside language but outside speech? Canetti is a traveler whose knowledge of many languages might have made him rather "at home" in many places, but not happily so in Marrakesh.

Canetti calls forth his own inadequacy to the cultural encounter at the crossroads; he even thrills to it. But is he in any less heartless a state than those who set out eager to name and find difference rather than stay awash in the liquid of prematurity? If there is no urge toward self-mastery because it is known to be a fiction, then is it possible that mastery where others are concerned becomes the more urgent matter? Is what makes the heartless traveler also the good traveler his knowledge of seduction as a play with and within domination? Is he, therefore, any more careful in his heartlessness? Or merely more haunted by melancholy in his thoroughly self-conscious and awkward relation to elsewhere?

Some answers to these questions may be found when we look in on Canetti, the good traveler, as he encounters the holy men and the mostly veiled women of Marrakesh. If the blind beggars are the "saints of repetition," then the marabout is their high priest:

> I resolutely watched him chewing. . . . I had never seen a man chew so heartily and so exhaustively. I felt my own mouth begin to move slightly although it contained nothing that it could have chewed. I experienced something akin to awe at his enjoyment which struck me as being more conspicuous than anything I had ever seen in association with a human mouth. His blindness failed to fill me with compassion. He seemed collected and content. Not *once* did he interrupt himself to ask for alms as the others all did. Perhaps he had what he wanted. Perhaps he did not need anything else. (27)

What the marabout is chewing are coins. Canetti can hardly bear his mixed reaction of disgust and awe. Unable to "read" the labor of the marabout, a holy man, Canetti is as if struck dumb, and this is confirmed for him through the eyes of others:

> I must have presented a ridiculous spectacle. Possibly, who knows, I was even gaping open-mouthed. . . . Only now did I notice that behind every stall there were two or three pairs of eyes trained on me. The astonishing creature was myself, who stood so long uncomprehending. (29)

Having just homogenized the blind beggars as saints with their "unchanging" singular cry, we come to the marabout, the blind beggar who will single himself out to Canetti—the traveler as itinerant benefactor—for the way that he mouths the proffered coin, which makes Canetti's "disgust immediately dwindle," transforming it into awe. With that transformation, the giving of the coin mutates, too. The marabout "had something to give away that

men needed much more than he needed their coins." After talking obsessively about this man for some days and returning to the square where he
had seen him, we learn that "exactly a week later" Canetti "saw him once
more," and this time he feels prepared to receive the marabout's "blessing,"
which is of a "friendliness and warmth . . . as I had never had a person be-
stow on me before."

Like countless Occidentals before him, Canetti is lured by the garments
of the women in Marrakesh, garments that both hide their wearers and gape
even if only the eyes are revealed. In a country of covered women, the
woman who shows herself at the window is known by all, including the
passing schoolchildren, to be mad. As with the marabout so with "the
woman at the grille"—Canetti cannot take his eyes off her. He keeps pre-
tending to move away only to return obsessively. And once again, he is
caught looking:

> Veiled women coming up the street towards me took no exception whatever
> to their compeer at the grille. . . . I did sense, though, that they gave me dis-
> approving looks. What was I doing there? Why was I standing there? What
> was I staring up at? (36)

Indeed. Neither the holy nor the mad is legible to our heartless traveler. And
try as he may to countenance only what he *hears* for its affect, which he
wishes to believe comes without differentiation, as with most travelers the
eyes are greedy, voraciously making meaning for lack of a common tongue.

In posing the problematic of identities and differences, we cannot do so
only in the context of the symbolic, although that has been the privileged
and presumed site of *identity*. If, however, we take another look, we are
obliged to recognize that in the process of *identification* comes the moment
of misrecognition that goes by the name of the mirror stage. And we know
as readers of Lacan and Freud that the invisible but inevitable "human or
artificial" support needed by the infant tends to be the arms of a woman,
and if not a woman herself, then her extension in the realm of caretaking,
perhaps even the hands of a man. But the casting of the moment is one in
which that prematurity of the infant is absolute and necessary to its jubilation, and where the drama/tragedy will be replayed. Porter speaks of this as
the déjà vu of travel (12). And the uncanny is, in Freud's terms, an encounter
with the radically other where we nevertheless have been before—the maternal body, that first home. This would also help to explain what Porter follows so well—the want and craving of so much travel writing, where desire
is laid bare in ways uncommon to "public" discourse, although extremely

appropriate for genres such as the autobiography. Once again, the blurring of genres that we contend with here is not part of the problem but rather part of the solution.

If we read the mirror stage as a moment of formation of the I, we must also, following Jane Gallop and the demands of a deconstructive reading, read it simultaneously as a moment of the dissembling of the I. For, as Gallop makes clear, in her reading of the temporality of the mirror stage, to grasp jubilantly the I, the one grasping also then knows with a shock the not-yet-I, the fragmented body, the body in pieces.[3] What unites our narrators of time spent elsewhere is their rather insistent hunt for and openness to moments that demand repeated negotiations with the I/not I—as if this repetition would serve finally to stabilize and even bring some closure to an interpsychic drama.

Canetti presents us with a version of this dramatic scenario in his repeated visits to the Mellah, the Jewish quarter of Marrakesh. Here is where he finally gains entrance to a personal residence, after staring longingly into dark corridors, getting only fleeting glimpses of bright courtyards beyond. Like Segalen's near mystical meeting with his younger self, Canetti in the Mellah has "come home" to himself:

> I had the feeling that I was really somewhere else now, that I had reached the goal of my journey. I did not want to leave; I had been here hundreds of years ago but I had forgotten and now it was all coming back to me. I found exhibited the same density and warmth of life as I feel in myself. I *was* the square as I stood in it. I believe I am it always.
>
> I found parting from it so difficult that every five or ten minutes I would come back. Wherever I went from then on, whatever else I explored in the Mellah, I kept breaking off to return to the little square and cross it in one direction or another in order to assure myself that it was still there. (45)

Canetti offers a near perfect description of the mastery of integration and separation that characterizes the infantile play with the moves toward and away from the mother—what Freud translated as fort-da. It is no accident or coincidence that this takes place in the Jewish quarter.

Here, more than elsewhere in Marrakesh, Canetti is after a sense of being that becomes personified in the square, what he calls the "heart" of the Mellah. For all his fascination with the market and the beggars who crowd the entrance to the Jewish cemetery, it is the homes that compel his wanderings: "Peace flowed out of them over me. I would have loved to step inside but did not dare, seeing no one." With a vacillation between what he imagines to be reciprocal desire and dread, he continues: "I would not have known what to

say if I had suddenly come across a woman in such a house. I was myself
alarmed at the thought of perhaps alarming someone" (45). On the next
day's return to the square, Canetti resolves to "set foot inside one of the
houses . . . not to leave the Mellah this time without having seen a house
from inside. But how was I to get inside?" (53). Here is the heartlessness of
the traveler who insists on intrusion; as a pretext, hearing many children's
voices, Canetti pretends to take a house for a school and enters the court-
yard. What draws his gaze, however, is a "young, dark, and very radiant"
woman.

The woman he is finally permitted to observe is a new bride, and he
imagines again with an odd sense of reciprocity that "my curiosity about her
was as great as hers about me" (56). There had just been a wedding the previous day in the home of the Dahan family, Sephardic Jews like Canetti's
own family. In a spirit of welcome, the family invites yet one more individual into their home. In French, Canetti and the younger unmarried Dahan
son strike up an acquaintance, but it is the silent newlywed woman who
arouses Canetti's unflagging interest. Because she is not Muslim, they may
look at each other more freely than was possible in Marrakesh until this
moment.

> It had been her eyes that had drawn me into the house, and now she was
> staring at me in steadfast silence. . . . [A] quite absurd hope filled me. I hoped
> that she was mentally comparing me with her groom, whom I had liked so
> much; I made a wish that she would prefer him to me, his simple nobility
> and easy dignity to my presumptuous foreignness, behind which she may
> have imagined power or wealth. I wished him my defeat, and his marriage
> had my blessing. (57)

The young woman never does speak to the stranger, and Canetti imagines,
with characteristic vacillation, that when she hears him reply to her
brother's question that he is, like them, "Israélite," she is "slightly disappointed." Instead, the younger brother, who shares Canetti's name, Elie, becomes a rather constant companion to him, insisting that the European
traveler find him a job. Canetti has come to Morocco with two friends involved with a filmmaking company, and to the young Dahan son he *is* a
powerful figure who, with one letter, can surely find Elie a job with the
"Americans." Dahan's persistence is matched perfectly by Canetti's wish to
know this family and their everyday life circumstances. The key moment in
this growing acquaintance comes when he is introduced to the father of the
family; this comes nearest to Canetti's earlier dream because the father
speaks no French, and Canetti speaks no Arabic. They merely stand and re-

gard each other at great length, and Canetti perceives himself to be in the presence of wisdom and generosity—thus experiencing another kind of homecoming, such as he had found in the square. In the meeting with the father there is a coalescence of earlier moments in Marrakesh, not just some return to an earlier imaginary scene but also an admixture of awe, as in the presence of the marabout, that is now converted to shame in the presence of paternal authority. The homecoming figured in the square in the Jewish quarter and refigured in Canetti's visits with many family members of the Dahans reaches an apogee when Elie Dahan says to Elias Canetti:

> "Je vous présente mon père." . . .
>   "Père" sounded positively majestic in his mouth. . . . I shook the man's hand and looked into his laughing eyes. . . .
>   "E-li-as Ca-ne-ti?" the father repeated on a note of interrogation. He spoke the name aloud several times, pronouncing each syllable distinctly and separately. In his mouth the name became more substantial, more beautiful. He looked not at me but straight ahead of him, as if the name were more real than I and as if it were worth exploring. I listened in amazement, deeply affected. In his sing-song voice my name sounded to me as if it belonged to a special language that I did not know. . . .
>   He was standing there as if he wanted to say: the name is good. But there was no language in which he could have told me. I read it in his face and experienced an overpowering surge of love for him. . . . Awed, I remained perfectly silent. Perhaps I was also afraid of breaking the wonderful spell of the namechanting.

This meeting leads Canetti to say about the man's importunate and bothersome son, "Because he was the son of that magnificent man . . . there was nothing I would not have done for him" (75–76). Finally, the letter in triplicate that Elie had been begging Canetti to write so as to secure him a job was written, and the young man himself was "praised to high heaven," as was his cousin, who was also in search of work. The expansion of self that Canetti experienced as awe or wonder in the presence of the marabout and the senior Dahan comes full circle and produces a sense of diminishment when Elie "brought me an invitation from his father to Purim." Now the lack of shared customs produces not the cultural work of the good, if heartless, traveler; rather, the earlier "tribal" kinship of Canetti as a Jew is now reinscribed:

> I could imagine his father's disappointment at my ignorance of the old customs. I would have got most of it wrong and could only have said the prayers like a person who never prays. It made me ashamed to face the old man, whom I loved and wanted to spare this distress. Pleading work, I brought

myself to turn down the invitation and never see him again. I am content to
have seen him once. (76)

With this sentence, the longest chapter, "The Dahan Family," ends. Canetti
feels no shame, only strangeness, when he chants "Allah" repeatedly to himself upon returning to Europe, trying to reinvoke some state he experienced
when among the blind beggars. And just as he had imagined various forms
of reciprocity between himself and the Dahans' new daughter-in-law with
no name, here he imagines the disappointed father, whose "distress" he must
avoid at all costs. The love he feels for this man and the love he felt coming
from the Muslim holy man we can only understand as one of the forms that
wonder can take in the presence of persons as opposed to places. Wonder in
relation to place is more recognizable in the scene of coming home, homing
in on the square, as a place he had been before—that primal site of the maternal warmth and loss of self-presence through the sensed presence of another's welcoming environment.[4]

The marabout mouthing Canetti's coin, the Dahan father mouthing the
syllables of Canetti's name, these are two of the moments when a kind of
synesthesia takes over in the traveler's impressions of Morocco—not a
synesthesia of confusion, but amalgamation. For the mouth performs what
the ears and eyes take in and process in amazement. Canetti listens as
"greedily" as he looks, and his closing chapter is called "The unseen." For
Canetti, who is pleased *not* to share a tongue with most of those he meets in
Marrakesh, this final encounter comes to embody all that is a merging of
human and animal in sound and cry.

Canetti has regularly visited the main square of Marrakesh, the Djema el
Fna. Among the sights and sounds that keep taking him back there is a
"small, brown bundle on the ground consisting not even of a voice but of a
single sound" (100). Unwilling and unable to discern the form of person
under the garment, Canetti is haunted by its unfailing presence every
evening: "How it got there and how it got away again were matters more sacred to me than my own movements" (102). Heartlessness and goodness are
revised in response to the "creature"; the traveler's never-to-be satisfied curiosity causes him shame: "I never waited until it got up or was fetched. I
slunk away in the darkness with a choking feeling of helplessness and pride"
(102). Both emotions are his own; however, the former he takes on quite
fully as the helplessness of the outsider who "had a dread of its shape" but
"could give it no other" and whose "temptation [to touch its hood] always
succumbed swiftly to [his] helplessness." The pride he feels, on the other

hand, is projected or ascribed to the one covered by the garment: "proud of the bundle because it was alive" (103). Speculating on its feelings and capacities, Canetti closes the chapter and the book thus:

> I never saw it pick up the coins that people threw it. . . . Perhaps it had no arms with which to reach for the coins. Perhaps it had no tongue with which to form the "l" of "Allah" and to it the name of God was abbreviated to "e-e-e-e-e." But it was alive, and with a diligence and persistence that were unparalleled it uttered its one sound, uttered it hour after hour, until it was the only sound in the whole enormous square, the sound that outlived all others.

Where the marabout's blessing uttered six times and the Dahan father's repetition of Canetti's name place this traveler in the position of the child receiving love and goodness, the encounters with the "bundle" shift Canetti's place in this drama in such a way that he becomes the proud parent of this creature whose presence is known to all in the square, and whose message is encoded only in the imaginary projective space that Marrakesh has provided Canetti.

~

Casablanca Revisited

Caryl Phillips's *The European Tribe*

Before I explored Europe there was one other journey I felt compelled to make: the journey back to the Caribbean of my birth. The discoveries that I made there were both deep and profound, but I still felt like a transplanted tree that had failed to take root in foreign soil. The direction in which my branches had grown still puzzled me, for the forces that had shaped their development were not to be found in the Caribbean. I found this disturbing, as I hoped that the Caribbean might furnish me with answers to urgently felt questions. In fact, all that happened was that my Caribbean journey heightened an already burning desire to increase my awareness of Europe and Europeans.
The European Tribe

In this chapter I explore some of the changes rung on the figure of the young European white man on the grand tour when that young man is Caryl Phillips, black-skinned, born in the Caribbean, raised and educated in England, and traveling to the Continent and North Africa for the first time. Phillips's own speculations on his formation through the effects of European racism will be briefly juxtaposed with the work of Frantz Fanon, who, as a revolutionary and a psychiatrist, theorized some of the knots of race and madness. Both Fanon and Phillips are well aware of the operations of racism through the looks exchanged between strangers. My analysis will concentrate on the look in the psychoanalytic setting out of which Fanon is sometimes speaking and the cinematic setting that marks Phillips's cultural translations in one especially rich scene. Both Fanon and Phillips are students of the theatrics of racism and offer vignettes in which the masks of color are in motion, as if they were the work of a cultural quick-change artist.

Schooled in the great narratives of European literature and liberalism, Phillips and Fanon draw on the characters of Othello and Caliban to display how European knowledge of men of color is codified by narratives of difference. The force of the desire for recognition with its simultaneous distortion is further complicated for the man of color when such encounters repeatedly provide evidence of the mistakenness of identity and the ever-frustrated efforts at identification. The psychoanalytic dialectic of loss and desire is recast in ways that Phillips and Fanon make poignant and clear in their roles as readers of the scenarios among men, in particular when they try to inscribe a relation to authority. In the spectacle of men of color seeing and being seen, Phillips and Fanon want their readers to see both the mask and the invisible man that it bodies forth at the same time. I am watching in this chapter for the relay between the look that instantiates race as a category and the toll it takes on subjectivity, to which Fanon's entire work attests.[1]

When Caryl Phillips starts out on the journey recounted in *The European Tribe*, his advance scripts are not only those provided by life and books, but by cinema as well. One key moment of mistaken identity occurs in the bar of the Hyatt Regency Hotel in Casablanca when he is brought to take account of his position as traveling black Briton of West Indian birth, mediated as much by the place as by the Hollywood film that has left its mark both on the place and on Phillips's consciousness. Phillips understands himself also to be preceded by Frantz Fanon as a Caribbean educated in Europe and coming to fuller consciousness of the vagaries of race and its imprints under the skies of northern Africa.

Phillips was brought to Britain as an infant by his mother, and this formative immigrant experience has written him into a script that risks erasing his Caribbean past. Race and ethnicity battle for Phillips's sense of his soul; nowhere in Europe will he be allowed to forget or disclaim his color, and at the same time, everywhere the assumptions of others that he is either African or American displace his West Indian place of birth. Uprooted, he will live out the "cultural confusions of being black and British."

Stepping into his narrative, Phillips, like so many traveler narrators, situates a (painful) moment of childhood as both memory and driving force for the journey that has now become his book. This memory centers on "racialism" and its emergence in the form of jokes and humor among those he had taken to be friends. Phillips recounts a scene from the everyday life of a schoolboy—a ten-year-old friend tells him an ethnic joke about Pakistanis that neither of the young boys "gets," but Phillips finds he cannot laugh as required by the triangulated ritual of the joke. However, he does understand this moment to be the end of a friendship, and it is this he recollects as he sets out in this "narrative in the form of a notebook" to investigate what it meant to him to be "of and not of" this so-called tribe. Another joke, made by his English teacher who is explaining the origins of his pupils' last names ("Phillips," he mused, "you must be from Wales"), leads Phillips to say years later, "If the teaching of English literature can feed a sense of identity, then I, like many of my black contemporaries in Britain, was starving" (2). As Phillips comes to recognize while still a child, local attachments are premised upon his willingness to attempt to efface his color from social interactions. For Phillips as a boy, books will come to stand in for the lost consolations of friendships that foundered on the question of race.

Travel and its reunions with the imaginary are realized in the spatialized pilgrimage "back" to the infantile wish and belief in a magical whole self, back to the bliss of the mirror. Phillips calls up the moment of contact with Europe at the "portable age of twelve weeks," when he was brought to Britain. And once again, with Gide's cradling image in mind, we need to remember that that mirrored self is held together by and in the arms of another—conventionally, the mother. Bliss and exile are irrevocably mixed for Phillips, and the agent of their blending is the mother. This figure of the displaced mother with child is a recurring motif in all Phillips's work.

An encounter as a university student at Oxford with a "crazy black American, Emile Leroi Wilson, from Watts, Los Angeles, who became my closest student friend," marks a new phase in Phillips's education in matters of race. One of the commonplaces of racism is what brings these two young men together; that is to say, while each is isolated as a black man at Oxford, they are nevertheless "mistaken" for each other by the porter who tries to give Phillips a letter addressed to Wilson. The porter assumes Phillips knows not only *who* the proper addressee is, but also where he is.

The subsequent meeting with Wilson leads Phillips to take an impulsive trip to the United States. There, within a couple of days, he is ignited by the freedoms and constraints—police question him in Detroit and Chicago simply for being out on the street, and bookstores lure him with copies of *Invisible Man* and *Native Son*. The "explosion" that the reading of Wright's book sets off not only intensifies Phillips's understanding of the workings of racism, but also leads him to choose the life of a writer, an option he resents discovering for the first time, ironically enough, in America.

The travel Phillips does in his year abroad is a repeated lesson in the forms of European racism and its particular blind spots. The return to the West Indies he left as a child is narrated in Phillips's fictions. *The Final Passage*, a novel published in 1985, opens with a scene of a young black woman with an infant in her arms waiting to board a ship for Britain (the reversal operates in *State of Independence*, published in 1986, when a young man looks out the window of a plane onto the island of his birth after a twenty-year absence). The sight of a woman queuing up is a repeated motif in *The European Tribe*, and the scene of a woman boarding a ship haunts Phillips, as we see in *Cambridge*, published in 1992, which opens with a young white British woman sailing to the West Indies.

In *The European Tribe* Phillips recounts a scene of winter in Moscow. It is written from the racial flashpoint of South meeting North, and we can see in it a doubled identification for the narrator. This doubling opens a door onto understanding that woman in the queue who "was" his mother and the fate she sealed for her son who is telling this story:

> Out in the street an African woman pushed hard at a pram in which a small baby was wrapped up like an Eskimo. . . . How would the child's mother retell the tale of her Soviet sojourn and her struggle with six-month long Soviet winters, once back in her native Angola or Mozambique? After all, the child would have to live forever with the distinction of having to write Moscow, USSR, under place of birth. (113)

Here is Phillips's own "urgently felt question" to hear the story his mother would tell in order to reread her own and her son's story. This desire is not to be satisfied, however. Only the son will do this work in his writing life. In fact, the fictive mother in *State of Independence* is supremely uninterested in the sense of estrangement that haunts her recently returned but long-absent son.

> As we moved away the legion of negro people gawped and suspended whatever activity they had been engaged in. They exhibited a savage curiosity.
> I believe it was I who was the object of wonderment upon which their eyes were riveted, but soon we were lost from view.
> Caryl Phillips, *Cambridge*

The narrator of *Cambridge* is a young white woman arriving on an unnamed West Indian island to do the work of her absentee landlord father.

We are once again among those curious savages shown to be oh so interested in the imperial subjects who survey their lands. The young woman's presumptuousness is an easily assumed cover for *her* wonderment and inability to stop her own uncivil (savage) staring. When Phillips is followed by a "crowd of waifs" in the Casbah, he feels the pressure of real and imaginary eyes upon him: "It occurred to me that everyone was watching, but they were not." His own sense of being seen is similarly overexcited by the sense of alienation, and, like Canetti earlier, his superfluity to the scene is clear: "For this was a tragically familiar scene. Eventually if you do not give in, they disappear to hold on to another sucker's waistband-conscience" (13).

In the chapter called "Hollywood's *Casablanca*," all the resonance of the place for a tourist of Phillips's generation is mediated through the film, which is reframed in the decor of the bar of the Hyatt Regency, a set piece meant to evoke just such textual reminiscences for the leisured classes who pass through. As this scenario plays itself out for Phillips, we find a key piece of textual evidence for a clear sense of one colonized body and its affects and apperceptions:

> As time has gone by, I am sure that very little in Hollywood has changed, and if there were profit to be made Warner Brothers would remake *Casablanca* . . . with Michael Jackson singing songs to Jack Nicholson's command, and Meryl Streep playing the lead female interest. But that still leaves the question of who will play Nuhammad, or the one-legged beggar, or the woman who tried to give me her child? The same invisible people who played them in *Casablanca*, perhaps.
>
> Why the film continues to exercise a grip on the collective consciousness of generation after generation of movie-goers still puzzles me. . . . [P]olitically the film is crude propaganda for the Allies. In fact, with hindsight, parts of it can even be considered offensive. Can we really believe now that Paul Henreid, dapper in a Savile Row suit, has been released from a concentration camp? And when Ingrid Bergman describes the middle-aged Dooley Wilson as "the boy who's playing piano" a shiver runs both ways along my spine. (17–18)

In that "shiver [that] runs both ways" we can locate a track, a route through which we might be able to read the plasticity and multiplicity of moments of dis/mis/identification. Phillips embodies the spectator Hollywood doesn't even imply; nevertheless, through the powerful training apparatus of the cinema effect, he knows how to become its ideally constructed (white male) spectator as the shiver runs one way—the lure of the imaginary where the viewing subject may "be" any and all of the moving figures; and then, as that shiver runs the opposite direction, fear and terror violently relocate his identification with the figure of Sam, the piano player, a grown black man made boy.[2] The "boy" who will play the tune, the figure of spectacle, is, in the final moments, erased by the specter of America and Europe walking off into the mist, arms locked, two white men, displacing both the heterosexual couple and the eunuchlike figure of Sam accompanying their forbidden romance. This profound and concretely marked embodiedness that Phillips feels or recalls in the bar of the Casablanca Hyatt Regency is a repeated moment in his travels. Such moments pose the question of what it means to be comfortable in one's own skin for this man of color as he moves across the globe.

How are we to take in the phenomenology of journeying? The one who sets out appears inevitably, sometimes rather explicitly, to be in flight and in search of some sense of framing that will make the contours of the body in the world more fitting. When Phillips takes off on his sojourn all he knows is that Britain, which has recognized his gifts, has not and may not be capable of recognizing him as he might wish to be seen. Some of the most significant mirroring that occurs in Phillips's narrative is through the eyes of other black men in life and in literature.

In a chapter called "Dinner at Jimmy's," which recounts a visit to James Baldwin, Phillips is haunted by a sense of his own insufficiency as interlocutor for the "great man" Baldwin has become in his own eyes and those of the world, as evidenced by his being listed on the Provence "Tourist Coach" itinerary. This is a visit to a hero, to one "larger than life." To complicate his visit further, it coincides with the Nice Jazz Festival and a get-together between Baldwin and Miles Davis—a "spiritual fix" that Phillips realizes is an all-too-rare occurrence for Baldwin in those last days. Feeling he would "only have been in the way," he leaves before the meeting of the minds/men.

> The reasons for my departure may seem a trifle feeble now, but I felt them intensely at the time. Part of me desired, however naively, access to whatever conversation they might have on more equitable terms than my age and status would allow, but the more important reason lay in the heart of Jimmy's talk the previous evening. . . . [H]e needed to be alone with someone who could relate fully to all the nuances of his predicament, past, present, and future.

Phillips longs for much the same kind of camaraderie; however, errant in the village of Saint Paul de Vence, it is clear that outside of Jimmy's there is nowhere he will find it. After an embarrassed display of awkwardness about his solitude, his place, and his manners at a local bar, he overtips the waitress and ventures into the night. This is not Chicago or Detroit; this is the France to which traveling and displaced Africans and African-Americans for a time emigrated for another sense of what it might be like to live inside their own skins. Nevertheless the scene is a repeated one in Phillips's narrative; it is a scene of harrassment that will propel him from one town, city, and country to another when the despair at misrecognition becomes burdensome, as it always does:

> Across the road four blue-suited gendarmes eyed me suspiciously. . . . They scowled in my direction—French policemen seldom smile. I heard another laugh from inside the house, then one of the perched policemen turned to the others and passed a comment. "*Les nègres, ils sont très jolis, n'est-ce pas?*" ["Those niggers sure are pretty."] Perhaps he did not say that, and I simply imagined he did. Either way I did not care. I ambled on past the gates and down the hill. Up above the firework display began. Later, much later, I would sneak in unobserved and unheard. Like a naughty schoolboy, I slipped quietly into bed and listened to the old men's laughter until dawn broke.

The tension between Phillips's sense of self in the presence of the gendarmes who seldom smile as opposed to the comfort of the unseen but laughing old men leads him to draw out a scenario of anguishing impossibility in terms of what it will take for him to find some confirmation of where he must *be* in order to feel part of some "tribe," although not the European one. The eyes of the white men, in their blue suits of discipline, harbor scorn, racism, and homophobia, as witnessed by the narrator, who even allows us to see his own paranoia when he notes that they might not have said what he thought he heard. Still and all, his very projection tells us enough to begin to appreciate the distortion and impoverishment in the forms of intersubjectivity to which a young-black-man-abroad like Phillips is subjected. The poignance of this particular scene lies also in the fact that he had denied himself access to a kind of recognition that would embrace him and tie him to a line of black male kinship of "star" quality. It is precisely his sense of the psychic costs of Baldwin's stardom that makes him decide to leave Baldwin and Davis to themselves, feeling himself excluded from their histories, their memories, their shared American cultural dialogues. And yet it is through the eyes of black America once again that Phillips comes to understand his own displacement.

What he perhaps overlooks is the cost to himself of denying and mistrusting the very appeal of this kind of mirroring and recognition. Everywhere he goes Phillips is looking for and at other black men. This is, after all, the manchild who was brought out of the Caribbean in the arms of his mother. The oedipal scene is always waiting to be played out, as it is imaginatively done in Venice where he sees "only one other black man" but imaginatively reinserts the Othello he long ago learned about onto the European stage. Here is Phillips, the Oxford scholar, now roaming the Continent as young men were long expected to do, musing on Othello:

> The problems of justifying his ascent from slave to revered and contracted soldier . . . dominate his mind. He cannot help but be overwhelmingly aware that his origins are out of tune with his present position. And naturally enough, the colour of his skin means that he cannot disguise this fact from others. In short, he feels constantly threatened, and is profoundly insecure. . . . [A]t every turn he is reminded that he is working within the parameters of an authority he is not quite sure of, for unlike Cassio who is simply "a foreigner" Othello is an alien, socially and culturally. Life for him is a game in which he does not know the rules.

How is Phillips to render himself the subject of the well-educated gentleman's grand tour when it was a ritual not constructed for subjects such as himself? Yet he manages to read into the European tribe moments such as those provided by Shakespeare. There he spies a spot on the cultural canvas where he can connect some of the threads of his own sense of broken kinship.

This moment in Venice will come to mark what Gayatri Spivak speaks of in another context as the "violating yet enabling convention" that makes discourse between colonized and colonizer full of the seams of signification; it is where the holes in language are more than the fabric; it is the shreds of meaning that a speaker/writer like Phillips finds among the detritus of the tribe he studies.[3] Phillips is helped in reframing Othello through a reading of Fanon's work with "the 'abandonment-neurotic' . . . the essence of [whose] attitude is 'not to love in order to avoid being abandoned' " (50). For Phillips, among Othello's fatal errors is to have forgotten even if only temporarily that he is black, for as Phillips remarks, "He has to play by Venetian rules, and historically the dice are loaded against black men in the European arena" (50). He will continue in this chapter, titled "A Black European Success":

> Othello was the Jackie Robinson of his day. He was a black first. The first black general, not in Verona or Padua, but in the major league, Venice. He fought his way up from slavery and into the mainstream of the European nightmare. His attempt to secure himself worked, but only as long as there was a war and he was needed. . . . He relied upon the Venetian system, and ultimately he died a European death—suicide.

The prize of membership in the tribe comes at too high a cost in Phillips's appraisal (both of Othello and of Baldwin), and yet the isolation Othello feels undeniably resonates for Phillips, the young black tourist in Venice.

What will his outstanding qualities bring him, and what will they erase of his own dislocated histories?

The Shakespearean tapestry provides figures against whom both Phillips and Fanon work to untangle the knots of colonized identity and postcolonial identities. Some of what makes the knots so complex has to do with the disjuncture between blackness and Africanness for Fanon, for Phillips, as for Othello. When Fanon was working to construct a psychoanalytic of the colonized through his experiences in the Blida-Joinville psychiatric hospital in Algiers, he was thinking through a critique of Octave Mannoni's *Prospero and Caliban*.[4] Mannoni's clinical fieldwork in Madagascar in 1948 led to this work on questions of race and psyche. Fanon was sparked by the work of the French colonial doctor to reread and rewrite this diagnosis through his own skin and the imprints on the minds and bodies of those he saw daily in his clinic, where the complexities of madness and race were enmeshed and ensnared.

A tribal model of kinship rooted in a place is what Phillips both critiques and desires. His own European self finds no easy mirror in those whom he meets; they are blinded as if by the sight of him—what he polemically asserts in closing his book, echoing Fanon's warning in *The Wretched of the Earth*, is that those who are comfortably of the European tribe must recognize their kinship with him and others of his tribe if they aim to avoid endless repetitions of tribal clashes. His moment in Venice recurs when closing his book:

> I looked down the Grand Canal and realized that our permanence in Europe no longer relied upon white European tolerance . . . for we, black people, are an inextricable part of this small continent. And Europeans must learn to understand this for themselves, for there are among us few who are here as missionaries.

Phillips came of age during Britain's first notable waves of urban racial violence in the early 1980s. He knows what willful European ignorance of the mixing of the tribes can and does produce. Like Fanon, his formation by the "metropolis," whether London or Paris, is indelible, but only legible by those who can read the skin with all its imprints dark to light and back again. Color blindness is not the aim; the aim is rather the acknowledgment of not only the "fact of blackness" but also of whiteness where there had only been light.

~

From Snakes to Ice

Tété-Michel Kpomassie's *An African in Greenland*

> There is yet another soul in man. . . . During sleep it leaves the body and
> "goes travelling." . . . So the background of all our dreamt exploits is
> provided by the lands and places, known or unknown,
> which this wandering soul explores.
> Tété-Michel Kpomassie, *An African in Greenland*

Reversing the conventional geographical polarities of the young man setting out on the grand tour is the account published in English in 1983 by Tété-Michel Kpomassie, *An African in Greenland*. As its title makes plain, this is a travel narrative of desire and transgression that borrows from the seeing-man trope and sets it askew. Kpomassie is not the first black man to set out for the North Pole; Admiral Peary's companion, Matt Henson, holds that place in cultural history. But he may be the first contemporary African citizen who comes to stay in the northernmost reaches of the earth out of an obsession with landscape—one formed from the reading of a book.[1]

As a youth in Togo, Kpomassie had been traumatized by an encounter with a snake. The snake had slithered over his body as he was climbing a coconut palm, and rather than reencounter the snake, which he could see was on its way back up the tree trunk as he was climbing down, Kpomassie hurled himself to the ground and lost consciousness. He was subsequently promised by his father as an initiate to the sacred snake cult whose practitioners had saved the young boy's life. Wanting more than anything to flee this fate, he decided, at sixteen, to run away from home as soon as possible. During his recovery from this trauma he had bought a book from the local missionary bookstore that told picturesque tales, in the manners-and-customs mode, of Eskimos in the land of ice and snow.[2] Captivated, even obsessed, by these tales, he began to dream of "eternal cold," and the name Greenland took on the function of a fetish. This was represented as the land where the "child is king," and his only worry was whether he would be able to tolerate eating raw fish. Kpomassie decided to leave Togo, first for the home of extended family members on the Ivory Coast, and later for African cities newly independent from colonial rule. His idée fixe was to get to the North Pole and live among people utterly unlike those he knew. It was absolute difference as an imaginary construct that lured this traveler, not so different from many others who set out for China, the Orient, the New World, Africa.

Like Polo arriving at the court of the khan, Kpomassie was to find eyes and doors opening wide at his approach as he became the object of another's encounter with the uncanny. By freezing the frame of this encounter in the cold, perhaps we can see again the culturally dislocated exchange through which a self is constructed. Perhaps we can try to discern the multimirroring plays of identification that occur when subjects who carry names and histories with them come into contact. What is the spin on mistaken identity in *these* scenes? How has the emperor been redressed? By whom? Who is pointing fingers? What does the crowd behold?[3] In terms of naming and mirroring that occur in the foreign scene, Kpomassie's book will furnish us with material that is startling for the ways it forces our confrontation with the commonplaces of the genre—the ethnographic discourse tracked so clearly by Mary Louise Pratt—and for the even clearer way in which certain elements of the form remain structural and generic while being rewritten idiosyncratically.

"The Call of the Cold" recounts in several chapters Kpomassie's arrival in Greenland. It is an encounter that moves from self-presentation to self-parody to narcissism and finally to fiction through a kind of realization that occurs among those travelers who let themselves go to the meeting with others . . . finally naked:

> I wondered what their first reaction would be on seeing me, a black man, leave the ship. They had never seen a man of my race, except perhaps in newspaper photographs. Like an actor carefully preparing for his first entrance, I took my time dressing in my cabin . . . and then, with my hands in my pockets, I made my entrance.

As soon as they saw me, all talking stopped. So intense was the silence, you could have heard a gnat in flight. Then they started to smile again, the women with slightly lowered eyes. . . . Some children clung to their mothers' coats, and others began to scream with fright or to weep. . . . Like children the world over, they spontaneously spoke their minds about me. . . .

The crowd opened to let me pass. It was then that I distinctly heard a woman speak the word *kussannâ*, a flattering term that I didn't understand at the time, but which means "handsome." Handsome in what sense? For the children I was a fearsome supernatural being who came to exterminate the village. Besides my being black, it must have been my height—five feet eleven— . . . that contributed to the fear I inspired in the children, whose parents were little more than five feet three. . . . So my height impressed them, but in different ways according to their age. It spread terror in the children, astonished the men, and was attractive to one woman who at that moment was probably summing up the opinion of all the other women. Two days later the radio station in Godthab, the capital, announced the arrival of an African in the country in these terms: "He is a very tall man with hair like black wool, eyes that are not slanting but arched, and shaded with curling eyelashes."

. . . All the children left their parents' sides and followed us. . . . [S]oon I had such a procession of them behind me that K'akortoq's scanty police force was obliged to follow us in a patrol car moving at walking pace to keep the children from trampling the "foreigner" underfoot. The scene made me think of the Lilliputians surrounding Gulliver. I had started on a voyage of discovery, only to find that it was I who was being discovered. (80–81)

What we find in this passage is a movement in, around, and through subject and object positions that are grammatically and visually performed or imagined. The mirror is refracted and displaced in the word. The speaker/ author is doing his best to offset and predict a set of reactions that he has been led to expect from previous history (each time he has told a white person that he intends to go to the North Pole) and that makes up his own cultural baggage. The looks and the looking are so frank, so full of inarticulate wonderings that he and his soon-to-be hosts engage in a kind of mutual gaze that we normally associate with the merged bliss of the maternal, or alternately with the transgression of taboos on staring. It is a kind of gazing permitted to children and "savages"; note also the women who momentarily cast their eyes down. But at this moment he and his hosts are filled with readings, soundings, images that will begin to construct a narrative of how these gazes can continue to meet. Surprised beginnings will give way to a dailiness where such looking will not continue to be sanctioned as it is in this moment.

In our more culturally located moments such bold gazing is variously expected, allowed, and forsworn. It is a moment of a breakdown and -through of taboos, possible only when humans confront each other in their visceral forms of marking, territorializing, naming each other for a moment, for a time. Rituals, reunions, strangers sometimes sanction such uncivil staring. This is looking before the senses have been educated in shame, when unconstructed wonder still prevails. In a new place we are, for a time, returned to that era when we did not yet know that the relay between shame and wonder needs to be negotiated with caution so that we cast our eyes down, if only briefly, before staring once again at that which captivates our gaze.[4]

How did the unknown reaches of the North come to resemble and reframe what Kpomassie would and could call "home"?[5] For Kpomassie realizes early that in going to the north the indigenous people he will encounter are, like himself, people of color whose conditions of existence have been shaped by white dominance—by Scandinavians, more specifically. And he will be very attentive to how the cultural practices that are indigenous and therefore seem strange to him resemble aspects of his own culture left behind.

There is a passage in Roland Barthes's *Mythologies* that points toward ways of reading and knowing that have been thickened by the languages of cultural studies. In the defining essay, "Myth Today," Barthes presents a theoretical and methodological approach to reading signs—the ones Homi Bhabha says we take to be "wonders."[6] Of the move from an earlier paradigm of symbol and meaning to sign and form, Barthes says:

> The meaning will be for the form like an instantaneous reserve of history, a tamed richness, which it is possible to call and dismiss in a sort of rapid alternation. . . . It is this constant game of hide-and-seek between the meaning and the form which defines myth. (118)

Hide-and-seek is one way of naming the work and play of myth; for Barthes myth also becomes a "sort of constantly moving turnstile," an alibi, a "relation of negative identity" until "reality stops the turnstile revolving at a certain point" (122). One of those stopping points occurs in Barthes's barbershop reading of the *Paris-Match* cover photo of "a young Negro in a French uniform [who] is saluting, with his eyes uplifted, probably fixed on a fold of the tricolour" (116). This image becomes emblematic for Barthes of the operative myth of colonialism—the young African soldier represented as if he had consolidated his identity with that of the dominant nation.

Kpomassie recounts a scene that we might read as the perfect inversion of that which arrested Barthes's readerly gaze. It takes place close to the end of

Kpomassie's sojourn in Greenland. The penultimate chapter is named after the man who becomes Kpomassie's last host, "Robert Mattaaq," a man recognized by his neighbors as eccentric.

Finding no regular cargo boats leaving for Thule, long the ultimate "true north" of Europe, Kpomassie had compromised and set sail for Upernavik, "the second most important town on the northern coast."[7] Echoing Gide's infantile images of rocking and seasickness, yet rewriting them for a solitary adult psychosexual script, Kpomassie ponders the act of travel itself:

> What's the point of flying over a landscape? Wasn't it a hundred times more worthwhile to sail through this natural grandeur, to feel its overwhelming power? . . . [E]ven though on every sea voyage I make, however short, I suffer from seasickness, a long boat trip is the form of travel I like best. That inner psychological war with the elements which one feels one is waging at sea provides me with a good cure for the indefinable sense of anxiety, or the powerful sexual drive, that the lone foreign traveller often develops so intensely in the idleness of Greenland villages. After all, this inner mental struggle may also amount, by transference, to a sexual act . . . (266, final ellipsis in original)

Two days later as he scouts out the new town, in the voice of the conventional traveler, "he spots a cottage made of turf . . . the only one left in Upernavik." He wonders, "By what miracle had it survived the axe of the GTO [the Greenland Technical Organization, a state construction agency who works to replace these habitations 'in the name of progress']?" (268). This hut is unique in the landscape, but it "reminded [him] of an African mud-walled hut; despite its dilapidated appearance, and probably because it aroused some personal memories, I felt an irresistible desire to share the life of its occupants." This turns out to be Mattaaq's home. Kpomassie enters the dwelling, crouches through its corridors, encounters "two eyes peering" at him and hears a woman scream:

> Finally the door swung open, and I found myself facing a squat little creature whose sex was indeterminate at first sight. It was covered with thick black hair, from which emerged a round face set in a hard mask. Long locks of tangled hair hung down its back. . . . Closer inspection revealed that the creature in front of me was an old man, though with quick and lively gestures. . . .
> His rheumy eyes stared impassively up at me, and he said: "I've heard about you on the radio since you arrived in the south. I've been waiting to see you for over a year." (268–69)

The walls of Mattaaq's turf house are papered with layers of pages, articles, and photographs from magazines. It is the closest thing to a library Kpomassie has seen in a personal dwelling.

We were drinking our second round of coffee when, learning that I was a
French-speaking African, he told me:
   "Somewhere in my 'library' I have a photo of one of your country-
men."
Turning to the wall over the bed, he pulled out two rusty drawing pins, ex-
amined the pages underneath them, replaced the drawing pins, and pulled
out two others further on.
   "Rebekka! Do you remember where I pinned up the photo of that big
   Qashlunak about two years ago? . . ."
Finally Robert found what he was looking for. You can imagine my stupefac-
tion when, instead of a photograph of a black man, I saw on the yellowed
page of some magazine a picture of General de Gaulle!

Barthes's revolving turnstile of myth stops abruptly and with *our* stupefac-
tion at the reproduction of myth on several levels at once. In a glossary at the
back of *An African in Greenland* are terms mostly in Inuit, the language of
the Eskimos of Greenland, and others in Mina, Kpomassie's native language.
For the term *Qashluna* we find the following: "usually translated as 'white
man,' but also applied to Kpomassie, so more correctly 'foreigner.'" In a
footnote accompanying the text Kpomassie explains further that it had been
translated by one Greenlander as "he who comes from the south," but there
were others who disagreed, and like most etymologies its "correct meaning
has apparently disappeared because of an incorrect translation." In the same
note Kpomassie goes on to tell us the Eskimo words for white, black, and
red, but points out that they are used for objects, landscapes, or the colors of
a dog's coat, but "are rarely used for a man" (92). In this moment of stopping
to read the semiological spin of myth, race is displaced onto ethnicity, language, and nation, as it was in Barthes's masterful reading of the magazine
cover photo of the African saluting the French flag, with everything such an
image conjured up of embattled but still imperial France in the mid-1950s,
when Barthes's essays were composed. In Kpomassie's inversion of the myth
where he becomes conflated with de Gaulle, and even tries seriously to answer Mattaaq's question about the health of the one "who thinks a lot," some
of the "revolving turnstiles" of myth have come to a stunning halt, while
other meanings and forms of myth are proliferating and spinning wildly.

As its title, *An African in Greenland*, suggests, this book is one where a singular individual will recount, in the ethnographic present and in what
amounts to a manners-and-customs discourse, his experience of place.
Nothing remarkable there. And yet even this self-recognized postcolonial
knows he is undertaking a kind of voyage that bears telling because of his re-

peated encounters with whites who are startled to hear the intensity of his obsession to get to the lands of ice, and later with the encounters in the idealized space/place itself. His host, Mattaaq, senses that he and Kpomassie are kindred spirits. For he, too, in the forms made possible locally, has plotted his path globally with his bibliographically decorated home. Mattaaq will not need to unpack his library for he is not going anywhere, but the palimpsest of his wallpapered room nevertheless permits him many journeys. This encounter is reminiscent of the scene between Gauguin and Jotepha earlier; this eager and curious questioning between Kpomassie and Mattaaq is an intersubjective encounter where modes of decorum and civility are almost comically mismatched, but in this very fact, the codes and manners themselves are for a moment discarded. For Mattaaq as for Kpomassie, at this particular juncture the African newcomer can speak from some identifiable relation to France about the well-being of the military hero and political leader. Kpomassie gets to represent himself as courtier if not the king himself. Unable to accede to the highest status in his Mina culture due to the continuing rule of primogeniture, his membership in the snake cult would have nevertheless gained him the highest rank possible as his father's sixth child and fifth son. By leaving home, his experiences away from his family will gain him some glory and even passing fame, but they will not assure him the lifelong reverence that this priesthood would have.[8]

The inscription of difference by way of the category of race is one of the many aspects of that loaded signifier that leads to its marking in scare quotes by Henry Louis Gates Jr., editor of the collection *"Race," Writing, and Difference.* In that discussion race remains part of our ideological baggage, even as we discover that it is a fully, if differentially, constructed category that may momentarily fall away.[9] Kpomassie, a fellow who comes to Greenland by way of Europe, has already been thoroughly instructed in the ideology of race as marker. But that is not what is at play in some of the more startling moments he narrates. For instance, in the example above, it is the knot of nation and language that is invoked by his host as it is misunderstood by both Kpomassie and Mattaaq; Kpomassie understands the term "countrymen" to include another African; Mattaaq means by this a speaker of French. Language, not borders, names collectivities and communities. And language is not all that passes through the mouth:

> Food is something we can see, smell, taste and, in our mouth at least, touch.
> Food is a more or less piquant form of foreign substance that we openly
> admit into our own body, normally with the expectation of a new pleasure.

Consequently, that classic question of the male traveler—What are the women like?—is, if anything, less common than What is the food like? Eating in a foreign land is an "adventure" in the mouth that, under certain conditions, may stir memories of our remotest psychic past. (Dennis Porter, *Haunted Journeys*)

It would be true to say that, aside from all political disagreements, the persistent hostility that divides our country's tribes is often caused by food taboos. Though it may not appear so on the surface, our relations are often governed by the saying, "Tell me what you eat and I'll tell you who you are." (Kpomassie, *An African in Greenland*)

When we recall how Lévi-Strauss's work on myth made so clear the extent to which culinary boundaries may be more firmly installed than political and territorial ones can ever be, we can more fully appreciate how the senses inflect the experience of the elsewhere.[10] So much about life in Greenland reinscribes Kpomassie's body in space and time—from the disproportionate nature of darkness and light in the Arctic to the demands of cold to the redistribution of both domestic and exterior space—those polar distances that are traveled with difficulty if at all at certain times of year. But if ingestion and consumption are fundamental in reconfiguring identity, as he already knows from life in Togo, then Kpomassie "becomes" in remarkably little time a man of the North. How is his going native in culinary terms to be understood? He is not collecting data, ethnographic or otherwise; he is not pleasure-seeking and then returning whence he came. Neither a Gauguin nor a Malinowski, neither explorer nor colonial entrepreneur, Kpomassie has come to stay as he is compelled farther and farther north in Greenland itself. The prominence he was to have as leader or healer among his Mina kin has been radically transposed. Instead he has brought with him a relation to authority, power, and distinction that leads him not to chafe at all under the gaze of those who see him for the first time. The extent to which he has gone elsewhere to spare himself the looks of those who might have mocked him for his fears—of snakes, for example—speaks to Porter's model of travel as transgression and flight from paternal authority. Kpomassie is pleased to reembody the one who is looked upon with awe—the fate that had been assigned him at home but that he felt driven to take on only as far away as imaginable.

The "adventure" of food that may stir archaic psychic waters and the reasons for venturing so far away from home recombine in the narrative of Kpomassie's decision to return to Africa. Now he can go back to his father's and grandfather's village as the storyteller of "this glacial land of midnight sun and endless night" who will "help the youth of [a now decolonized] Africa open their minds to the outside world" (291–92). Mattaaq insists that Kpomassie will be one of those few who return to this, his new home (and he will), but bids him farewell recognizing that "you don't know what's become of your own folk." While Mattaaq acknowledges Kpomassie's continuing *dis*location even in the face of having become a "true Greenlander," Kpomassie recognizes the degree of his *re*location here, and the recognition comes through the realization of what he may now eat. On the morning of his last breakfast at Mattaaq's home he says:

> These seal intestines . . . were tough. . . . They were especially prized when eaten with seal blubber, that yellowish, bloodshot fat which had turned my stomach on the day—now so long ago—of my arrival in Greenland, but which now seemed to me a choice side dish for dried meat and fish. Now that I had been sharing these people's lives for sixteen months, their food no longer disgusted me. (292–93)

Like any tourist, Kpomassie repacks his gear to make room for those accoutrements of Greenland culture that he wishes to keep near him and to display for the folks back home; the uncured animal skin outerwear must be left behind, but not a miniature kayak and sled, dolls in local costume, and a dog whip. As a parting gift from Mattaaq, his wife strings a polar bear claw and tooth from a hunt of his much younger days for Kpomassie. Kpomassie knows that because of his finances, his return to Togo will take years, as did his trip to Greenland; in fact, the book closes with a chapter title that quotes Mattaaq: "Your Place Is Here with Us," but its last line places the writing in "Clichy, September 28, 1979."

There is a melancholy that haunts this final chapter of Kpomassie's book. It is the melancholy of oscillation between the forelonging that has brought him to the farthest reaches north, and once he has arrived there, the simultaneous and slowly growing nostalgia for home. Robert Mattaaq is the transferential figure of this transitional moment for Kpomassie, in a scene that is constitutive of the traveler's sublime. For Kpomassie this scene calls him home to the father. As for the place of the mother in Kpomassie's life history, it is worth noting that at the moment of being attacked by the snake while climbing the coconut palm and all during his long recovery, Kpomassie's mother was away from the village visiting her kin, and the first wife who functioned as his aunt stood in for her during this episode. Perhaps he would have framed his travels in much the same way, talking of "our African women" and the women of Greenland, whose only function is to mirror his fully dressed masculinity; recall the whispering women of his arrival scene.

In any case, at a crucial moment, the mother is absent, missing, and the father promises his son to a woman (the snake healer) who frightens him. This promise, a gesture of thankfulness on the father's part, was nevertheless experienced by the son telling the tale as a betrayal, a repudiation, a sacrifice. And hence, perhaps, his flight.

The meeting with Mattaaq has functioned not only to close the book but also to open the question of his reception (by his father, among others) on his return to Togo. An overdetermined meeting for both these men—Mattaaq, the avid, even fanatic reader of periodicals brought to him by family members since he rarely ventures out, comes face to face with the "Qashlunak," the foreigner he had been awaiting; Kpomassie, having reached his ultimate destination, finds a dwelling that becomes his last home in the North, the home of a man whose story will travel south even if he never does. (Kpomassie mentions hearing about Mattaaq's death after his arrival in Copenhagen.) A most unconventional father-son pairing is what clearly motivates both Mattaaq and Kpomassie, the eager young questioner, who wants to hear stories of custom, manners, beliefs, and burial practices—and tales of the sea goddess. Acknowledging that one has at best a "semblance of reasons" for traveling elsewhere, Kpomassie ends his tale with a set of clear reasons gathered only in the traveling itself: to bring that elsewhere into contact with his African past. These contact zones are not only geographical but also representational; they will produce neighboring narratives of Greenland (once the storyteller is back) in Africa. And as the storyteller, come from afar, his unspoken hope may be that the shame of denying his patrimony will be overwhelmed by the wonder his stories evoke in his audience, gladdened and perhaps even startled by his return.

~

From Travelers to Ethnics;
or, Looking for America

Imagine the first two substantives of this title as ends of a spectrum along which we might locate the prismatic effects of identities formed in circumstances of dislocation—the traveler, dislocated by choice, so to speak, and the ethnic at some personal-historical moment dislocated by force. The metaphor of a spectrum is crucial because it opens a range for speculation about processes of differentiation without suggesting a telos. There is mobility to identity across this spectrum that is arrayed not as a color chart, but a prism. To move from travel writing to the immigrant genre shifts the theoretical figure and ground, so to speak, of the self-conscious narratives of border crossings.

Displacement is a concept with different valences depending on the perspective of the speaker: we might be talking about political refugees who are stateless; we might be talking about victims of violent crime whose wish to forget leads them to see the enemy within rather than outside themselves; we might be talking about the dream-work where symptoms we cannot own are inscribed onto imaginary sites. And all three "we's" of these possibilities might be the same speaker at different moments in time.[1]

Consider the term *travel* as a verbal substantive that means not only leaving home for *some place else*, but also calls up the capacity for movement, a lack of fixity, a knowledge of shifting grounds. Travel would then suggest an affirmative sense of groundlessness, while displacement would suggest another side, an underside of a dynamic—that moment when the headiness of motion turns to anxiety, disavowal, the abyss in the ground. The travel writer moves across borders with papers all in order and language in place. The young man abroad (as we might image this exemplar, and as Paul Fussell, among others, has anatomized him) speaks many languages, but even if he does not, he speaks the imperial tongue, and others will translate on his behalf. Even if he is found deficient he will not be shamed—it is his hosts who will bear the reversed humiliation; their language will be found wanting. This gendering of the traveler as male or masculinized has been critical in my readings thus far, even when the traveler in question has been female.[2] Alongside this theoretical assumption, let us feminize the ethnic writer, and we will find an entirely other scenario in place as s/he confronts language and difference. Again, gender not as polarity, but as spectrum, and one of the troublesome sites of identity formation.[3] The phenomena of displacement and dislocation are inscribed in the history of the ethnic writer as the one who brings old tales to light, tales of world and family politics—politics of language, location, and identity.[4] For the ethnic, borders have always already been crossed.

For the traveler, the sanctioned regression of travel may carry the phantasm of unmediated bliss, wonder, solitude, and wordless communication; for the ethnic any regression may have been imposed or enforced, and the encounters with border crossings bring instead the reality of complex mediations of shame, fear, despair, loneliness, and the disempowered experience of an unshared tongue. Where the ethnic writer tracks passages marked by those whose history is somewhat similar, going where others like herself have been, the traveler's impulse is to set out alone, blazing new trails. Where the ethnic finds some pieces of identity within a group, the traveler leaves group, family, ethnos behind, seduced by elsewhere, lured by xenophilia. In the model of American or cultural studies we could reframe a distinction made between the new world types of the pioneer and the settler. As the pioneer may, at a certain moment, choose to become a settler, imagine also that the traveler and the ethnic could be one writer in differing voices or positions while "traveling."

As with so much of the language of differences, our terminology is derived from those who name, not those who are named as they might name themselves.[5] If we follow the trail of uses of the word *ethnic* in a descriptive dictionary, its Eurocentric history first names those not converted to Christianity, the "gentiles"—the ones who fill the margins and have not yet been brought into the center by the "Greco-Roman-European" namers. Moving from a designation by belief, we find the word signifying differences of language, race, culture, nation, and, perhaps most problematically, character.[6] Translation is a crucial question in this problematics of differentiation. Travelers are translated into the foreign space in ways that may remain unnameable, unspeakable: clothing, bearing, tones, gestures will speak (for) them. Nevertheless they remain in possession of the master's tongue; native will translate as "less" whether couched as noble or savage.[7] For the ethnic, translation moves in another direction: it will always be translation into the master's language from the native/mother tongue. The longing that has been at work in the narratives of seduction, that desire to surrender to the elsewhere, will be rewritten under the sign of suspicion and fear when narrated through the dislocations of ethnically mediated immigration.

Dennis Porter's *Haunted Journeys*, an elegant and provocative study of European male travel writers contextualized through a psychoanalytic model,[8] differs from my project in the dialogical texts we read. As I noted earlier, Porter situates the writer in an im- or explicit struggle with the father/land. My focus, also psychoanalytic, is informed by feminist psychoanalytic theory, which would read both traveler and ethnic also in a struggle with the mother/tongue. If we are to read these texts as exemplifying aspects of the construction of identity, then what they display are lifelong processes of oedipally marked dis- and mis-identifications—textually revisited sites of coming into language and self. It has been my contention throughout that the dislocations of border crossings reawaken and restage these processes of identification and differentiation.

Travel, or mobility between here, there, and elsewhere, seems to seduce new selves into being, refracting more facets of the prism named identity. When we shift our inquiring glance from travelers to ethnics, different inflections of displacement emerge. This is particularly true in the passage from wonder to shame that I have traced and have called the traveler's sublime. For the traveler, it has by now become obvious that the status of outsider tends to be more colored by wonder, whereas, for the ethnic, it is too often colored by shame. As I suggested in opening, while the affective and phenomenological dimensions of wonder and shame both render the subject reduced or diminished, wonder carries with it a positive charge, while shame is fraught with negativity.

The vacillation between wonder and shame can be usefully read in tandem with the fluctuation among possible and potential identifications that occur when the writing subject is on the road. For identifications occur not only enmeshed with other persons but also with other places. It is generally agreed by many contemporary writers on the subject that psychoanalysis has not produced a thoroughgoing theory of shame; rather it may be the case that shame is a strong feature of the repressed of psychoanalytic theory. This may help to explain the virtual explosion of writings on shame in the last decade. One of the leading theorists in this discussion, Silvan Tomkins, is unique in suggesting, perhaps counterintuitively, that "shame is in no way limited to the self, to the other, or to society" (153).[9] Furthermore, Tomkins supports my thesis on the intimate relation between wonder and shame as they adumbrate identity formation when he continues thus:

> A once beautiful place, where one lived, and which is now ugly, for whatever reason, may cause the head to bow in regret and shame on being revisited in hope of recapturing idealized memories. But, as is characteristic of shame, one may also bow one's head in awe and shame at the unexpected grandeur and beauty of a sudden view of an ocean or mountain, never before encountered, that overwhelms by its beauty rather than by its ugliness. In such cases there is often an invidious contrast with the self as unequal to such beauty and grandeur, as in the confrontation with parents or parent surrogates who make the self feel small and unworthy by comparison. (153)

Whereas most theorists assume the presence of an other for shame to exist, Tomkins's theories of affect and emotions presume shame as a transhistorical phenomenon; in this same essay, which offers an overview of his own work, he asserts, "The history of shame is also a history of civilizations" (156).

While it is frequently the case that a gendered or sexed body may become the precipitating site of shame, Tomkins, in what is offered as an example or an aside, opens the door on a discussion of the "raced" body as scripted by shame—a discussion that would entail our reading Tomkins with Fanon. This is particularly potent in thinking back to a traveler like Caryl Phillips, who occupies a position somewhere between traveler and ethnic/immigrant and is therefore rather more subject to being shamed on his journey precisely because of his skin color than was Gide or any of his countless white colonial forerunners. The following passage from Tomkins is remarkable both for its insistent ambiguity and its evocation of the intersubjective knotting of shame:

Feelings of shame or of shame as guilt may be experienced either as coming from without or from within. . . . Further, I may feel ashamed because *you* should feel ashamed or guilty but do not. I may feel ashamed or guilty because you feel ashamed or guilty but *should not*, as in the case of my sanctioning slavery reluctantly. (154; emphasis in original)

The sudden and unexpected appearance of slavery as an exemplary source of shame strikes me as a symptomatic eruption of the social in the theoretical context of this paragraph and the entire essay from which it is taken. And yet, if we recall his earlier rather totalizing statement about the history of shame and civilization, we can glean in Tomkins a political subtext—one that speaks against the means that some civilizations have adopted to occasion shame, slavery and its various manifestations.

Shame as an affect may be irrevocably with us as human subjects; nevertheless, it is one that travels intersubjectively along very specific byways. Some of these paths include scripts about bodies and their boundaries and about which ones may or may not be subject to trespassing. As we observe more closely the shame side of the dynamic of displacement, we can trace out some of the specifics of the construction of the shamed, enslaved, dominated body and its experience of border crossings and identity checks—encounters with authority, sightings of the emperor. What is very apparent in the Tomkins quote above is the slippery nature of shame, a kind of intersubjective hot potato, a cultural confrontation that leaves subjects momentarily turned to stone. The place where we are arrested by shame is that place where the narrative of the emperor's new clothes abruptly finds closure. One of the reversals operated by this tale is that the figure of authority finds himself caught out, and by one (the child) who is not socially located to make the accusation. The pointing finger signifies "You should be ashamed," but these are not words permitted to travel from child to adult, father, ruler. This reversal or inversion of the place of adult and child is a trope of the immigrant genre and experience. These texts suggest what might take place if the fairy tale did not stop where it does—if the burden of shame were spoken, held in view long enough to map some of its hidden and healed injuries.

The immigrant genre, following Rosemary George's naming, presents readers with the repeated coalescence of wonder and shame in relation to one's place in a given culture. What speaks to the victory of wonder over shame is the ethnoautobiographical text itself as a document of having claimed a place, culturally speaking. Yet the narratives of this coming-into-place are replete with the brutal lessons of shame, even as they recount the exultation of instants of shamelessness. In the texts that constitute this section we will see the twisted nexus of wonder and shame in three writers as they work through this dialectic. Hurston will exemplify some of the movements through race and class as scripted unabashedly; Sandra Cisneros will map out some of the relations between place and class in her evocation of a neighborhood; and Eva Hoffman will self-consciously take up the thorny issues of language and class as they map North America for her. Class inevitably calls up stratified, hierarchical structures; its metaphors work, as it were, to give depth and density to the surfaces of my refractive prism of identity and authority, wonder and shame. These three writers move between classes in various directions. They are not simply telling tales of upward mobility. As travelers, they are sometimes deciding on their own itineraries, as immigrants or ethnics they are at other times pushed along by the so-called choices of others.

Travel writing, immigrant autobiographies, and also concentration camp memoirs (the subject of the final part of this book) provide a textual unfolding of the relation between wonder and shame. Each of these narrative forms shows writers differentially placed along this axis. How they are positioned is dependent on their relation to power and language as they move from place to place on their journeys of arrival and departure. I think that an analytic eye on this writing gives evidence of the profound stake we seem to have in differences as they have been bound up with hierarchy, and shows the insistence with which encounters at the crossroads necessitate the making of distinctions and differentiations. To examine an array of psychic and political positions on the spectrum from travelers to ethnics demonstrates the complex knot of shifting subjectivities that haunt narratives of dislocation in time and space. We must understand this insistence, and its performance in writing, as a need, desire, and demand for orientation in time and place. Then we can follow the way this orientation is colored by idiosyncratic genealogies scripted by the material of everyday life as it sets in motion the dynamic of authority and autonomy.

~

Going North

Zora Neale Hurston's *Dust Tracks on a Road*

> Once I found the use of my feet, they took to wandering.
> Zora Neale Hurston

Zora Neale Hurston is widely acknowledged as occupying a place in American and African-American letters that is unique from many perspectives. One of those is her early childhood in Eatonville, Florida, a town governed by and for black people. Hurston's much-debated autobiography may be productively read as a contribution to the immigrant genre and its tales of crossing cultural borders. Eatonville will provide Hurston with a context much different than the America she will find elsewhere. Hurston is determined to make her way in the (outside) world in ways that resonate with the passion and cultural confusions often found in more conventionally framed immigrant autobiographical tales. For Hurston it will be the passage from the South to the North that maps her movements toward somewhere other than the America she knew as a girl awaiting interlocutors foreign to Eatonville while perched on the gatepost.

Nellie McKay reads the novel *Their Eyes Were Watching God* as autobiography and travel story; let us consider then the cultural travels that *Dust Tracks* narrates of Hurston's "life as a journey" (34).[1] Elsewhere McKay notes the patterns of women's and other minority writers' autobiographies, in which "the importance of group identification repeatedly surfaces" (175).[2] This particular pattern I would insist is integral to Rosemary George's attempt to anatomize the immigrant genre.[3] It underscores as well my earlier point that where travelers seek out the unfamiliar, dislocating space, immigrants or ethnic writers begin by finding themselves already amid the unfamiliar, already dislocated in relation to some site of beginnings, if not origins. To read Hurston as an ethnic or immigrant writer opens potentially new ground for the discussion of African-American texts in relation to the postcolonial rewritings of ethnicity, race, and even nationality.

Hurston's early life among African-Americans provided her with an unquestionably affirmative relation to her own skin and color and value. Nevertheless, significant stories recount her regular contacts with whites from outside Eatonville during her childhood. Hurston tells readers of her autobiography that she was "grannied" by a white man who arrived in time to cut the umbilical cord for her mother, laboring alone. From this man, who is never named, who helped her to be born, and who returned from time to time to take her fishing, she was to learn about the norms of class behavior through the lens of race. His voice is set by Hurston in contrast and somewhat in contest with her father's discourse on race. Both men—one black, one white—will offer her ideas about desire and pride, limits and knowledge, and her power or lack of it.

It is crucial to ask what comes embedded in these fatherly lessons about class and race in relation to Hurston's gender and her proper assignation in that category. We can read Hurston as we did Phillips, as a transitional figure moving between traveler and ethnic at certain key moments. In doing so, ethnicity complicates further what is frequently written under the sign of race.[4] Following McKay, if we read *Their Eyes* as Hurston's text presenting the contradictory wisdom on relations between men and women, *Dust Tracks* and its many frustrated commentators attest to *this* text as the significant, if troublesome, piece of Hurston's literary legacy on the knotty problems between black and white in the United States.[5]

The fourth chapter of *Dust Tracks*, "The Inside Search," does a great deal of work to locate Hurston's sense of agency outside the family while asserting her sense of powerlessness within. It is here that we see the young Hurston

> on top of the gate-post [watching] the world go by. One way to Orlando ran past my house, so the carriages and cars would pass before me. The movement made me glad to see it. Often the white travelers would hail me, but more often I hailed them, and asked, "Don't you want me to go a piece of the way with you?" (45)

To her grandmother such "brazenness was unthinkable" (46). This tenacious and bold temperament lifts Hurston up—her head and her ambitions with it. Yet the punishment that it sometimes brings provides the background of this first extended scene. Imagine this as an intrapsychic stage on which the black and white "fathers" figure the potential horizons of this daughter's world.

> Papa . . . asked us all what we wanted Santa Claus to bring us. . . . Suddenly a beautiful vision came before me. Two things could work together. My Christmas present could take me to the end of the world.
>
>   "I want a fine black riding horse with white saddle and bridles," I told Papa happily. . . .
>
>   "A saddle horse!" Papa exploded. "It's a sin and a shame! Lemme tell you something right now, my young lady; you ain't white. . . . I don't know how you got in this family nohow. You ain't like none of de rest of my young 'uns." (38)

The statement "you ain't white" is asterisked, and Hurston explains to her implied white readers, "That is a Negro saying that means 'Don't be too ambitious. You are a Negro and they are not meant to have but so much'" (38). Ever the worker of the imagination, Hurston tells us that although she was "sucking sorrow," she made one up (a black horse) and rode to "far places." Hurston's mother had wished to believe that "a woman who was an enemy of hers had sprinkled 'travel dust' around the doorstep the day [Zora] was born" rather than connect this to a tendency inherited from Zora's father; like him, she would wander off at the slightest instance, even if only in her thoughts, as with the desired horse.

Competing with this parental/paternal discourse about skin color, class privilege, and the privilege of dreams is an anecdote that characterizes her relation to the first of her white fathers.[6] He gives her one of her nicknames and offers her an axiom for living that will require yet another asterisk for the benefit of her readers: "He called me Snidlits, explaining that Zora was a hell of a name to give a child. . . . 'Snidlits, don't be a nigger,' he would say to me over and over. 'Niggers lie and lie!'" At this point Hurston breaks in: "The word Nigger used in this sense does not mean race. It means a weak, contemptible person of any race" (41). Finding her just as she has lost a fight to a few other children, he repeats:

> Now, Snidlits, this calls for talking. Don't you try to fight three kids at one time unlessen you just can't get around it. . . . And while I'm on the subject, don't you never let nobody spit on you or kick you. Anybody who takes a

thing like that ain't worth de powder and shot it takes to kill 'em, hear? (41–42)

A few paragraphs later, Hurston comments, "I knew without being told that he was not talking about my race when he advised me not to be a nigger. He was talking about class rather than race" (43). As if to convince those she takes to be dubious white readers—and these days, equally dubious black readers—she hastens to vouchsafe this judgment of the white father, allowing that he "frequently gave money to Negro schools" (43). It is precisely this kind of ambiguous, even obsequious, discourse on race that has made *Dust Tracks* a controversial and problematic text for many of Hurston's readers. If we redirect our attention, this symptomatically ambivalent discourse rehearses the tension that Hurston negotiates years later when she narrates her childhood—a tension that speaks her indebtedness to those who helped her learn to live, while remaining aware of her own extraordinary capacities to make others of all sorts take notice of her and make way. This dynamic between the girl her own father thought she ought to be and the person whom the white father thought she could become would set the scene for some of Hurston's passages through difficulty and disorientation during her early life.

Hurston's life seems charmed by its fortuitous encounters with men and women who help her find her own wandering way. Orphaned at ten by the death of her mother and figuratively by the loss of her father upon his remarriage, when he sent his offspring to dispersed family members throughout the South, Hurston learns to listen to the words of those who can help her. Her sense of where to ask for help is uncannily developed, a trait that may mark those who cross borders, whether they start out from the centers or margins—as travelers or immigrants. To pose the very question is to acknowledge helplessness, yet again reminding us of the archaic psychic structures that any of us bring to such an encounter with a stranger.

In the "Voodoo and Fetish" chapter we saw Hurston's discursive practice as a forward-looking ethnography in contradistinction to Gide's nostalgic traveler's glance. I also read Hurston together with Kingsley for their fearlessness as travelers and ethnographers. I now want to read Hurston's efforts for her shamelessness as ethnic autobiographer, all the while keeping in mind that the positivity of shamelessness is, of course, derived from a negativity that is abjected, or rejected. From childhood on and well into her later years, situations that for other narrators would be highly inflected by the bowed head of shame instead spur Hurston toward defiance, irreverence, and audacity. She is bold in turning the tables on conventional or contextual expectations.

Two further examples will underscore my point and will thicken the discussion of race and gender that came through the scene of the fathers. Later in the same key chapter in *Dust Tracks* Hurston recounts a visit to her school by two white women from the North. A visit of this kind by strangers to Florida was a regular occurrence for which the children knew the routine and obedience exacted on such occasions. This, however, was an unscheduled visit, so the usual "close inspection of every one of us before we marched in" did not take place that day. Hurston, ever the performer, figures out which paragraph she will have to read when her turn comes, and she takes the time to rehearse while the other fifth graders begin their recitations. Confident in her skills, she does not focus anxiously on her potentially and usually unkempt self. Rather she observes

> our visitors, who held a book between them, following the lesson. They had shiny hair, mostly brownish. One had a looping gold chain around her neck. The other one was dressed all over in black and white with a pretty finger ring on her left hand. But the thing that held my eyes were their fingers. They were long and thin, and very white, except up near the tips. There they were baby pink. I had never seen such hands. It was a fascinating discovery for me. I wondered how they felt. (48)

In later years and less reverent moments whites are sometimes referred to as the "pink toes." But in this instance we see recorded not only the young girl's perception of well-dressed older women of a certain imposing stature, but also the manicured hands of white leisure. The semiotics of class, race, gender, and power are alloyed with the sense of discovery that I spoke of earlier in Hurston's discourse as traveler.

After her triumphant reading of the myth of Persephone being abducted by Pluto's black horses, when the teacher and the visitors begin to speak and look her way, Zora remembers herself:

> They glanced my way once or twice and I began to worry. Not only was I barefooted, but my feet and legs were dusty. My hair was more uncombed than usual, and my nails were not shiny clean. Oh, I'm going to catch it now. (49)

But Zora is asked to come shake hands with the women, and lies appropriately and partially:

> So I said yes, I *loved* school.
> "I can tell you do," Brown Taffeta gleamed. She patted my head, and was

lucky enough not to get sandspurs in her hand. Children who roll and tum-
ble in the grass in Florida, are apt to get sandspurs in their hair. (50)

Once again, what could all too readily be couched as her own inadequacy to
the scene is reversed when the outsider is "lucky" not to be bothered by what
is integral to the lives of local children. The outsider is awesome but remains
outside—Brown Taffeta brushing up against sandspurs. And sandspurs constitute the norm. When the two women invite Zora to their hotel in the
neighboring white town of Maitland, the foods they offer are "strange
things." She reads aloud for them again, and they photograph her and give
her a mysterious gift, which turns out to be a roll of new pennies: "Their
gleam lit up the world. It was not avarice that moved me. It was the beauty of
the thing. I stood on the mountain" (52). The gift can enrich her without simultaneously evoking any shame over the impoverishment or scarcity that
moves the giver. This first of many gifts that were to arrive from the women
gave Hurston "such joy" that years later the comparison most apt is the arrival of "the telegram accepting my first book." The books the two women
send her later give her a more sustaining pleasure than the pennies. And yet
their tales of heroism produce a very particular conflict for the young
Hurston:

> My soul was with the gods and my body in the village. People just would not
> act like gods. Stew beef, fried fat-back and morning grits were no ambrosia
> from Valhalla. Raking back yards and carrying out chamber-pots, were not
> the tasks of Thor. (56)

Versions of heroism are mixed with loss. This young girl who aspires to the
"tasks of Thor" also regrets the end of her childhood, marked, she claims, by
twelve visions of what will constitute her wanderings and exile, which had
not yet begun in earnest.

Hurston's wandering is first cast in a mode of desire for new people and
their stories; however, after her mother's death this wandering is recast for
some time as a kind of "vagrancy" (114). She describes a decade of being
without a stable home or family, and says that the first five years were the
worst. During this time her father remarried, chose a new wife who was not
liked by the younger children, and ended up driving both his daughters
away. Zora felt less love lost than did her sister, Sarah, whom Zora rescued
when even she—the father's favored child—was slighted and shamed by the
new stepmother.

Hurston had felt a certain ineffectuality when she insisted that she was
privy to her mother's last wishes ("not to let them take the pillow from

under her head until she was dead. The clock was not to be covered, nor the looking-glass"), and was ignored, as a child might be, by her father and her mother's women friends (86). This wound had been festering. The failed promise to her mother is fulfilled in the rescue of her sister as she, Zora, becomes successor to her mother's deeds. Sarah was the oldest of John Hurston's daughters and much wished for after the birth of three sons. She was pampered and petted: "She had a gold ring for her finger, and gold earrings. When I begged for music lessons, I was told to dry up before he bust the hide on my back" (99). Among all his children, the father had never struck this one, until after the new stepmother "insisted that Papa put Sarah out of the house . . . go over and beat Sarah with a buggy whip for commenting on the marriage so soon after Mama's death" (97). After this incident

> neither Papa nor Sarah ever looked at each other in the same way again, nor at the world. Nor did they look like the same people to the world who knew them. Their heads hung down and they studied the ground under their feet too much.
>
> As for me, looking on, it made a tiger out of me.

Hurston cannot stand even the sight of shame in those she loves. She will physically insert herself to take shame from those upon whom it has landed and remove it to its more proper place. Her fury leaves her lying in wait for the moment when she will be able to return the humiliation in kind:

> And six years later I paid the score off in a small way. . . . [M]y stepmother threatened to beat me for my impudence, after vainly trying to get Papa to undertake the job. I guess that the memory of the time that he had struck Sarah at this wife's demand, influenced Papa and saved me. . . . Old memories of her power over him told her to assert herself. . . . The bottle came sailing slowly through the air and missed me easily. She never should have missed.
>
> The primeval in me leaped to life. Ha! This was the very corn I wanted to grind. Fight! Not having to put up with what she did to us through Papa! Direct action and everything up to me. (100–101)

Hurston counts the stored-up rage chronologically, and even when the fight is over she feels frustrated that she "had not beaten more than two years out of her yet" (103). Nevertheless there is the satisfaction of the women in town who "had been praying for something like that to happen" (104). And like the father and daughter whose heads had been bowed by her orders, the stepmother now "went on off with her lip hung down lower than a mason's apron" (104).

What is important in this extended scene is its relation to Hurston's deeply ambivalent discourse about her father; he is both revered and adored for the likeness they are said to share, while in her grandmother's narrative legacy he is simultaneously reviled and dismissed as the young man from "over the creek," mismatched with her daughter. This scene also asks to be read for its very dense display of the knotting of gender and generation. A child *is* being beaten here; one daughter steps into the fray to spare the shame of the other daughter. In doing so this daughter, Zora, rewrites the memory of her dead mother, and remedies the father's shame of his submission to the whims of his second wife. These are matters of family and class—both the father's and mother's place in the town are reclaimed. Zora's deeds also reinscribe the words of men, those designated to rule over the life of the young woman-to-be. It is no small matter in this instance that it was Hurston's father who wrote the laws of Eatonville in its early days.

I want to shift this discussion of gender, identity, and shame back onto the ground of race, and that moment later in Hurston's life when she worked as a manicurist pampering white men. This occurred during a crucial transitional time when she was in her first semester at Howard University and got a job supporting herself in one of George Robinson's black-owned barber shops for whites only in downtown Washington. Hurston was aiming to "be worthy to stand there under the shadow of the hovering spirit of Howard" and also learning "things from holding the hands of men" who took her into their confidence, revealing personal and political secrets. Her place in this microcosm of black and white, power and service, taught her as much as the lessons of Howard. She became a liaison in a network of delicate loyalties to different customers. On one particular day a black man entered, sat down in the manager's chair, and demanded a haircut and shave. Banks, the manager, apprised him of the fact that "Mr. Robinson has a fine shop for Negroes on U Street" (162). In the confusion that followed, all the black employees were "helping to throw the Negro out" in spite of his demands and insistence on constitutional rights.

Hurston reflects with full ambivalence on the incident—the self-interest of the employees, the sanctioning of Jim Crow practices, the sense of threat of loss of livelihood, and the irony of another black man "wrecking George Robinson like that on a 'race' angle" (165). In a utopian mode she imagines:

> Offhand, you might say that we fifteen Negroes should have felt the racial thing and served him. He was one of us. Perhaps it would have been a beautiful thing if Banks had turned to the shop crowded with customers and announced that this man was going to be served like everybody else even at the

risk of losing their patronage, with all of the other employees lined up in the center of the floor shouting, "So say we all!" It would have been a stirring gesture, and made the headlines for a day. (164–65)

But the bright picture dims almost immediately as she continues in the dystopian mode of everyday life for herself and her fellow workers: "Then we could all have gone home to our unpaid rents and bills and things like that. I could leave school and begin my wanderings again" (165). This incident brings out the deep ambivalence of Hurston's politics and the complications of how race matters operated then and still now. She admits her intellectual defeat in not knowing just how to absorb such a moment:

So I do not know what was the ultimate right in this case. I do know how I felt at the time. There is always something fiendish and loathsome about a person who threatens to deprive you of your way of making a living. That is just human-like, I reckon. (165)

I daresay that Hurston might be a less disquieting voice on the problematics of race if we could read in her not just dissembling, but competing desires, alive and struggling to be satisfied—desire for recognition and the desire that her wisdom not single her out because of her race alone.

Furthermore, what I take to be Hurston's refusal of shame throughout her life may be a crucial piece in understanding her politics, particularly her utterly flexible positionality on matters of race. If, recalling Tomkins, the history of civilization is a history of shame, certainly the history of African-Americans demands that the dominant white culture recognize a history of institutionalized humiliation. Hurston will have none of this as her burden, even though she comes to know this history well once she leaves the safe borders of Eatonville. Like so many African-American autobiographers, she will say about her experience in a new town subsequent to her mother's death: "Jacksonville made me know that I was a little colored girl" (94).

There is in the coming-to-consciousness of those in a racial minority another mirror stage, one in which that which is already perched in the unconscious comes to inhabit the everyday. It has been said that the assumption of sexed subjectivity allows us to gain meaning at the expense of being. We can only also assume that the ideological imperative to assume a raced subjectivity exacts a further psychic toll in a script that is even more assymmetrical than the script of gender. This awareness of racial difference we must understand not as a difference with no valence; rather it is a sense of difference that is fraught with negativity, the kind of psychic weight that Fanon made visible, audible, sensible for his readers. Fanon's masks of race are worn to cover scars, pain, rage, despair—they are, so to speak, masks of the tragedy of racism and its shameful imprints. Hurston's masks, I would venture to say, are worn with a kind of verve, nerve, and sass; this attitude nevertheless does not prevent her recognition, also while a girl in Jacksonville, that there was "just a jagged hole where my home used to be" (95). The emotional and economic destitution she experiences when she leaves the family leads her to realize that "having nothing, I still did not know how to be humble" (117). She persists in her refusal to become tainted by the smell of death that poverty gives off; she will not be one of those "people [who] can be slave-ships in shoes" (116). In this utterance Hurston casts off a history of shame and the civilization that traded in the currency of humiliation. Hurston sometimes refuses to speak *for* her race, while she often speaks quite easily *of* her race, and yet elsewhere she aims to deny the significance of race in her speaking. However, for my reading, Hurston's degree of ambiguity and difficulty helps to locate some of the complex coordinates of identity troubles.

Caryl Phillips's text showed how being or not being at home in one's skin may produce a complex relation to the power to speak and to be heard. In addressing the questions of power *to* and power *over* that are conferred by a sense of self in (relation to) place we can read the shifting function of place both as grounding and as condemnation, a sentence pronounced. That particular knot of identity we saw much less of in the discourses of Hurston or Gide, for example, where recognition was much more tied up with a sense of discovery, even wonder. If Gide knew shame it was depersonalized in terms of his nationality, and displaced onto France and its colonialist sins. Hurston refused shame—for her womanhood, for her ignorance of Caribbean or northern ways—and instead searched for history in her voyages out and back.

"Where Do You Live?"

Sandra Cisneros's *House on Mango Street*

> That sentiment accompanying the absence of home—homesickness—can
> cut two ways: it can be a yearning for the authentic (situated in the past or in
> the future) or it can be the recognition of the inauthenticity of all homes. In
> the context of the immmigrant novel it is the latter that usually prevails.
> Rosemary Marangoly George

In the autobiographical narrative of ethnic identity formation a thoroughly
articulated position in relation to the past and future of the self often surfaces. The traveler, ethnographer, or anthropologist, no matter her relation
to her subjects of study, is in a position of having chosen her place, her
routes, her questions. The displaced autobiographer finds herself dislocated
and needs to blaze a trail that will lead her out of an imposed, not chosen
loss of place and self. However, the traveler and the autoethnographer will
share the desire to make the writing of their displacement lead them to a re-
shaped sense of self. Writing will lead them back to a new home.

Sandra Cisneros is a writer who, while sorting through the affects of ethnicity with longing, also remains unsentimental, albeit not heartless, about
her search for a home. Rosemary George further explains that for the immigrant writer, "making oneself at home is a project that may not be completed" (79).

For Cisneros, a Chicana writer, storytelling is about an exploration of
place and belonging. Esperanza, the fictionalized and autobiographical nar-

rator of *The House on Mango Street*, describes herself as a girl "who didn't want to belong." Not to Mango Street, although she has come back to tell its stories, which are her own whether she wants them or not: "I write it down and Mango says goodbye sometimes. She does not hold me with both arms. She sets me free." Not just the house, the entire street is embodied as mother whose strength is in letting her daughter go, but the girl who wants desperately to leave with her "books and paper" addresses her farewell to all those "friends and neighbors who will say, What happened to that Esperanza?" (101).[1]

Esperanza will take quite a long time before she believes that her place on Mango Street may represent a gift as well as the burden she has known it to be. In this narrative of living the urban "borderlands," a Mexican neighborhood in Chicago, the knotting of recognition and shame becomes particularly legible for the girl child whose urges to leave home and to write are what will enable her to work shame into the power of language and knowledge.[2] Cisneros carves out a self shaped in being named through the eyes of another. The following is from the opening scene, where Esperanza is bound to the task of street historiographer:

> Once when we were living on Loomis, a nun from my school passed by and saw me playing out front. The laundromat downstairs had been boarded up because it had been robbed two days before and the owner had painted on the wood YES WE'RE OPEN so as not to lose business.
>
> Where do you live? she asked.
>
> There, I said pointing up to the third floor.
>
> You live *there?*
>
> *There.* I had to look to where she pointed—the third floor, the paint peeling, wooden bars Papa had nailed on the windows so we wouldn't fall out. You live *there?* The way she said it made me feel like nothing. *There.* I lived *there.* I nodded.
>
> I knew then I had to have a house. A real house. One I could point to. But this isn't it. The house on Mango Street isn't it. For the time being, mama said. Temporary, said Papa. But I know how those things go. (8–9)

The nun, a figural amalgam of church and state, confers upon the girl, through questions and a pointing finger, a place because she appears not to have one; the house to which Esperanza draws her eye is not within the realm of possibility for the teacher—she cannot delineate this space called home by the girl. To the nun's senses it appears only as undifferentiated poverty of dwelling. The unnamed nun, who is also an ambiguous figure of authority, brings Esperanza to a recognition of herself through a relation to place whereby she learns to deny an identity, to disclaim until she can re-claim it—"I have gone away to come back."

This opening scene of the nun pointing her finger at Esperanza's house inverts and displaces the scene of identities taking shape—that moment where the child notes the emperor's nakedness and thereby claims a vision, an insight that must be recognized by those who surround her and who marvel at her audacity. Here, however, when the relations of identity and authority are moved around, such that it is the child whose identity is laid bare, we have the classic moment of shaming the self mediated through the home—house and street as the outermost layers of the outfitted subject.

Esperanza's long road to self-authorization or agency is rationalized as a space traversed "for the ones I left behind[,] for the ones who cannot get out" (102). To those around her—relatives and childhood friends—Esperanza will become Mango Street, the voice of its inhabitants who only pass from the oral to the written through her stories. While this moment of claiming identity romanticizes marginality, still, the identity thereby claimed is not that of discrete autonomous selfhood, the self of American discursive liberalism;[3] rather, this is an identity formed as a burden whose weight is only learned as it is taken from her, by her, into herself. In living her hope (Esperanza), she makes the past live for her, rather than letting it continue to live off her. Only in becoming Mango Street can she let Mango Street go. This self must first gather its dispersion before it can forgo coherence. Then it can remake the parts, the partial identities that were fighting the nun's pointing finger, the girl who didn't belong "there," who didn't want to live "there," but who had to live somewhere. In the repetition of "there" we can read the depth of the tie between place and self, how a self, even one as dislocated as Esperanza, becomes forced to take root in foreign soil. Even if the place she is put is ill suited, she must accommodate herself to it. Not a real home, but her home. Not a good home, but her home. And wear it she will.

This is an identity formed in community—heavier than the weight of a child, a burden whose weight is only learned as it is taken from her shoulders into herself, the one who can return to take the others with her, within her. When she enfolds it, it will no longer hold her back. First comes a self-knowledge through ethnicity, gender, language, and only later might she elect the postmodern fashion of questioning identity.

When "The Three Sisters" read her palm—"yes, she'll go very far"—they seem to know her silent wish to leave this world. Papa may have the deciding voice about where "there" will be, but mother, grandmother, aunts, sister, and female friends are the ones who shape with Esperanza what "there" will become in her. The women are the ones in whom she will have to recognize herself, and through whom she will have to learn to become someone else, someone they may not recognize before she can come back to them:

> A circle, understand? You will always be Esperanza. You will always be Mango Street. You can't erase what you know. You can't forget who you are.
>   . . . It was as if she could read my mind, as if she knew what I had wished for, and I felt ashamed for having made such a selfish wish. (98)

Cisneros must recover from shame to inhabit an identity she may begin to put into question after having disclaimed and reclaimed it, mistaken though it may be.

In the chapter called "My Name" Cisneros mixes two ethnic traditions in order to strengthen her budding hopeful self:

> It was my grandmother's name and now it is mine. She was a horse woman too, born like me in the Chinese year of the horse—which is supposed to be bad luck if you're born female—but I think this is a Chinese lie because the Chinese, like the Mexicans, don't like their women strong. . . . (12)
>   At school they say my name funny as if the syllables were made out of tin and hurt the roof of your mouth. But in Spanish my name is made out of a softer something like silver . . .
>   I would like to baptize myself under a new name . . . (12–13)

This shame and pride in the name is a topos of the immigrant genre. Cisneros's use of this dramatic moment recalls the tension created by Maxine Hong Kingston in her exemplary text of the immigrant genre, *The Woman Warrior*, where the narrator, Maxine, also a young girl, must constantly negotiate the meanings to be made of two opposing stories of femininity told by her mother. There is the unspoken shameful history of the paternal aunt, No Name Woman, who drowned herself and her newborn daughter in the family well in order to erase her child's illegitimacy and her own adultery; but there is also Fa Mu Lan, the warrior woman of the title, who leaves her family to save her village and is brave in battle even while pregnant. Esperanza wants to redeem her grandmother's name while rejecting her legacy, a familiar one among the married women, young and old, whom Esperanza studies—"she looked out the window all her life, the way so many women sit their sadness on an elbow" (12).

Countering the sadness of the grandmother is Aunt Lupe, who is dying slowly but reminds her "to keep writing, Esperanza. You must keep writing.

It will keep you free, and I said yes, but at that time I didn't know what she meant" (56). This aunt's death occasions a very specific inquiry into the shifting place of shame. The chapter is called "Born Bad," indicating the lasting guilt Esperanza feels for the game she and her sisters often played, which on this particular day coincided with her aunt's death. As a charade the children usually imitated a famous person, whose identity the others had to guess, but on this day they chose instead to imitate the aunt they knew. Once a woman in "her Joan Crawford dress and swimmer's legs," she had become blind from her illness. Visits to her house inspired revulsion and disgust:

> I hated to go there alone. The six blocks to the dark apartment, second floor rear building where sunlight never came. . . . She never saw the dirty dishes in the sink. She couldn't see the ceilings dusty with flies. . . . I can't forget the smell. Like sticky capsules filled with jelly. My aunt, a little oyster, a little piece of meat on an open shell for us to look at. Hello, hello. As if she had fallen into a well. (56)

There is the inarticulate shame of the child who is watching the grown woman's body disintegrate and disappear, and the shame at her own disgust and ignorance.

Esperanza came to read to Aunt Lupe; one day when she tried to show her a picture in *The Waterbabies*, the aunt revealed her blindness, intensifying Esperanza's shame. Her aunt's last act, as it were, was to bless Esperanza's talent for writing. But the last act of the visiting nieces that day was to imitate her limp, blind body: "We didn't know. She had been dying such a long time we forgot. Maybe she was ashamed. Maybe she was embarrassed it took so many years" (57). The strands in the tangled knot of shame include not only a sense of filial betrayal for having ridiculed the aunt's infirmities, but also, irrevocably bound up in it, Esperanza's blessed talent, now nearly cursed by this unfortunate congruence. Certainly her writing will necessitate the betrayal of family secrets, which in immigrant life often have as much to do with *being* as with *doing*—one of the simpler distinctions often made between shame and guilt.

I began by talking of the house, street, and neighborhood as externalized accoutrements of the shamed, because *dys*located, self. If we shift the discussion onto the more familiar terrain of the body, particularly the female adolescent body, we come upon minefields of shame. In Cisneros's acute representation of femininity under construction we find our attention drawn to shoes (and the feet they hide) as anchors of the awkward body. When the mother in "The Family of Little Feet" offers Esperanza and her friends, Lucy and Rachel, three pairs of high heels, a pubescent comedy of female manners

is all too quickly transformed into the everyday vignette of street sexual harrassment that girls learn very early to negotiate more or less well:

> It's Rachel who learns to walk the best all strutted in those magic high heels.
> She teaches us to cross and uncross our legs, and to run like a double-dutch
> rope, and how to walk down to the corner so that the shoes talk back to you
> with every step. Lucy, Rachel, me tee-tottering like so. Down to the corner
> where the men can't take their eyes off us. We must be Christmas. (38)

The thrill of being admired is undercut moments later "Bum man says, Yes,
little girl. Your little lemon shoes are so beautiful. But come closer. I can't see
very well. Come closer. Please." Running away, back to Mango Street, the
narrator somewhat breathlessly says, "We are tired of being beautiful," and
when Lucy's mother throws the shoes away, "no one complains" (40). This
passing thrill comes rarely to Esperanza, who is more likely to watch from
the sidelines as older girls she knows take on the visible burdens and imaginary pleasures of men and sexuality. Two more typical moments of ill-fitting
femininity appear in "Chanclas" (old shoes or slippers) and in "The Monkey
Garden." The first recounts a family baptismal party in the Precious Blood
Church basement where

> everybody is laughing except me because I'm wearing the new dress, pink
> and white, with stripes and new underclothes and the new socks and the old
> saddle shoes I wear to school, brown and white, the kind I get every Septem-
> ber because they last long and they do. . . . Meanwhile that boy who is my
> cousin by first communion or something, asks me to dance and I can't. . . . I
> shake my head no. My feet grow bigger and bigger. Then Uncle Nacho . . .
> who is a liar says you are the prettiest girl here, will you dance . . . and, yes,
> we are dancing. . . . My feet swell big and heavy like plungers, but I drag them
> across the linoleum floor straight center where Uncle wants to show off the
> new dance we learned. And Uncle spins me and my skinny arms bend the
> way he taught me and my mother watches and my little cousins watch and
> the boy who is my cousin by first communion watches . . . until I forget that I
> am wearing only ordinary shoes.
> All night the boy who is a man watches me dance. He watched me dance.
> (45–46)

Here the two-page chapter ends. All the shivering anguish and delight in
being looked at, a key aspect of what has long been taken to be properly constructed femininity, is exposed in this scene. In "The Monkey Garden" the
anguish is aroused by the ambivalent gendered identity of early adolescence
when Esperanza tries to rescue her friend Sally from Tito and his friends,
who demand a kiss each before returning Sally's stolen keys. Esperanza can
hardly differentiate clearly the mixed, clotted emotions she feels one day

when the usual pleasures of the garden—an abandoned house and yard formerly inhabited by a family with a pet monkey—turn sour:

> Who was it that said I was getting too old to play the games? Who was it I didn't listen to? I only remember that when the others ran, I wanted to run too, up and down and through the monkey garden, fast as the boys, not like Sally who screamed if she got her stockings muddy. (89)

The familiar games of the garden are suddenly no longer Sally's and Esperanza's; Sally has turned to play with the boys. And Esperanza experiences their laughter as an outsider: "It was a joke I didn't get" (89). From isolation to anger, Esperanza explores the path between the shame and pride of her gender trouble:

> I . . . ran back . . . to the garden where Sally needed to be saved. I took three big sticks and a brick and figured this was enough.
> But when I got there Sally said go home. Those boys said, leave us alone. I felt stupid with my brick. They all looked at me as if *I* was the one that was crazy and made me feel ashamed. (90)

In an earlier chapter called "Beautiful and Cruel," Esperanza assumes this same dislocation in relation to gender expectations as a guerrilla girl, or woman warrior-in-training. This one-page chapter begins: "I am an ugly daughter. I am the one nobody comes for." It closes thus:

> In the movies there is always one with red red lips who is beautiful and cruel. She is the one who drives the men crazy and laughs them all away. Her power is her own. She will not give it away.
> I have begun my own quiet war. Simple. Sure. I am one who leaves the table like a man, without putting back the chair or picking up the plate. (82)

To refuse the versions of femininity available to her, Esperanza imagines borrowing the garments of domestic masculine privilege. She will defy femininity's goodness and loveliness (of which she feels already dispossessed), as well as its fiercer, laughing Medusa variations. The rudeness and crude weapons of boyhood seem more accessible, although they leave Esperanza feeling rather disembodied—those feet again. The shame of the monkey garden sent Esperanza running, hiding, and finally crying. The partly grown girl tries to soothe and erase her own pain, saying:

> I read somewhere in India there are priests who can will their heart to stop beating. I wanted to will my blood to stop, my heart to quit its pumping. I wanted to be dead, to turn into the rain, my eyes melt into the ground like two black snails. I wished and wished. I closed my eyes and willed it, but when I got up my dress was green and I had a headache.

> I looked at my feet in their white socks and ugly round shoes. They
> seemed far away. They didn't seem to be my feet anymore. And the garden
> that had been such a good place to play didn't seem mine either. (90–91)

Cast out of her Eden, Esperanza would choose to leave her body, the weighty
anchors of those shoes, and the earth itself. Heterosexual femininity and the
sexuality that follows in its wake leave Esperanza feeling betrayed by Sally in
this chapter. What follows it, "Red Clowns," presents the further betrayal of
Sally's lies, but also the lies of "storybooks and movies" about playing with
the boys. Esperanza becomes the object of unwanted kissing, groping, and
threatening words of seduction while she waits for Sally, who has gone off
with another boy at a carnival. Esperanza's anguish at her first unwelcome
encounter with boys—"You lied, you lied. He wouldn't let me go. He said I
love you, I love you, Spanish girl"—is rapidly transformed into her own refound truths.[4] For in the very next chapter Sally has become the wife she
longed to be—"She met a marshmallow sales man at a school bazaar and she
married him in another state where it's legal to get married before eighth
grade"—and is just as rapidly becoming one of those women who "sits her
sadness on her elbow" because "she is afraid to go outside without his per-
mission. She looks at all the things they own. . . . She likes looking at the
walls, at how neatly their corners meet, the linoleum roses on the floor, the
ceiling smooth as wedding cake" (95).

Just as Esperanza would not become the house or the street that ought to
have been hers to call home, she will not become the women who inhabit
these houses and streets. Nevertheless it is to the women that this book is
dedicated. And, as is evident from this discussion, it is the women who sustain her even as they disappoint her with the impoverished nature of the
choices they appear to be making. The difficulty of packing up her own bags
filled only with paper and books is so overwhelming that Esperanza can for-
give the women she loves for their dreams that are nothing like her own.
Their dreams nourish her imagination and its embellishments on the possibilities of daily life. In this text Esperanza is the only one who leaves, whereas
in Cisneros's next book, *Woman Hollering Creek*, we read about some of the
women who break out of their immobility at the windows of houses and
lives that have become too small.

~

Careless Baptisms

Eva Hoffman's *Lost in Translation*

It seems a simple affirmation of justice, of rightness, of reason that Jews are
human the way other people are human. After all, I see that with my own two
eyes, and I'm too young yet to believe that the emperor is wearing clothes.
Eva Hoffman, "Paradise"

Eva Hoffman's 1989 memoir serves as an example of a highly self-conscious
study in living on borderlines, as do many other recent autobiographical
texts by women and postcolonials. Hoffman's stance in her text, that of the
outsider, makes it possible to read this work, plainly one of passage through
identities, as speaking the language of the ethnic, the traveler, and the survivor. What Hoffman must learn to do, she acknowledges in the closing
pages, is give up the position of outsider and let herself live in the language
that has nevertheless become her when once it had fit so badly. Language is
clothing, a linguistic transvestism; not the emperor's clothes, which remain
invisible and fraudulent, but garments that take on pattern and shape at the
moment we enter speech. Identities can be seen, then, as things we bear and
wear—being as donning; a newly mastered language becomes another skin
over our own but one on which we also learn to feel the breath of encounters
with other tongues.

Hoffman's text is divided into three parts: "Paradise," the time of childhood in Cracow, Poland; "Exile," the years in Vancouver, British Columbia,
and later in college at Rice University in Houston, Texas; and "The New

World" of Cambridge, Massachusetts, where she completed graduate school at Harvard, and her later move to New York City. Each space marks life in a "new" language. In the first instance she is learning her mother tongue; what follows is a passage of childhood recollection:

> I want to tell A Story, Every Story, everything all at once . . . and I try to roll all sounds into one, to accumulate more and more syllables, as if they might make a Mobius strip of language in which everything, everything is contained. . . . I want articulation—but articulation that says the whole world at once. (11)

We can hear in this passage the utopian longing for a "universal" syllable, childhood's metaphysics of language and its capacities. But we can also hear in this the later acquired wisdom that language will not do all.

When in "Exile" the language in question becomes English, there is more than resignation and longing, there is a sense of not being able to emerge in her syllables even though she will take pains to enunciate more clearly than native speakers. Her early urge and wish to make language say everything is rewritten when she is given a diary as a birthday gift by one of her first new world friends:

> If I am indeed to write something entirely for myself, in what language do I write? . . . Writing in Polish at this point would be a little like resorting to Latin or ancient Greek—an eccentric thing to do in a diary, in which you're supposed to set down your most immediate experiences and unpremeditated thoughts in the most unmediated language. . . . I finally choose English. If I'm to write about the present, I have to write in the language of the present, even if it's not the language of the self. . . .
>   This language is beginning to invent another me. However, I discover something odd. It seems that when I write (or, for that matter, think) in English, I am unable to use the word "I." I do not go as far as the schizophrenic "she"—but I am driven, as by a compulsion, to the double, the Siamese-twin "you." (120–21)

The young girl, long disabused of the possibility of language saying everything, telling every story, still hopes for, but is denied by her circumstances *in* language, an unmediated route to something she calls the self. Even with a recognition of the thoroughly mediated texture of language, still Hoffman will contend that "we want to be at home in our tongue" (124). However naive we may understand such a desire to be, if we know language as prisonhouse or temporary shelter, still we also recognize the phenomenon Hoffman is alluding to. If we have ever tried to master a new language and then been in a position to make use of it we know how un-at-home, how *unheim-*

lich, that can feel. If, in fact, we have achieved a degree of fluency in a new language, it is an experience akin to discovering a new home. And even so, there will inevitably come moments where the subtleties of this newly mastered tongue will elude us and remind us of how great is the distance from our "native" tongue.[1] If language, like clothing, is meant to protect, the best kind of clothing in language would make us invisible, not recognizably *from elsewhere*.

Hoffman's most poignant transformation is the one from Polish girl into American woman, just to peel back two layers of the ways that an ethnicized gender identity must be refashioned in the new home. The critique of femininity, itself a contested cultural space, has taught us to recognize the mobility, plasticity, and mimicry involved in becoming a woman.[2] Hoffman notes the cultural differences in the "allegory of gender" and realizes her lack of landmarks for negotiating these paths. Here are some of the inflections of nationality, ethnicity, and gender and the knots they make:

> I can't become a "Pani" [Mrs.] of any sort: not like the authoritative Pani Orlovska, or the vampy, practical Pani Dombarska, or the flirty, romantic woman writer I once met. None of these modes of femininity makes sense here. (189)

It is not merely the complex set of questions about how to make herself learn to speak this language—North American English—well, but also how to make its practices of embodiment hers: Will she make up? shave her legs? kiss the boys? None of these dilemmas remind her of what she had begun to understand in Poland about the lives of women among men. There are expressions that find no echo here about what kind of woman one could be. Coming to Canada at age thirteen, Hoffman's is a story that asks to be read as one version of the adolescent reinscription of the oedipal parable of psychoanalysis—that thoroughly self-conscious assumption of heterosexual femininity. Hoffman surrenders herself to the work of psychotherapy at the end of her book almost as if this were finally a wholesale acceptance of the culture she had tried so hard to enter or, at moments, keep at bay.

Perhaps because of the self-consciousness of Hoffman's text, it serves up nodal moments of the complex set of transactions that constitute aspects of identity construction. Hoffman, once a graduate student of English literature, knows just how contested the sites of identity formation and construction are and have been for late-twentieth-century "Americans." As an outsider, she has accumulated some impatience, if not disdain, for this constant clamoring for identities. However, the tracks of her own life have marked her as one who must, in very obvious ways, reclaim and discard bits and pieces of herself scattered across the globe.

An early moment that will mark her path with some subtle detours is when she and her sister, four years younger, are quite casually and carelessly renamed in order to be registered for school in Canada. Names she has never heard become theirs, her surname sounds nothing like before; she recounts how her mouth struggled with the syllables of this new set of names, and how in later years the sisters made their separate accomodations to the new world names. Reentering this moment she says, "Nothing much has happened, except a small, seismic mental shift" (105). She reflects on her experience of being a "living avatar of structuralist wisdom" who knows

> these new appellations, which we ourselves can't yet pronounce, are not us. They are identification tags, disembodied signs pointing to objects that happen to be my sister and myself . . . names that make us strangers to ourselves.

The problem with this "wisdom" about the break between referent and sign is that it is "without any of the consolations that wisdom usually brings"; rather it performs a "desiccating alchemy. . . . It is the loss of a living connection" (107). Hoffman is on familiar, even intimate terms with nostalgia and its Polish variant, which, inevitably, summons more of what she wishes to signify, *tesknota*, or homesickness. So we can read her as already recognizing how the immigrant's classic tale that she has to retell is cast in metaphors of irremediable loss. But we overlook the repetition of this motif in such narratives at the risk of missing some of the crucial elements at war and at play in the contemporary struggles over identities. Hoffman recognizes that "speech is a class signifier," and she recounts that she learns to discern the diacritical marks of class in speakers on whom she eavesdrops through "the extent of authority that shapes the rhythm of their speech" (123).

Words *are* things, although certainly not the things they name. And to be dispossessed of them, or shamed in the use of them, or unable to share in their currency may be akin to that moment when the emperor cannot seem to notice that he has been exposed. The one left outside the verbal loop operating in specific circumstances mimes comprehension and hopes to remain undiscovered, like the emperor stiffening at the truth of the child's words. However, at such a moment in a narrative like Hoffman's, it is the child who is masquerading, who is trying to pass so as not to lose whatever footing she may be tenuously and tenaciously guarding in order to make a new name and place for herself.

The child's wish for the universal syllable is never fully forgone. Approaching her conclusion, Hoffman recalls and realizes once again:

> The tiny gap that opened when my sister and I were given new names can never be fully closed up; I can't have one name again. My sister has returned to her Polish name—Alina. It takes a while for me to switch back to it; Alina, in English, is a different word than it is in Polish. . . . When I talk to myself now, I talk in English. English is the language in which I've become an adult. (272)

Realizing that her psychotherapy is in large part "translation therapy," Hoffman notes that the "wholeness of childhood truths is intermingled with the divisiveness of adult doubt." For her own autobiographical self this divide is marked not only in the change from Poland to Canada but also all that this change brings in its wake that is best carried and most easily lost in words. Forsaking "childhood unity," Hoffman gains experience that translates as "style, and style, in turn, creates a new woman" (273). We know style to be an adaptation, a garb, an idiosyncratic borrowing from the available markers in order to pass sometimes noticed, sometimes unnoticed. In adolescence it is her style that makes her awkward, that leads various girls and women to "make her over" into a proper girl-becoming-woman; in her adult life style is precisely what will allow her to pass rather less noticeably as the outsider she once was. She will have regained a sense of humor, if not the one she might have constructed without the break in tongues; for humor, too, is a medium in which dislocations once lived as pain are translated into laughter, for the one juggling the words and for the audience.

Where Hoffman will examine what it felt like to be sometimes caged by language, other writers of this experience of border crossings will anatomize the contours of silence in the face of cultural dislocations. But even the documenting of silences comes to us finally in words, texts, that attest to the salvaging effects of language that once seemed a sealed house.

Hoffman's closing pages circle toward the statement that "dislocation is the norm rather than the aberration in our time" (274). The preoccupying questions of my work are those that investigate just how this norm is lived and told, and how the shifts whereby "every competing center makes us marginal" are variegated according to histories that may be idiosyncratic but also emblematic. For Hoffman the bureaucratic designation of immigration, "resident alien," comes to embody her sense of herself as "hybrid"; only when she returns to her family home in Vancouver as the successful writer does she feel herself returned to an "oxymoron." While she tires of the fetish of identity-talk that she encounters in the United States, still she knows "on her skin" that this sort of talk *is* her experience of self and place, self in place. She wonders if, perhaps, she has "acquired a second unconscious, an American one," which would help to explain her "incompletely assimilated" status (220–21). The writing of memoirs like Hoffman's represents the work of excavating and cataloging strata of consciousness and the unconscious through the medium of a new, "second" language.

In a vocabulary that differs notably from Denise Riley's "skating" across identities, James Clifford, in the introduction to *The Predicament of Culture*, says, "Identity is conjunctural."[3] Assuming a subject who knows *how* to skate, there would be great pleasure to be taken in the motion produced by this activity of identity-making and identification, but that is a very different perspective from the "conjunctural," which focuses attention on circumstances and their weight on the subject. If we look briefly at Hoffman's representation of her mother, we read the mother's difference from her two daughters through metaphors of mobility and circumstance; Hoffman notes that "when she sees Alinka break into a sprint . . . she says regretfully, 'I've never done that. I've never run.'" Eva, the narrator, continues to wonder if her mother finds her daughters somehow "monstrous" since

> such rapid and independent movement surely did not belong to the female side of the equation among the traditional Jews of Zalosce, and my mother has never swum, or skied or skated, or taken a trip entirely on her own.
>
> Alinka and I move around on our own as if the globe were a large toy to play with. (250–51)

Hoffman is the ethnographer of her own exile as adolescent castaway who opened her memoir with the recollected sense that the ship's departure signaled to her that "life is ending" (3). Thirteen-year-old self-dramatizing, perhaps, but also the beginning of the life-writing that would turn conjunctural fate into play with the world, with the words of the world: broken syllables salvaged, language made new, a suit of clothes that fits once again, like new.

Hoffman wishes to have language fit her so well that invisibility will disguise her "fear that no one will ever recognize me as one of their own"; this wish coexists with the visible struggle of her immigrant odyssey in which she feels called upon to display instead a "compensatory, counterphobic immigrant bravado" (244). She explores the ramifications of this demand when she says:

> Immigrant energy, admirable name though it has gained for itself, does not seem a wholly joyful phenomenon to me. I understand the desperado drive

that fuels it. . . . As a radically marginal person, you have two choices: to be
intimidated by every situation, every social stratum, or to confront all of
them with the same leveling vision, the same brash and stubborn spunk.
  I too am goaded on by the forked whip of ambition and fear. (157)

We can hear in Hoffman's speculative and theoretical disquisition on desire, drive, and ambition both the boldness and "spunk" of Hurston's version of "immigrant energy" and the whip of Cisneros's young "bullish will
to gain a foothold in some modest spot," which Hoffman realizes is "fueled" by "insistence, and ignorance, and obliviousness of the rules and social distinctions—not to speak of 'your own place'" (157). A self that has
grown so self-consciously is eternally vigilant, alert for contextual markers
that those who take themselves for the center may not ever learn to discern.
Before Hoffman learned to speak English to her own satisfaction she had
educated her ears to the misspeaking of others, whether the Polish immigrant Jews of Vancouver whose accents she finds harsh or the new musical
intonations of her Texas college friends. She will get it right; she will learn
to speak and finally dream in this new tongue until it no longer twists and
breaks her thoughts, her speech, and her emotions. Finally a dream comes,
with a voice speaking poetically, in English, and fills the void of that space
and time before sleep when Hoffman often felt especially wrenched from
the place of her birth. With this dream and its subtle words and meanings
she realizes she has become some kind of "American" ("eaten enough words
so that English now flows in my bloodstream"), just as she realizes with regret and some resentment that her own focus on her identity is no mere
cultural borrowing. She is as plagued by the questions of her time and place
as she might have been if she had never left Cracow, but in the new world
they are other questions. To have only contempt for such forms of introspection is to deny just how far she has come from Cracow, and how her
political consciousness has continued to develop according to history: just
as Stalin's death, announced in somber and momentous tones by the school
principal in Cracow, cemented an early layer, Kennedy's assassination in
Dallas during her freshman year at Rice University ("so close by that it's as
if the shot had been fired in the neighborhood") added another stratum to
this genealogy of political identity.
  To imaginatively construct identities in archaeological terms allows for a
clear sense of multiplicity and simultaneity. What I have meant to do with
my earlier metaphors of the prism and the spectrum is to add mobility to
the picture. This would render the images of identity holographic rather
than photographic, thereby releasing us from notions that are all too fixed,

even if only momentarily. Now, I have also said that to study this process of mobility, simultaneity, and multiplicity we need to freeze the cinematic frame. What is equally important to this study is to recognize its captured, captive objects of inquiry in all their subjectivity. In the passage below we read Hoffman attempting to do just this kind of work in reading herself:

> It is I who will have to learn how to live with a double vision. Until now, Poland has covered an area in my head coeval with the dimensions of reality, and all other places on the globe have been measured by their distance from it. Now, simultaneously, I see it as my classmates do—a distant spot, some- where on the peripheries of the imagination. . . . The reference points inside my head are beginning to do a flickering dance. I suppose this is the most palpable meaning of displacement. I have been dislocated from my own cen- ter of the world, and that world has been shifted away from my center. There is no longer a straight axis anchoring my imagination; it begins to oscillate, and I rotate around it unsteadily. (132)

The "flickering dance" of identity that Hoffman describes as oscillation and rotation give a fairly clear sense of how a relation to place is constructed and how truly palpable the anchors of imagination and belonging become. Hoffman's memoir speaks from the multiple positions of traveler, mastering the new world, and immigrant, obliged to endeavor mastery. While telling a tale that is resolutely tied to specific historic circumstances, we also come to see how her narrative shares some features with the other texts in this book. Insisting on her loss of anchor and the pain of such loss, she nevertheless recognizes that her own displacement does not isolate her from those she meets. Rather it connects her disparate strands of the self with aspects of her history that are shared by many, although always idiosyncratically. Her par- ticularity calls up a generality among those with whom she shares a post- modern situation—the vexed politics of location. Here is Hoffman on the futility of the exhortations to particularity in certain ongoing debates in the domain of identity politics:

> How, with this bifocal vision, does one keep one's center? And what center should one try to keep? The cherishing of our particularity seems as out- moded as the wearing of many skirts. (213)

Hoffman may not be prepared to give up the language of margins and cen- ters; indeed we seem quite thoroughly lodged in this discourse still. But it might slightly stir this political pot in new directions if this discourse were imaged in at least a three-dimensional fashion—a cauldron, not a map, of people in places and the knowledge they may gain there.

Perhaps a successful immigrant is an exaggerated version of the native. From now on, I'll be made, like a mosaic, of fragments—and my consciousness of them. It is only in that observing consciousness that I remain, after all, an immigrant. (164)

The immigrant (female) child dare not do more than point at the figure of unclad authority. For in the instant of her recognition she will apprehend that the others surrounding her do not see what she sees. To learn to see as they seem to see will be an essential part of her obligation in mastery. Her success will be measured in the exactitude of the exaggeration of the native. In the immigrant genre the native has been relocated as master of the discourse through the eyes of the displaced resident alien.

~

Survival Elsewhere

What we have lost we cannot, and must not, help recalling, though it remains
to us only in the guise of its absence. Even as we are parted from it—and
because none of us are so innocent as to be merely the passive victims
of terror, ourselves incessantly depart from it—our vision of
another world returns to us, as trace, as testimony.
Chris Bongie, *Exotic Memories*

Just as we "know" language in its inadequacy, it is all we have as a medium of translation between and among speakers and subjects (and subjectivities). And just as we "know" identity formation to be a naming that dispossesses as often as it confers being or meaning, still it is the process through which we learn to inhabit a variety of subject and pronominal positions. To enter into language is both to gain and to lose meaning—to risk recognition of a partial kind and cede a sense of being that may seem full but remains inchoate, inarticulate. It is the bargain of the social, the negotiation of need, demand, desire—an economy, an exchange. This negotiation subtends daily life in a manner often unremarked and unremarkable until the bargain can't or won't be made. What happens at such a moment of negotiations breaking down is a phenomenon that will be repeated in some textual examples that follow so we can try to discern the details of how identities and identifications get made. To temporarily isolate such moments is the only way to lift them out of their life-pool for study.

Narrative may refuse us an answer to the question of who speaks, but theory must assume it will come to know something of the speaker and the speech. The audience is in the process of giving itself over to the storyteller while preserving the right to cut off her head if the tale she tells should stop. Walter Benjamin reminds readers in the opening of his essay that the storyteller comes from afar, and he remarks on the intimacy of the tie between journey and narrative impulse.[1] Michel de Certeau remarks that "tout récit est un récit de voyage."[2] Benjamin diagnoses the decline in storytelling as contemporaneous with the loss of experience and wisdom, forms of exchange prior to "information" and its postmodern hybrids. De Certeau is working with the effort to rediscover in daily life the forms now taken by those earlier demands for stories from afar.

The stories we will be listening in on here, and doing our best to take in, are tales of fracture that ask to be heard when the daily structures of exchange have irreparably collapsed. In this set of tales of dislocation I will turn my attention to what I call postmodern captivity narratives—concentration camp memoirs. In taking this turn what we bring along is all we have seen before about how the phenomenon of dislocation forces to the surface a set of discursive demands to say who we are and who we are not. We have read the shifting frames around the responses available to this demand that emerges in the unknown scene. Here the alien landscape raises questions not of seduction or of mastery but of survival.

Lawrence Langer's *Holocaust Testimonies: The Ruins of Memory*, a book on survivors' videotaped accounts, is an "anatomy of melancholy for the modern spirit," which ends with an impassioned reply to and critique of Charles Taylor's *Sources of the Self: The Making of the Modern Identity*. Langer is irreconcilably and understandably dismayed by Taylor's insistence that "doing without frameworks is utterly impossible for us" (200); what Langer has spent the entire space of his text doing—a text that he and his attentive readers have entered in agreement that they forsake comfortable, familiar moral values and assumptions—is working through the utter lack of frameworks possible for taking in the Shoah. My sole corrective effort comes as a wish to shift Langer's dissatisfaction with Taylor and to suggest that the *modern* spirit has about it a kind of sanity, a sanit*ized* quality that is foreclosed to those who wish to gain access to history as mutilated by the Holocaust and to those who gained access to such history against their will. Taylor will not do for Langer or for my purposes in investigating identity and its formations because this world-historical calculated incineration of millions is a defining feature of *post*modern identies and their unmaking—and in this Langer recognizes his own work as the opposite of Taylor's. Langer wishes to engage his readers and hearers in what he calls "unreconciled understanding" wherein "the Holocaust does little to confirm theories of moral reality but much to question the reality of moral theories" (198). For, continuing to work Taylor to his own compelling ends, Langer notes that Taylor's "goods which command our awe," such as "family devotion and unity, parental care, filial affection, sibling loyalty . . . suddenly collapsed on the ramp at Auschwitz" (199).

If we understand this collapse to be collective as well as individual we might begin to be able to reread certain features of the debates on subjectivity in view of the Holocaust. Dominick LaCapra makes this point as well in his most recent book when he suggests that

> much recent debate in critical theory and historiography is recast if one takes the Holocaust as at least one more or less repressed divider or traumatic point of rupture between modernism and postmodernism. In this light the postmodern and the post-Holocaust become mutually intertwined issues that are best addressed in relation to one another. (Chap. 6)[3]

LaCapra understands the work he is doing as a project in which theory becomes partner to the psychoanalytic process of working through, a process that remained undertheorized in Freud's own work. More thoroughly understood and exhibited was the process of acting out or repetition compulsion. LaCapra recognizes that theory in postmodern times must become critical and self-critical in order to escape the double bind of an " 'all-or-nothing' frame of reference [in which] . . . the only alternative to deceptive transfiguration is disfiguration" (24). I am aiming here to avoid precisely this abyssal sense of "mistaken identities" where identity becomes a zero-sum game. Consider instead the paradox that although the voices gathered in this part of the book all take themselves to be deeply and permanently displaced, yet they must speak and remember and be heard; in an often-quoted statement, Charlotte

Delbo reminds her readers in a biographical afterword to her memoir, "I am no longer sure that what I have written is true, but I am sure that it happened."

Langer's book, subtitled *The Ruins of Memory,* presents us with a new archaeology of memory, one constructed through the subtle distinctions made necessary by the discourse both written and oral of survivor victims. He names five kinds of memory and the self that each helps to (mis)shape: deep memory—the buried self; anguished memory—the divided self; humiliated memory—the besieged self; tainted memory—the impromptu self; and unheroic memory—the diminished self. While Langer's structure means to sort out these variously operating forms of memory and does so quite stunningly, it also becomes clear that all operate simultaneously. So the diminished self of unheroic memory, for example, shares a barely beating heart with the besieged self of humiliated memory, and all the others. Langer ends by calling up a model of multiple identities, not as pathology and certainly not as fashion, but as descriptive of what living on has come to mean for those whose memories are crammed with the shreds of their own pasts and the pasts of those whom they lost, encountered, and outlived, those who would have no futures.

At a certain moment in an ongoing discussion of how rhetoric and grammar fail in their efforts to distill the "tyranny of the actual," borrowing from Nietzsche, Langer considers his dissatisfaction with the very word *survival.* Having coined terms and phrases earlier to try to find some adequation between the story and plot, so to speak, of Holocaust testimonies, he asks whether he might speak instead of *surmortal,* for those whom he has spent countless hours watching, interviewing, and hearing have not only been witnesses to lived reality, but also to "died reality."

LaCapra also discusses Charles Taylor's *Sources of the Self* as a "massively redemptive master narrative" (17), recognizing in it nevertheless an "admirable desire to affirm a needed existential shift in response to basic problems that would help overcome cynicism" (18). What makes such a shift impossible to locate in Taylor's project is an emphasis on a synoptic view of the modern and the historical through insistently Eurocentric, neoromantic, and Protestant Christian glasses. From such a perspective, what LaCapra characterizes as the "insistently counter-epiphanic literature of the Holocaust" is for Taylor read symptomatically as "just a step towards the new kind of epiphany" (Taylor, 487). LaCapra makes the point that the "benevolently bland and judicious 'just' . . . is typical of the manner in which Taylor's own approach to problems and his very subject-position, notably including his use of language, tend to remain untroubled by the dislocations, challenges, and 'inner' turmoil he notices in modern works" (18). I might add that Taylor would wish away the unsanitary nature of what the postmodern/post-Holocaust would have us understand about the loss of epiphany as redemption.

The Theater of Shame

Langer theorizes (from the experience of those who have made of him a secondary witness) that "among the many victims of the Holocaust was the classical ideal of the beauty of the human *form*" (101). This "disabling erosion," to reframe his discussion, is another aspect of how camp narratives present us with the very tight fit that existed in this de-written time and space between the "physical and metaphysical that [Jean] Améry described as one of the legacies of the camp experience" (101). There is no longer an emperor whose subjects are in awe, except for that innocent one who notices what no one else will acknowledge. In the camp world there are instead those countless moving figures inhabiting bodies that are corpses. This utter loss of a self was concretized particularly for those consigned to extermination who were naked in body and rendered less than human in the shaving of heads; the resemblance to idealized, let alone, real human forms was stripped as much as possible by the institutionalization of shaming rituals—tattoos, collective showers, lack of water for washing, public latrines—rituals of wartime taken to their extreme and massified.

Langer's work takes up the testimonies of those who survived in the camps and elsewhere. One of the stories he retells is of Menachem S., who was separated from his parents at age five and spent the next two years until the war was over living among "orphaned or vagrant children [and] intermittently with various families" (111). Before their separation, his mother had given him her high school identification card so that he would remember her. But, although his parents survived the camps, they were unrecognizable to the then seven-year-old, who said in his testimony, "I was like 70. Like an old man" (111). Langer speaks to the ruins of the human form that shocked this son as the photos and films of the opening of the camps shocked the world, for the human form had been ravaged, reduced to its skeletal essentials:

> The "reunion" between Menachem S. and his parents is a traumatic meeting that violates all traditional notions of closure and afflicts consciousness with an overpowering sense of the *im*possibility of restoring interrupted family unity. His father, more than six feet tall, weighs eighty-eight pounds. His rotted teeth are hanging loosely from his guns. Menachem S. looked at him and didn't recognize him as his father. His emaciated mother did not resemble the woman in the picture she had left with him. "I just couldn't believe they were my parents," he reports. Although he had waited two years for this moment, "When I was confronted with those disfigured people I just couldn't force myself to make any contact with them." He says that logically he knew they were his parents but emotionally couldn't feel close to them. For some period after that, he called them Mr. and Mrs. S. instead of mother and father, unable to restore continuity to the disrupted story of his life. (111)

Menachem S. himself had not been part of the ravaging effected in the labor camps, and especially in the death camps, and so could not make a connection to these two crippled human beings. Such changes followed on a daily basis were equally devastating but allowed those interned in this alternate universe to adapt their criteria for who looked more or less well or ill, able to work or ready to die. Without the parameters enforced by the camps themselves we see in this son's reaction—he who had waited to love again—an aspect of the reaction of the world that watched the evidence pile up as those inside had watched the bodies pile up, and both those inside and those outside had enormous difficulty believing that what they saw was real. Only those inside know it on their skin and in their veins; for them this impossible but necessary knowledge is what has poisoned their memory. It has left them with an "unresolvable conflict between shifting identities" (Langer, 111), which may sound like the latest "vogue emanat[ing] from Paris" (Taylor on deconstruction, cited in LaCapra) but which is anything but a chosen change of skin, dress, name, hair, way of life. It is in this sense that the postmodern and the post-Holocaust must be seen to be coexistent in our time. This is what Langer describes as a world of "choiceless choice" in which those who survived to tell lived and died on.

If we follow the suggestion that shame is the repressed of psychoanalytic theory and LaCapra's suggestion that "the Shoah has often been in the position of the repressed in the post–World War II West" (chap. 6), we might recognize the return of this repressed in the form of ever-proliferating monumentalizing gestures—most recently the Washington, D.C., museum—and note that the repressed returning does not equal working through but may instead constitute further incentives to acting out, or even repeated forgetting.[4] I hope in this final section to offer some examples of what it might mean if we could understand, not intuitively but viscerally, so to speak, what Tomkins opens up in the statement with which I have framed this book, that the "history of shame is a history of civilizations." For in memoirs of internment and confinement we have narratives that offer the possibility of further theorizing the workings of shame, if we can bear to hold it in our intellectual grasp long enough to be touched, perhaps contaminated by it. For if we cannot or will not, it will return as it has in contemporary Europe, where many in the West believed it could never do so again. We need to comprehend both the wonder and the shame of mastery—that what humans *can* do they *will* do.

I don't wish to sunder shame from wonder, but to polarize them by the nature of their affective charges—the negative to the positive, and back and forth in between. The camp memoirs take us rather immediately to a site of shame as the scene of knowing and misrecognition, and the quiet dark places where this form of comprehension is staged. When we read Langer on oral testimonies, my earlier metaphor of the prismatic character of identity is rewritten to suggest not the varieties of white light but the indistinguishable variations on what we may see through a prism, darkly.

~

Speaking Memory

Charlotte Delbo's *None of Us Will Return*

An extraordinary Sunday because it was a rest Sunday and we were permitted
to sit on the ground. All of the women were seated in the dust of the dried
mud in a pitiable swarm that made one think of flies on a dung hill. No
doubt because of the smell. The smell was so strong and so fetid that we
thought that we were breathing not air but some thicker and more viscous
fluid that enveloped and shut off this part of the world with an additional
atmosphere in which only specially adapted creatures could move. Us.
A stench of diarrhea and of carrion. Above this stench the sky was blue.
And in my memory spring was singing. Why had I alone of all these
beings kept my memory? In my memory spring was singing.
Charlotte Delbo

In her memoir, Charlotte Delbo laments the survival of memory at
Auschwitz from the time before, as she sits writing at a café table in Paris,
years later, where the lamentation is rather for the memories of her internment—memories that refuse to recede in time. Delbo's memoir forms the
centerpiece of this chapter, but I will also be drawing on her play *Who Will
Carry the Word?* and two oral histories by other survivors of Auschwitz.

Before the Nazi occupation of France, Delbo had been studying philosophy and working in the theater with Louis Jouvet, a film actor and dra-
maturge. She had believed this would be her life's work. However, she became an active member of the Resistance during the occupation, and it was
this political work that led to her imprisonment in Auschwitz. The con-

fluence of her chosen and enforced paths did not come until some years later when she began to write plays of a specifically political sort. The concerns of her work center on the loss of language to represent the terror and suffering that occur under systems of political oppression and genocidal bureaucratic structures.[1]

Interwoven with a reading of Delbo's memoir and play are moments from narratives that are less easily placed; these come from three other speakers who are survivors of Auschwitz. One is a memoir called *Auschwitz: True Tales from a Grotesque Land* by Sara Nomberg-Przytyk.[2] The two other speakers are women who have borne witness in oral histories gathered by the Fortunoff Video Archive for Holocaust Testimonies at Yale University.[3]

In bringing together the work of imagination and memory it is crucial to keep in mind both the historicity of the events and their transfiguration and disfiguration of our thinking universe. All too often in the everyday talk of the Holocaust there is a kind of embalming called commemoration. But there is also real memory work, and working through, as suggested by LaCapra, that must be done by "obsessed witness bearers," in the words of Eli Pfferkorn and David Hirsch, the editors of Nomberg-Przytyk's *Tales*.

In a fragment called "The Lovers of Auschwitz," Nomberg-Przytyk tells a tale that survives in several forms—a myth from the camps, if you will. Tadeus and Mala, whose names vary according to different versions, are devoted to each other and are doomed in their joint escape attempt. Their story, Nomberg-Przytyk suggests, would make a "tragedy written in a barbarous age"; the romance under barbarism is a tale of mutual strength dedicated to resistance. What Delbo writes are also tragic reports from a barbarous age in which women manage to forge a collectivity in a setting where the rituals of privacy have been nullified. Narratives that address this period are not dramas of the bourgeois self; rather they are epic plots that render the *Bildung* of a generation, and are often cast in an allegorical frame.

In Delbo's play *Qui rapportera ces paroles?* (translated as *Who Will Carry the Word?*, it makes singular what in French is plural), the signs and gestures of women witnessing, expecting, and surviving mass and random dying are those a post-Holocaust audience knows how to decode. Stage directions indicate "a barren, snowy place or a barren, dusty place" with "only one exit" and an action "without intermission." The author's note tells us we are "nowhere . . . a place that no one can imagine." The prologue is delivered as a soliloquy (by Françoise) and voices both recalcitrance and compunction:

So why should I speak?
For the things I could say
will not be of use to you. (273)

This complex and conflicted relationship to utterance—its necessity and its inadequacy—is a topos of camp narratives that nevertheless give voices and words to the unspeakable. Delbo's dystopia (the "bad" place, in this instance the death camp) overturns utopian (the "good" place, which is also "no" place) conventions in the inverted world of the camps—a world not beyond but "*below* good and evil," as Jean Améry has written—but dramatizes the same oppositions: between wish and dread, hope and fear, desire and doubt.[4]

In Delbo's memoir we enter a universe where the structures are those of everyday death that permit and enforce survival, and where the dystopian moment is felt to be the "never before" in contrast to the utopian "not-yet."[5] Most testimonies and texts raise the question of recognition and its distortions as a central feature of the psychic deformations of the camp universe. In the videotape of Edith P. from Czechoslovakia, she says of her first days in Auschwitz, "One million women looked all alike." But out of this anonymous sea one day a hand touches her shoulder; it is her sister-in-law who had been deported some time earlier. Edith is shocked when she says hello and explains that other members of the family are here. "Come and live with us," are her words—simple, mundane, yet comforting beyond belief, and a thoroughgoing denial of what living means here, a tenacity that insists on connection and community. Three days later most of Edith's former block is sent to the gas; it is then that a resolve forms in her when she says: "From that day on I knew, I am a survivor. I am going to survive and tell the story one day."[6] This resolution to survive comes in the face of the arbitrariness of death, and functions as a way to take responsibility and to work against the "drastic guilt," in Adorno's words, of those spared. Helen K., who lived through the Warsaw ghetto and worked in the camp resistance group at Auschwitz, finds her resolve after her younger brother has died in her arms. She says, "They wanted us to die; I must be the only one to live . . . to defy Hitler."

On this question of recognition and kinship Helen K. speaks simply; married at sixteen in the Warsaw ghetto, she and her husband were separated, but both survived. When they rediscovered each other after the liberation she said, "He was not the same man; neither was I the same woman." But their differences cannot be used to separate them again, because she goes on to say, "He knew who I was, there was some connection," repeating,

"He knew who I was." This chance to maintain a sense of self and continuity while fully within a knowledge of irrevocable rupture outweighs all the other burdens of freedom. Delbo's play formulates this question in the following scene:

> CLAIRE: Don't you recognize me?
>
> FRANÇOISE: Now I recognize your voice. Voices are different to recognize. . . . It's even more strange when you don't recognize those who are close to you. The hair, the walk, the silhouette. Is it enough to have your hair shorn to no longer be yourself?
>
> YVONNE: If the men who loved us could see what had become of us.
>
> GINA: We'll soon get used to these others that we have become and we'll recognize each other. (275)

In order to survive, what has never been before must become the everyday; the paradox is the one described by Améry, that to accept death is to preserve life. The dead are those whose "skin is a color no one has ever seen before," the suffering of "a limit no one reached before." In certain utopian contexts language loses the capacity to name what no longer exists: poverty, rape, war; in the camp dystopia there are also words that must be jettisoned: coquetry, cowardice, choice. Primo Levi points out that in camp slang the words for "never" were "morgen früh," or tomorrow morning, a radical compression of temporality that both denies a future and renders the unthinkable quotidian.[7] Delbo captures this warping of temporality in a haunting passage in which the repetition of "yesterday" becomes a death knell and an already ritualized remembrance of these lives lost:

> The women who are lying there in the snow are our companions of yesterday. Yesterday they were on their feet at roll call. They stood in rows of five on either side of the Lagerstrasse. They went off to work, they trudged toward the marshes. Yesterday they were hungry. They had lice, they scratched themselves. Yesterday they gulped down the dirty soup. Yesterday they had diarrhea and they were beaten. Yesterday they suffered. Yesterday they longed to die. (21)

We read here of life reduced to the ability to scratch and the wish to die, and the past becomes as compressed as the future that can only be summoned as tomorrow morning.

In Nomberg-Przytyk's account in a section called "Old Words—New Meanings," she learns through a character named Fela an inversion of a familiar word—to organize. Nomberg-Przytyk, a political worker in the Bialystok ghetto before her imprisonment, notes:

For some people, Auschwitz was an ordinary term, but now the word has taken on a completely new set of meanings. An unusually interesting psychological study might result if someone could demonstrate the way in which meanings passed beyond the accepted boundaries of conventional significance. Why a psychological study? Because the new set of meanings provided the best evidence of the devastation that Auschwitz created in the psyche of every human being. No one was able to resist totally the criminal, amoral logic of everyday life in the concentration camp. To some extent all of us were drawn into a bizarre transformation of reality. We knew what those innocent words meant, such words as "gas," "selection," but we uttered them, nevertheless, as though there was nothing hidden behind them. Take the word "organize." Usually it is associated with such positive values as political, social, and cultural order and well-being. When we say of someone that he is a good organizer we usually mean that he is a constructive leader who brings sanity and tranquility to the whole community. In Auschwitz, however, "to organize" meant to improve your own situation, very often at someone else's expense by taking advantage of that person's ignorance or inexperience. "To organize" meant to procure for yourself, by any means, better clothing, lodging, or food. (72)

We can read here the end point of the economic structure of capitalism "raised to the degree of self-nullification, self-caricature, absurdity," to quote further from Améry. What then are the words Delbo wants to be carried, brought back? They are those of the "one who will return" and speak for the dying: "Haven't you heard them? [The dying,] who all say, 'If you return, you'll tell.' " An insistent messianism struggles with the apocalyptic belief that "none of us shall return." The memoir in fact closes with the avowal:

> None of us will return.
> None of us should have returned.

In this "will" the future tense encloses the assertion that those who did return/survive were not the "same" as they had been before deportation, and the "should have" speaks both of the genocidal intentionality that ought to have exterminated them all as much as it discloses the melancholia of the "ruined memory" that incessantly whispers through their lives after Auschwitz.[8]

Both the need for and denial of the others is absolute; Améry points to the "boundless solitude" in the midst of this "compression of human masses" (34, 29). In "A Visit," a poem by Irena Klepfisz, she tells us about her mother, who "during this time . . . learned survival / depends on complete distrust."[9] In Delbo's play it is Agnes who speaks this same verity:

It is only through blindness that we can hope. It's not courage we need, it's blindness or madness. Our only chance is for each to say to herself: "If there is one who returns it must be I." And it's madness to say that to yourself. And none knows why she must return. (286)

This was echoed by Helen K., who knew "I must be the only one to live." For Agnes it is not sufficient reason to live "to tell how the others died," for she believes "nothing will remain. If we live we will live without life." The materiality of life *and* death is cadaverous: "Here no one clings to life. It's life that clings to us," says Françoise on the daily disposal of the dead and the effect of such labor on the women who perform it and yet continue to live. The distrust with which the testimony of survival was sometimes met is figured as Delbo frames these words to be carried: the truth must be told to the fathers and "even to the mothers," but, realizes Françoise, "by returning we will deny our own story." This kind of "foreknowledge" of the invalidated voice of the survivor may be among the reasons that so many narratives of this experience did not get written, or in some cases published, until decades after the events, although such a lag is also common to the literature of war.

The urge toward and simultaneous lack of recognition is restaged throughout Delbo's war writings. An implicitly psychoanalytic structure, it rehearses that moment of constitution of the self through and in the eyes of the other, a moment that, whenever it recurs, also marks the place of the self within the family as community. It is also a scene dominantly theorized and lived out between the child and the mother. Delbo's writings offer multiple occasions to reenact such a scene, since the relationships among the women are cast, of necessity, in the family paradigm.

For Mounette this moment comes as a dream where the mutual gaze is denied:

Tonight I dreamed that I returned home and that my mother didn't look at me. Or rather I didn't recognize her face.

With increasing panic she continues:

My mother's face is disappearing. . . . I've lost my mother's face.

Serious Agnes offers innocent Mounette reason:

Look at Helene, who's with her mother. Each one suffers doubly. . . . For the mother, it's worse yet. . . . She sees her daughter being beaten, and lowers her head. And for the daughter! To see her mother beaten, naked, tattooed, shaven, dirty. . . . Next to them, you're lucky. (304–6)

Agnes speaks the zero degree of shame as simultaneously solitary, familial, and communal. In the memoir the mutual humiliation of mothers and daughters is rendered in the poem:

> My mother
> she was hands
> she was a face
> They set our mothers before us naked
>
> Here mothers are no longer mothers to their children. (15)

Tomkins theorizes that shame is among the first of the affects experienced in infancy, and that its instantiation occurs when the infant's gaze is not returned or in some way acknowledged by its caretaker; conversely, the returned gaze, the mutual acknowledgment in vision and voice, produces in the infant a sense of its own presence in the world, and in Lacanian terms, jouissance. This shared bliss of parent and child that can be sometimes refound for an instant in the mutual look of recognition, whether of someone's pride, pleasure, or pain, has been abolished in the camps. Instead, mothers and children are set before each other's eyes as "stranded objects," in Eric Santner's phrase—objects who are indeed no longer subjects, but who have been rendered abject.[10] We will see in the following chapter how the sight of old men naked sets off in Primo Levi a similar experience of shame that is his own as well as that of anonymous others.

In "Meditations on Metaphysics" Adorno says that at Auschwitz "it was no longer an individual who died, but a specimen" (362). This fact marks those who survive and characterizes what Langer calls humiliated memory; it also distinguishes genocide and its institutionalization from war mortality statistics more broadly speaking. Yet for those who survived to tell their true tales, it is often in the momentary acts of individuals that a sense of humanity—although without dignity—is salvaged. How to come to terms with the epistemic break of this conflagration? How to find a way through the rupture of the bourgeois social order and the myth of radical individualism to a sudden awareness of radical replaceability? The answer must come, at least partially, in the structures of kinship that are recreated, making replaceability not obscene but rather life sustaining. Nomberg-Przytyk, for example, speaks of Magda, a young woman miraculously ennobled, not degraded, in Auschwitz, and says that later Magda "became my camp daughter."[11]

In the netherworld of the camps the women are together and separated, perforce, and live under a regime of scarcity and deprivation. They learn to look "not straight ahead but far away." The spatial-temporal scheme is out of balance. The future is barred; the present teaches truths too horrible to live with; the past consoles, reminds, and belies. The myth of Persephone, one of the West's most powerful texts of female regeneration, must be read very cautiously when posing questions of gender about this period of time.

The separation of men and women from each other is extreme. A rare moment of women and men together occurs in Nomberg-Przytyk's account of New Year's Eve of 1945 when, through carefully made prearrangements, some women and men meet at the barbed wire separating them and join in singing the "International" in their various languages. A chapter in Delbo's memoir called "The Men" recounts another kind of stark encounter between men and women; it emblematizes what I would call the "metaphysics of bread":

> In the morning and in the evening, on the road to the marshes, we met columns of men. . . . They had the gait we all had. Head thrust forward, neck thrust forward. Head and neck drag the rest of the body along. . . . All intent on marching, they did not look at us. We looked at them. We looked at them and wrung our hands in pity. . . . There were so many sick people among us who did not eat that we had lots of bread. . . . One morning we took some bread out under our jackets. For the men. We meet no column of men. We wait impatiently for evening. On our way back we hear their tread behind us. . . . When they overtake us we quickly take out our bread and toss it to them. Instantly there is a scramble. They catch the bread, they fight over it, they snatch it from one another. They have the eyes of wolves. Two men roll over into a ditch after a piece that eludes their grasp. We watch them fight and we weep. The SS screams and sets his dog on them. The column regroups, resumes the march. Links, zwei, drei. They did not turn their heads in our direction. (24–25)

Although most accounts of the camps generally allow that women were treated worse than men, we see in this one scene the differences between political prisoners—who, although also dying daily of starvation and disease, have, for the moment, sufficient bread to spare for others—and the columns of men, who include Jews and other prisoners and are therefore more likely to be subject to extermination, and who are saved only by what narrow margin of "health" they are able to maintain because of youth, for example. But we may also read this passage for the gendering of the scenario of shame enacted; "all" have the gait where the hanging head of humiliation and hunger "drag the rest of the body along." But where the men and women differ is that they cannot meet each other's gaze; while the women may be behaving conventionally—like mothers, feeding others—the men are shamed by that conventionality in which they ought to be the ones to provide the bread in question, and are shamefully infantilized by being the ones who are offered the life-sustaining food, which they fall upon like less than children, like "wolves." What speaks additionally to the "health" of Delbo and her comrades is their ability to weep for the men as they watch them fight over the bread—converting some of the men's shame into their own inability to *be* those who can give anything worth having.

In terms of gender specificity and modes of survival, the question of women under conditions of extremity is addressed by Delbo in a play from the 1970s, *Maria Lusitania*, where she avows that "women are more in the habit of making do with nothing" ("Les femmes ont plus l'habitude de faire avec rien"). If women resist it is from their already inscribed situations as those who make do "with nothing." In them the possibilities for resistance are borne out of what is already internalized and experienced as limitation—resistance by those with less to lose.

Elizabeth Janeway's *Powers of the Weak* speaks of survival and resistance under extreme conditions. Among her many examples are Holocaust survivors, and her specific focus is repeatedly on women. The experience of distrust is basic for women, accustomed to living on a "minimum ration of hope" (210), and therefore it produces the ability to tolerate forms of shame and degradation that are more devastating to men, whose expectations begin and remain consistently higher. If Jews may be said to have internalized the otherness attributed to them, then Jewish women of the period were in a sense doubly othered. I turn to Janeway in order to caution against the essentialist privileging of women's endurance of conditions in the camps, and to suggest that such endurance may not *simply* be championed.[12]

A scene particularly apt for such misreading occurs in the third act of *Who Will Carry the Word?* It is cast in the conditional mode common to the grammar of utopia-dystopia that seeks to imagine a future.

DENISE: How will we live afterwards, if we come back so hardened?

GINA: I tell myself that if I could cry on my mother's shoulder, tenderness, weakness and pity would come back to me. (314)

What I wish to emphasize here are the elements of longing for emotions that are human, but coded through contact with the mother as the feminine; the longing is also invoked in face of the injunction against stepping into the feminine, that is, weak, position during this time. Denise answers Gina, saying, "You have a mother." And Gina makes the following offer: "If we come back, I'll share my mother with you." Here again I want to point out the refusal Delbo's play performs—here, where expectations are almost impossible to maintain, all that can be supposed is a deprivation attenuated only by the collective nature of the experience—the sharing of too few mothers.[13] But if we recall Janeway's argument and those of other feminist theorists of mothering, we can see in this offer of Gina's the extent to which in a patriarchal society female children are less well mothered than the male children, who are presumed to transcend the limitations of the mother's own lived reality, becoming thereby invested with more hope in their own futures.

In an exchange about the future, Denise remarks, "All our sentences start with 'if we come back.'" Gina knows they must begin to say "when we come back." But this temporal shift cannot be maintained for long. Gina notices "we never evoke anything but our childhood"—that period recreated as the site of plenitude and security. Edith P.'s testimony echoes this conversation when she says that the two worst things about Auschwitz were the hunger and lack of work: "We sat the whole day long talking about our past, and the humiliation of our souls."

The basic distrust that Klepfisz learned from her mother and that Janeway spotlights as the primary source of the powers of the weak is what Delbo doubts as useful under any conditions except those as dire as in the camp. The deep connection between trust and the mother, distrust and the lost mother's face returns:

> What use is it ever to read truth in a face? In life who needs to see through people to know in one split second if they'll share their bread or help others to walk? (316)

Such insight is the terrible gift of survival: a truth "without shadows," an "incommunicable knowledge." Such negative capability for those who survive turns against the "never before" and wishes hopelessly that life could resume "as if we had never been here." That these stories are too awful to be told and yet must be—this is the life sentence of survivors. It is a knowledge of shame gained shamefully. And it offers a wisdom few are seeking.

In the penultimate scene Gina (who is going to commit suicide in order to avoid an enforced sentence among the White Kerchiefs, those who bury children in mass graves) and Françoise (who in the first scene was dissuaded from the rationality of suicide) make a pact. Françoise must become the bearer of Gina's words written on her memory. She promises:

> I remember, I will remember. I'll try to carry back the memory. I'll do everything I can. I give you my word. (323)

But in the epilogue the words written on memory have become unbelievable even to those who must speak them:

> FRANÇOISE: words that say simple things:
> >   to be cold
> >   to be thirsty
> >   to be hungry
> >   to be tired
> >   to be sleepy, to be afraid
> >   to live, to die
>
> DENISE: . . . we no longer know how to say them with the meaning they had there. (324–25)[14]

The play closes with a question that supports and complicates the question of the title:

> Why should you believe
> these ghost stories
> of ghosts who return
> without being able to explain how? (325; my translation)

The arbitrariness of who would live or die comes to haunt and threaten the validity of the survivor's voice. And those who remain return with words and stories remarkably alike both in their quotidian and metaphysical speculations. The dreadful knowledge of the source of the *Smoke over Birkenau* (the title of two other memoirs)[15] makes clear what Adorno might have meant when he wrote that "the course of history forces materialism on metaphysics." He wonders if it is possible any longer to have a metaphysical experience. But what else is the recurrent telling of a red sky, a sun that destroys rather than sustains life, stars that sneer, or the spring mud that retains the smell of death and dysentery, another humiliating way to die? Edith P. marvels that "we took care of each other, that we didn't kill each other," and refers to those around her alternately as "colleagues" and "prisoners."

> It was a cold and dry winter day. One of those winter days when people
> say it would be nice to take a walk. People. Elsewhere.
> Charlotte Delbo

Not only was the elsewhere that was Auschwitz measured in the forms of intersubjectivity producing knowledge that was intolerable, unthinkable; as we have seen it also produced a relation to language that gave breath and words to the inconceivable. In a chapter called "The Farewell," Delbo illustrates how words and the realities they carry have been thoroughly wrenched from their past; note the parentheses needed for the uninformed reader.

> Two prisoners enter. At the sight of them the screaming grows louder than ever. It is the heaven commando. . . .
> (Members of the heaven commando have privileges. They are well dressed, eat their fill. For three months. When this time runs out, others replace them and see them off. To heaven. To the oven. And so it goes every three months. They are the ones who keep the gas chambers and smokestacks running.) (57–58)

The heaven commando have come to fill their truck with those women too weak to do anything but shiver and scream "these cries from the edge of terror" (57). These are the ones who have entered what Levi will call the "grey zone" of the drowned, not the saved. These women, about to die, are unable to offer anything to each other; they do not share the possibility of warmth to be had by placing their hands under the arms of the women in front of them, as was the practice at roll call when all had to appear in lines of five women each. And although they cannot resist this sweep through block 25, where those closest to death are to be found, still, to Delbo's amazement, once piled on top of each other in the truck, "they attempt to work their arms or their bodies free" (58). Delbo finally tells us that she turned away from this scene. The ability to be shocked by watching and seeing such daily occurrences is apparent; a series of short poetic chapters in the memoir end with the exhortation to readers to "try to watch. Try to see."

Literature of the Holocaust is shot through with this paradox of the need to say what will not be believed. The nowhere of dystopia, the living death of the camps, returns in the injunction to speak. As with other minority or marginal discourses, there is a faith in the voices speaking histories of oppression and the lifting of repression that is at theoretical odds with the poststructuralist critique of presence and the voice. In Delbo's work, as in much writing informed by the history of the Nazi regime, there is an internalized knowledge and recognition of both the power *and* the inadequacy of language and representation. In the texts I have arrayed here, from testimony to memoir to drama, the urge is constant to find language, words, and a way of telling that will be able to transmit, even as the speaker or writer comes constantly upon the failure to do so.[16] The memoirs and testimonies I've been retelling achieve a searing intensity that marks the reader-listener. We read and realize there are no adequate words; this process constitutes the necessary and unpredictable dynamic of numbness and receptivity of the cultural critics who work their way into absorbing and being absorbed by this history. Langer, LaCapra, and others acknowledge this dynamic; I expect its operation is also evident here in the move between texts and approaches to them. In a meditation on ashes as death of the letter, Jacques Derrida says, "Writing in a single stroke cancels and recognizes a debt."[17] There is in this writing of mine just such a wish, a similar paradox and dialectic that often exist when events are recently witnessed and allegedly unrepresentable. This same paradox recurs in the words of survivors themselves who write and in the words of those who write about what they have not experienced. But my self-criticism is not reserved for mere lack of experience; it is also meant to acknowledge what has been described as the protectiveness of the second generation vis-à-vis its elders.[18] This self-legitimation is in tension with a compunction, if not compulsion, to think, read, write, and speak through this history that permeates my memories and imagination and informs my reading of other postmodern, post-Holocaust, postwar texts and testimonies.

The urge to preserve a historical specificity in thinking the experience of those who knew the ghetto and the labor, concentration, and death camps vies with a desire not to set up hierarchies of victimage. Rather than maintain the position of the paranoid consciousness or spectator who always looks back, like Benjamin's angel of history, there must be a consciousness that will contemplate the present surround and speak of what it sees as repeating aspects of that which was never to be possible again. While nowhere minimizing or forgetting what has taken place in the name of that specially and problematically designated form of racism that is anti-Semitism, it is of equal if not greater importance to shift the ground of solidarity. Jean Améry points out in his essay "In the Waiting Room of Death: Reflections on the Warsaw Ghetto" that the solidarity of Jews has been founded on suffering and that the experience of the Holocaust has rendered that no longer possible—it must become a solidarity based on struggle. This dialectic of a reformulated solidarity may help us to think and work through some of the awful new histories being made and lived.

Time and the Other Laid Bare

Primo Levi's *Survival in Auschwitz* and Liana Millu's *Smoke over Birkenau*

> Forgetting seems ghostly, not because it has no force or weight (it presses
> against us heavily and constantly, and it may yet do us in), but because
> we are so unused to naming it that even those of us who realize
> its danger usually prefer to speak *for memory*.
> Jonathan Boyarin

To speak about identities in formation in situations of dislocation and not to speak about the testimonies of life in the Nazi concentration camps, those ephemerally forged sites of homelessness and displacement in the mid-twentieth century, would be to overlook the textual evidence of what tattered selves insist on weaving into some kind of cloth, if not whole, at least one providing a minimum of cover, warmth. We come back finally to the denuded emperor—or to one of his most eloquent if also most abject subjects.

In all of Primo Levi's works we are witness to a thinker who experienced the sudden disappearance of a kind of daily systematicity and organization in his deportation from Italy to Auschwitz, and yet who was in his very temperament wedded to systems. That is to say, Levi always found a way of making sense and system of the material of the world, whether by way of *The Periodic Table*, the materials of the chemist he was, or the elementary rules of social kinship that came to prevail in the camp system known as the Lager.

Stripped of physical (food) and metaphysical (work) sustenance, the subjects of these postmodern narratives of captivity are inevitably obsessively focused on moments of recognition and the affective realm of deep shame and humiliation that impinges with and without the evidence of another to witness our existence when it is so debased, or demolished, as Levi will say. Those who are the most shadowy figures in Levi's account are the ones who cannot look into anyone's eyes and will therefore be among the ones who die without even the slightest degree of dignity for they have lost all care for themselves; they are known universally in camp slang as "mussulmen,"[1] or those Levi designates as "the drowned" as opposed to "the saved"; this distinction forms one chapter of the memoir *Survival at Auschwitz* and is the title of a later collection of essays. In "The Gray Zone," the key essay in *The Drowned and the Saved*, Levi further explores the distinctions that were made among the saved about how their survival was purchased. The economic metaphor is neither accidental nor mistaken. For, as we saw in the earlier account by Nomberg-Przytyk, the entire project of surviving required certain basic forms of what must be called enterprise, a grasping onto life, that knew, in ways that were not required in life before and after the camps, *who* might be a likely co-worker.

Levi's hellish cosmology reads the questions of recognition in the Lager along a continuum moving from his repudiation of the "men in decay," with whom it is not worth speaking, to his commemoration of a few men—Jean, Charles, and Alberto, one of the few Italians who, along with Levi, vouchsafed his own survival. But before looking into the maze of shame that colors the Lager as lived and told, it is important to note that even in 1947, without the long work of burnished memory that comes to Levi's writing later, he understood the following about how humans would live their lives as *Häftlinge* or prisoners:

> Sooner or later in life everyone discovers that perfect happiness is unrealizable, but there are few who pause to consider the antithesis: that perfect unhappiness is equally unattainable. The obstacles preventing the realization of both these extreme states are of the same nature: they derive from our human condition which is opposed to everything infinite. Our ever-insufficient knowledge of the future opposes it: and this is called, in the one instance, hope, and in the other, uncertainty of the following day. The certainty of death opposes it: for it places a limit on every joy, but also on every grief. The inevitable material cares oppose it: for as they poison every lasting happiness, they equally assiduously distract us from our misfortunes, and make our consciousness of them intermittent and hence supportable. (13)

This passage is central to Levi's account of the journey to Auschwitz with which his narrative begins. If the imaginative and historical renderings of the middle passage from Africa into slavery in the Americas have as a motif of learned servitude the slave ship and its arrangements of bodies deprived of light and liberty, the memoirs of deportation under the Nazi regime are focused on the death trains that took days to go from a place that was home or near home to a place that was nameless and foreign, where it quickly became clear that no previous rules applied. The conditions on the trains of crowding and starvation began to do the work of dividing human beings among themselves in a struggle for breath, water, light, and any knowledge that might be gleaned from the "barking of Germans in command" (15) who "greeted" them on those intermittent occasions when the doors of the trains were opened. Further divisions were enforced when they were driven out of the trains onto the staging platform of the camp; this was often the place where family members were separated; it is also the moment where men and women were forced to go different routes. Later would come the "selections" by age, strength, expertise, caprice, or further misfortunes.

The savage and salvational effect of laughter emerges unpredictably in this tale of survival, and the ritual bond of laughter and shame is key here in these tales of necessarily mistaken identities. In this moment of arrival "on the bottom," Levi mocks his own and his comrades' ignorance, even as he exposes the cruelty of their captors in the ways of life that in just a few days will become routine:

> I had never seen old men naked. Mr. Bergmann wore a truss and asked the interpreter if he should take it off, and the interpreter hesitated. But the German understood and spoke seriously to the interpreter pointing to someone. We saw the interpreter swallow and then he said: "The officer says, take off the truss, and you will be given that of Mr. Coen." One could see the words coming bitterly out of Flesch's [the interpreter's] mouth; this was the German manner of laughing. (19)

Laughter has long been understood to have a curative effect, but this is the humiliating and poisonous laughter of shame. After the ritual of undressing, waiting endlessly for a shower, and being given other clothes, all the same clothes,

> there we are finally allowed to get dressed.
> When we finish, everyone remains in his own corner and we do not dare lift our eyes to look at one another. There is nowhere to look in a mirror, but our appearance stands in front of us, reflected in a hundred livid faces, in a

hundred miserable and sordid puppets. We are transformed into the phan-
toms glimpsed yesterday evening.

Then for the first time we became aware that our language lacks words to
express this offence, the demolition of a man. (22)

However, although shorn of all that "is" one's own, one's self, including a
name, prisoner Levi is nevertheless able, even compelled, to think his situation, to live it precisely with the assumption that soon he will die.[2] The self of
which he is being shorn would believe, contrary to all appearances of this
very moment being narrated, that humans cannot live as they are in this no-
place.

As one who is intimate with systems, Levi easily learns the "funereal science of the numbers of Auschwitz," as the prisoners learn to joke at their
own expense:

Everyone will treat with respect the numbers from 30,000 to 80,000: there are
only a few hundred left and they represent the few survivals from the Polish
ghettos. It is as well to watch out in commercial dealings with a 116,000 or a
117,000: they now number only about forty, but they represent the Greeks of
Salonica, so take care they do not pull the wool over your eyes. As for the
high numbers, they carry an essentially comic air about them, like the words
"freshman" or "conscript" in ordinary life. The typical high number is a cor-
pulent, docile and stupid fellow: he can be convinced that leather shoes are
distributed at the infirmary to all those with delicate feet, and can be per-
suaded to run there and leave his bowl of soup "in your custody"; you can
sell him a spoon for three rations of bread; you can send him to the most fe-
rocious of Kapos to ask him (as happened to me!) if it is true that his is the
Kartoffelschalenkommando, the "Potato Peeling Command," and if one can be
enrolled in it. (23–24)

Having been subject to and object of these forms of gallows humor, Levi is
quick to turn irony to critique and open the horizon for the forms of survival on "the bottom" (24).

It is worth stopping to look closely at what Levi narratively reviews; for in
the relay of looks, gestures, assumptions, and words of command and obedience we can garner an intimacy with the inmate that tells us much of what
we must know about estrangement and its relation to shame. What we come
to know with more eagerness about that end of the continuum concerned
with wonder and awe is recast here as that terrible side of the postmodern
sublime. If this appears to be an obscenely, unseemly aesthetic category to
invoke in discussing the Holocaust experience and its writings, let me cite
LaCapra from his introduction as both caution and spur:

One may be unable—or even find it undesirable—to overcome the allure of sublimity or the valorization of melancholy, particularly when they attest to an extreme situation and are combined with arresting insights that are otherwise denied or obscured. Indeed melancholy may be warranted by crisis and a traumatic past, and the sublime is a possible correlate of estrangement, uncanniness, and dislocation. But one may nonetheless question the role of melancholy and the sublime insofar as it becomes prepossessing, leads in dubious directions, or is fixated upon as the *ne plus ultra* of thought and action. (22)

My one modification of LaCapra's point would be to underscore rather than name as "possible" the relation between estrangement and the sublime. Indeed, to come to terms with the work in the last part of this book is to be willing to be "arrested" by the otherwise "denied or obscured" insights offered by texts such as the written and oral testimonies discussed here. Even Levi would welcome the category, I think. For is he not the one who asks us to contemplate that survival in Auschwitz was not perfect unhappiness? And aren't we taken aback that the passages above might even manifest for the reader a form of the sense of the humor to be exhumed from the horror? We also know that songs, fables, and myths were born there in the ashes as well as strict systems of economics whose rules were quickly learned before death might become one's companion. To return to Tomkins on some of the further workings of shame, he reminds us:

> While terror and distress hurt, they are wounds inflicted from outside which penetrate the smooth surface of the ego; but shame is felt as an inner torment, a sickness of the soul. It does not matter whether the humiliated one has been shamed by derisive laughter or whether he mocks himself. In either event he feels himself naked, defeated, alienated, lacking in dignity or worth. (17)[3]

This degree of lack, it must be remembered, became a routine aspect of everyday life and death in the camps. (I leave the pronoun masculine as found in the quote from Silvan Tomkins, but ask you, the reader, to recall here the women in Delbo's account of the same phenomena.) The primal affect of shame is better appreciated when we recall with Kaufman, commenting on Tomkins, that

> all societies, therefore, exercise varying degrees of control over affect expression, and particularly over the cry of affect. Societies in general neither encourage nor permit their members to cry out in rage or excitement, in distress or terror, whenever or wherever they wish. The open expression of affect is restricted beginning at an early age and strict control is exerted particularly over the voice. (18)

Among the prisoners at Auschwitz all sorts of boundaries that are generally invoked in social life have broken down; however, what even these men—in conditions that we have seen represented but still may not readily imagine, or can *only* imagine—cannot abide is the open cry of rage, terror, fear that comes at times from their comrades in suffering. Even here there are limits to what it is possible to endure while still maintaining a shred of (inter)-subjectivity. Reduced to circumstances we want not to be able to imagine, inmates still insist on some of the constructions of self that we demand children learn in order to begin to take up membership in the social, the civil.

That holding in of breath that is required so as not to cry out in rage, for example, may be costly even for those who survived. Levi does not, as some memoirists of the Holocaust do, wait very long to let go the withholding of voice and vision. His first book, *Survival in Auschwitz,* written many years before he became a writer, conventionally speaking, is the muted, tactful, poised speaking out about that which is continually equated with the un-speakable in the later part of the century. Levi may owe some of the power of his "teachings" on survival to his ability both to hold his tongue and to speak with matter-of-factness and with forcefulness. His preoccupation with the basics, the elements, is apparent in all his work, and he works his preoccupa-tion with deft and kind attention to the barbarism he knew and whose po-tential never left his consciousness.

Levi tells the two dreams that are shared by many in the Lager: they are of the story that will not be believed by those outside, and the vision of Tanta-lus who can never assuage his hunger. The metaphysics of bread in the camps is a thread through Levi's meditation on survival; it is the basic unit of currency and it shapes the days and ways among men in this setting. Within minutes of the reveille call just before dawn

> begins the distribution of bread, of bread-Brot-Broid-chleb-pain-lechem-kenyér, of the holy grey slab which seems gigantic in your neighbour's hand, and in your own hand so small as to make you cry. It is a daily hallucination to which in the end one becomes accustomed: but at the beginning it is so ir-resistible that many of us after long discussions on our own open and con-stant misfortune and the shameless luck of others, finally exchange our ra-tion, at which the illusion is renewed inverted, leaving everyone discontented and frustrated. (34)

In a chapter called, remarkably enough, "A Good Day," Levi returns to the "ever-insufficient knowledge of the complex nature of unhappiness" in order to situate the standards by which any experience may be judged by the prisoners:

> We have never seen each other in sunlight: someone smiles. If it was not for the hunger! . . .
> But how could one imagine not being hungry? The Lager *is* hunger: we ourselves are hunger, living hunger. (66–67)

Watching a "steam shovel's meal," Levi and his companions begin to fantasize about the food they remember at home. What Levi recalls is his "last meal," the one he and his partisan companions were sharing when they "suddenly heard the news that we would leave for here the following day; and we were eating it . . . and we stopped, fools, stupid as we were—if we had only known!" The certainty that emerges from this reminiscence is that "it will not happen to us a second time" (67). What makes this a good day, one better than others, is that Templer, "the official organizer of the Kommando," has managed to get hold of a pot of soup holding more than eleven gallons. This unusually larger ration for all makes it possible that the day should end thus:

> As we are all satiated, at least for a few hours, no quarrels arise, we feel good, the Kapo feels no urge to hit us, and we are able to think of our mothers and wives, which usually does not happen. For a few hours we can be unhappy in the manner of free men. (69)

Levi, like Delbo, Millu, and most memoirists of the camps, gives back names to those who were meant to be lost to history. They insist on the acts of individuals, whether victims or perpetrators, as crucial to the everyday operations intended to annihilate entire populations. Certain specific members of the collectivities of captives and of captors helped others to live another day or brought about their deaths. Levi never forgot and asks us to remember the work of Templer on that memorable day.

The miraculousness of survival and recovery is clear in the essay "My House," which opens Levi's collection *Other People's Trades*. If we did not know his fate under Italian and German fascism, we would never guess from the following:

> I have always lived (with involuntary interruptions) in the house where I was born, so my mode of living has not been the result of a choice. . . . Perhaps I owe to this static destiny the never satisfied love I harbor for travel, and the frequency that a journey appears as a *topos* in many of my books. (11)

Can it be that to begin anew, a new book, is to recall that first book and the journey it recounts again and again? Those discreet parentheses refer the reader who knows Levi to his earlier writings, which prepare us for the man he has become and whom he might never have become otherwise. The forge of his wisdom and generosity was an infernal space where he spoke to his comrades of Dante, for example, so as to get them to attend to a terrible task. Whether he would have become a writer without the experience of deportation and the Lager is moot; like so many of the texts and voices here it is the experience of dislocation and its transformation into narrative that gives us the task of reading how such "travels" demand that we reenact the entry into culture(s) and all that that entails of encounters with the figures and structures of authority and identity.

Liana Millu's *Smoke over Birkenau* is structured through six tales of the women's Lager of Auschwitz—Birkenau—where the crematoria stood. Each story recounts the death of particular individuals who had come to matter to the narrator during her time in the camp. Like Levi, she survived due to her ability to labor—in her case, in an arms factory. In an afterword to her book, she states the paradox of survival we have read here repeatedly:

> Today I realize that I owe my salvation to the fact that I already considered myself as good as dead. I was resigned, and that allowed me to do the unthinkable, such as look around, seek out a blade of grass amid the mud, marvel at the colors of the dawn. (200)

This unrelenting capacity to "marvel" or wonder at the continuity of nature in the midst of one of the great sociopolitical ruptures also keeps Levi wondering at the inability to maintain "perfect unhappiness." It is also what moved Delbo to tell the tale of "The Tulip." On one of the usual mornings when the women were marched off to dig ditches, she noticed:

> This was a direction that we had never taken before. . . . The chimney is smoking. Who can be living in this isolated house? It draws nearer. We see white curtains. Muslin curtains. We say muslin with a sweet taste in our mouths. And in front of the curtains in the space between the window and the storm sash, there is a tulip. . . . All eyes are trained on the flower. . . . All day long we dream of that tulip. Sleet was falling, sticking to the backs of our soaked and frozen jackets. The day was long, as long as every day. At the bottom of the ditch we were digging the tulip blossomed in its delicate corolla. On the way back, long before coming to the house on the lake, our eyes were waiting for it. . . . And during the roll call we said to comrades who were not with us: "We saw a tulip." . . . When we learned that it was the house of the

SS who was in charge of the fishery, we hated our memory and the tenderness that they had not yet dried up within us. (69)

Here is a moment when the capacity for wonder itself is the cause of
shame—hating one's memory. Where Delbo insists on resistance even as she
surrenders to feelings that were better extinguished, Millu sees her own
stance as one of resignation. In the face of resignation Millu is then able to
record her own and other's moments of "tenderness . . . not yet dried up,"
which lead nevertheless to death. Two of Millu's stories will help to make my
point; both are tales of what insistence on biological kinship accomplished
in these situations of extended emergency, and both are tales of women who
remain mothers in the camp—and who die as mothers. Millu does not hate
her memories; however, in the telling of these two stories there is a sense that
tenderness that is hoarded or misspent leads one to become one of the
drowned, in Levi's terms.

"Under Cover of Darkness" is the story of Maria, newly pregnant, who
managed to disguise her pregnancy rather than submit to an abortion upon
arrival at Birkenau. Maria became Millu's bunkmate for a time. Sleeping directly above them was Adela, an older woman, whose daughter had been
about to give birth when the family was deported. Adela revealed Maria's secret to Millu, who found Maria's behavior "utterly selfish," and wondered,
"Were the laws of nature still valid in a death camp? She refused to sacrifice
her right to be a mother, refused the pain of having the child stripped from
her, but why give birth to a creature who was doomed to feed the flames?"
(56). Maria, to avoid any extra notice, bound her belly with rags, and worked
"incessantly, never even trying to sneak away for a break" (57). Millu and the
other women taunted Maria for her assiduousness to distract themselves
from the exhaustion of their days, but Millu later recalled, "In the end I re-
coiled in shame from their weary eyes gleaming with malice and their
pinched mouths spewing out vulgarities, sick at the sight of what our misery
had made of us. . . . Soon I would be a true daughter of the lager" (58). Re-
sisting such hideous transformation, Millu identified with Maria's position
and allowed herself to become her protector and confidant. She realized that
she, too, would fantasize about the war ending in time for the baby to be
born in freedom, and participated in such fantasies with Maria: sexing the
child female, imagining a name for her, becoming the girl's godmother, fore-
casting future visits from afar, furnishing a room for her. But Millu's compassion was not reserved only for Maria; she recognized Adela's "desolate
hostility" as born out of the fact that the "two young lives that were all she

treasured on earth were taken first," so that this "solitary old woman, destined to die alone and uncomforted, must be in far greater pain" (64–65). Compassion existed side by side with primal and "shamefaced" hunger when Adela offered Millu her unfinished food, and Millu tried and failed to refuse such "undreamed of luck" (66). Later that evening, some of the women in the camp who remembered that it was Hanukkah gathered around eight candles someone had carefully "organized" for this event. Maria and Liana Millu went to the gathering, where most of the women took the occasion of ritual to weep through their grief and recite "all the names of those who would not see the sacred candles lit next year, nor the year after, nor ever again, for any holiday on earth" (69). When Millu suggested that it was time for them to leave, Maria

> stepped reverently to the improvised altar and, bowing her head, gazed down at the flickering, gleaming flame. I knew she was envisioning next year, when she would stand in front of her ancient Menorah holding little Erika in her arms, straining a bit under her weight, and give thanks for the emblematic light; the dismal barrack at Birkenau would be but a shadowy, long-gone dream. (69)

This mixture of temporalities in which Millu imagined what Maria might feel a year later held in it the wish for everyone's survival, the war's end, the child's healthy birth, and a forgetfulness that the text proves was unattainable.

The next morning Maria and Millu were given the task of getting the vat of weak coffee after reveille; when Maria tripped and fell, spilling much of the liquid, her dress "slid up, revealing a strip of blanket" (75). Erna, the *blockowa* (prisoner in charge of the others, therefore one step up in the hierarchy) noticed, and Adela, acting out her rage at the loss of her own daughter and unborn grandchild, exclaimed the fact of Maria's pregnancy to all within hearing. Erna, furious, could only think of herself, "caught in the middle," and turned her anger on Adela for not having told the truth about Maria sooner. But Erna and the other women in charge, to save their own skins, formulated a plan to hide Maria from others for as long as possible. She was "consigned to isolation" (79) and to the futile task of washing floors repeatedly, breaking her spirit. The women in charge took every occasion to brutalize, beat, and kick Maria, whose condition risked exposing their inattention and complicity. When Maria called out again and again for water, offering to sell her bread, it was Adela who recognized the beginning of labor pains. Acting now in full contradiction with her act of exposing Maria's lie, she instead became the experienced midwife who was delighted *and* crazed as she explained,

"It'll be born on the last night of the holidays. That's good luck" (85). Only Millu and a few of the other women seemed to notice that after the baby had been delivered, Maria was hemorrhaging "indefatigably" (88). Then

> suddenly the reveille gong sounded and the yellow lights flashed on. It was still night, but for us day was dawning, with its unvarying acts and imperatives, the harsh Birkenau day that acknowledged neither birth or death, only silence and obedience to its pitiless laws. (88)

To avoid discovery at roll call they covered Maria and her baby with blankets "in the darkest corner of the bunk," but when the roll call was over Millu discovered that Maria and her baby were, predictably, "*kaputt*," "all finished" (90–91). Only the story, Millu's story, would remember them, and would provide Maria and her child a proper burial and place to be recalled. Maria's pregnancy, which caused her death and that of her child, brought her nevertheless a form of recognition during her time in the camp—one that circles always back to the mother, who, as we read in Delbo, is the one taken to be most lost in this universe. There *are* no proper deaths at Auschwitz-Birkenau. There are only the haunted memories of those who witnessed life and death as they held sway over all who entered here.

The other story from Millu's book that emphasizes the terrible cost of degradation witnessed between mothers and children is called "High Tension," after the electrified fences that surround the camps—"those wires unmarked by any warning skull and crossbones. The entire camp was devoted to death. How absurd it would be to warn people against the lady of the house" (109). In this story Millu finds some comfort and reprieve working among other Italian Jews in a factory, glad to be indoors and not "outnumbered by hostile strangers calling me 'macaroni'" (95). Among the workers was Bruna, whose good fortune was that she knew her son was alive, if not well, because the women usually passed him on the road from the factory back to their barracks. Pinin, Bruna's son, worked the garbage kommando, and his birthday was imminent. One of the guardswomen sometimes averted her glance, and through this capricious and unexpectedly human gesture Bruna and her son were even able to hold each other and speak a few words in the midst of the rhythmic marching as they passed each other. On one such occasion

> the child clung to his mother's embrace. He was telling her something, looking quite disconsolate, while Bruna kept shaking her head, no, no. Meanwhile she adjusted the cap on his shaved head, straightened out his jacket, and kissed him. (100)

Bruna decided to trade her bread for additional food for Pinin, who looked ever more weak, and asked Millu to accompany her to the "'Redheads' barrack, the camp's official black market and trading post" because Millu could speak some German. En route there Millu learned the source of the boy's distress earlier: "He'd burst into tears, recounting how one of the boys had taunted, 'Hey you, Italian! Macaroni to the crematorium, get going!'" (102). The son's shame and terror led the mother to risk her own health and life, as she traded away her food to acquire some carrots and the extra unbidden gift of "a minuscule slice of onion," after fierce negotiations with Katia. From a perspective that reveals further how ethnicity complicates life among captives, Bruna asked Millu to sleep with the bundle that night, for her own bunkmate was a Greek: "It's so awful to sleep with a thief" (104). Millu agreed, "never imagining what an ordeal I had in store":

> The golden carrots and tangy onion danced behind my closed eyes. . . .
> I didn't want to steal poor Pinin's food, only to smell it, to savor the wonderful fresh, raw smell. I hadn't smelled anything like it since I was arrested.
>   It was all I could do to control myself, and in the end blessed sleep came to my rescue. I dreamed I was with Bruna and Pinin in a huge field of cabbages. I plucked a leaf and put it in my mouth, and it turned into a soft, sweet, fragrant slice of *panettone*. I could taste the sweetness of the cake melting in my mouth. Pinin was laughing because it was a holiday and the bells were ringing.

But as Millu explains, the bells of this Tantalus dream, which Levi had described as common among the prisoners, were only the "harsh gong of Birkenau sounding reveille" (105). This tormenting hunger and the blessed sleep that transformed the barely averted theft of a child's food into a dream of laughter and sweetness in the mouth—instead of raging emptiness—was not yet the final punishment that would come from attachments held perhaps too dearly under the circumstances. The next time that the women passed by the young boys hauling garbage, Pinin was not there. Bruna found out from one of the others that he was in the quarantine Lager, where rest was briefly available, but all who had been in camp any length of time knew that it was a rest that merely preceded certain death in the gas chambers, only to stoke the already choking fires of the crematoria. The women knew Bruna's anguish was inconsolable and feared for her sanity. The next day at work in the factory, a small regular act of sabotage—in which Costanza disarmed the machines so that the women could rest briefly while mechanics arrived to get them going again—became the scene of Bruna's acting out her agonized wrath. The usually morose German woman (herself in mourning for her family killed in an air raid) who acted as overseer, suspecting foul play, called in the *Meister*, who "ranted and raved, never pausing for breath, filling the pressroom with his guttural voice" (113). Bruna in her grief had kept working while the others had paused. The *Meister* threatened them all, "This time, everyone *kaputt*, understand?" but singled Bruna out as the "good girl" (114). But here is the totally unprecedented act of resistance that was nevertheless not uncommon—Bruna, when she understood the import of his words, did not feel spared and grateful. Shifting suddenly in her identification with her comrades, whom she had just been ignoring while lost in her sorrow over her son, she was filled with "outrage and loathing . . . radiating an infinite contempt," and "she deliberately spit at the huge man," who knocked her to the floor with kicks. Others who tried to explain her act to spare her, and only secondarily themselves, found that they, too, came under his boot. Millu is speaking:

> I looked at Costanza and could see the identical thoughts in her eyes. She too must feel rage and bitterness rising in her heart like a dark tide, flooding everything except fear of the unknown, fear of tomorrow, disgust, exhaustion. Over toward Birkenau, a few wisps of black smoke hung stagnant in the dense air. As I shifted around, trying to get the edge of my dress under my knees, which stung from the gravel, I felt a surge of anger. I was furious with myself and all the miserable creatures around me who prolonged their own suffering, eating themselves alive and leaving the Germans the final nuisance of setting them free.
>
> Why not get it over with ourselves, set ourselves free? But no, we were too cowardly for that. (115)

But Bruna, who had risked all, was no longer too cowardly. On the return from the factory, as the women passed the quarantine Lager, the marching rows were disturbed. Bruna saw her son seeing her, and ran toward the electrified fence, crying out, "Come to Mama!"

> The boy hesitated for an instant. But his mother kept calling until he rushed to the fence, entreating her, "Mama, Mama!" As he hit the wires, his arms melted into his mother's in an explosion of violet flames. A buzzing sound zipped through the violently shaken wires, and the pungent smell of scorched flesh filled the air.

After the ensuing commotion,

> the line reassembled and Hermine began marking time. I turned for one last look: Bruna and Pinin lay in their tight embrace, the mother resting her head on the son's, as if to watch over his sleep. (116)

Such scenes are etched in the memory of survivors, and we deny or obscure them at our own risk. But we read them and wonder, in our shaken leisure, at the remapped terrain of human experience that could render this moment a luxurious death in the world of choiceless choice that was the extermination camps.

The stories of Bruna and Pinin and Maria and her barely born Erika suggest that for different generations to witness each other's demolition at the hands of the captors was more than they could bear. It is common to read that sisters who survived together often escaped some of the worst psychic ravages of time in the camps, although Millu describes sisterly love as encompassing an "almost morbid attachment" (151). She also tells a story of sisters in "Scheiss Egal"[4] in which Gustine and Lotti have chosen opposite paths; Gustine risks the wearying and killing life of the Lagers, while Lotti takes the chance to volunteer for the Auschwitz *Puffkommando* or brothel, leading Gustine to deny her and consider her as good as dead. When Millu through coincidence meets Lotti, the sister who has "chosen" the comforts of clothing, cosmetics, mirrors, and men, Lotti has this to say to her:

> People think blood ties mean everything. But what good is being brothers or sisters or whatever, when you see things in such opposite ways? The differences create such a barrier that you have no more in common than total strangers passing on the street. Gustine and I are of the same blood, we grew up together, but now there is nothing left between us, because I was afraid to die and she believed God would save her. (173)

This chance encounter with the effaced sister in her surroundings of relative comfort brings Millu face to face with her own resignation and despair:

> It was all nothing but smoke. Smoke drifting over the lagers, the town, and the brothel; smoke drifting over evil and innocence, wisdom and folly, death and life. All of it "Scheiss egal." (175)

In a preface to *Survival in Auschwitz*, Primo Levi warns readers that "many people—many nations—can find themselves holding . . . that 'every stranger is an enemy'" and that "when this does come about . . . there is the Lager" (5). This last part of my book has shifted the earlier emphasis and allure of xenophilia to the most well—and awfully—witnessed aspects of the horrors of xenophobia. Estrangement, defamiliarization, alienation, displacement, and the subjects who undergo these affects and experiences have, as I have intended to show, myriad stories to tell and a compelling need to tell them. I have focused on Millu's stories last and their emphasis on situated kinship and recognition rather than familiarity grounded in sameness and blood because the dangers of that are all too clear here. Millu herself remarks in "High Tension" that

> words such as expiation, suffering, punishment were utterly beside the point. No one can atone for another's grief; all the combined suffering of the Germans could never make up for our own, not for a single quarter of an hour in the shadow of the crematorium, our teeth chattering in the cold, our eyes fixed on the curls of smoke drifting overhead. (108)

The impossibility of the law or justice coming to work history over is not all that Millu is asserting. In his ethnographic study of the "politics of Jewish memory," Jonathan Boyarin notes "the link between empathy and empire" and asks the pertinent question of the "possible alternatives . . . to the triumphalism of empathetic participant observation or empathetic historicism" (89).[5] Edward Said has provided eloquent and passionate models of the relations between culture and imperialism; reading Said, Boyarin has made a case for the further connections between genocide and imperialism in his "distinctions between [Europe's] Other within [the Jew] and the Other without [the savage], the Other in space and the Other in time, [which] collapse at the pinnacle of *modern* imperialism" (89). If the postmodern condition and ideal may be said to be that of diaspora, as Boyarin and others suggest, then indeed it would be necessary to make full contact with the underside of this "ideal" and to "reinscribe empathy more knowingly, with a critical awareness of the power relations and the tendencies to symbolic violence its usage implies" (90). Vain and problematic though it may be as a wish and regret, Isaac Deutscher spoke to some of the same troublesome history of Europe's legacy to the nationalist geopolitics of the twentieth century when he said, "I would have preferred the six million men, women and children to survive and Jewry to perish" (50).[6]

We do not need borders to mark strangers. The desperate grasping for marking frontiers, taking space, is occurring in Europe once more, although many thought it never again would, but then what were the iron and concrete curtains and walls inevitably intended to lead to once opened and fallen?

The mastery of the self in motion through a landscape offers the possibility of an affirmative deterritorialization in which the world may come to feel like home even while one is homeless. It is when this mastery is premised on the bondage of those fixed and figured in the landscape who may not move at their own whim that movement, scattering, and diaspora embody the potential for exile, or negative deterritorialization. Dislocation—forced, inherited, or chosen—asks that subjects draw on all their resources for recognizing their need for and dependence on other subjects. What any of us may find in the moment of encounter with the stranger depends on a mastery over ourselves in which all our senses can participate in order to write anew the shameful history of civilizations as we have known them.

~

Speaking of Travel . . .

In opening this book, I spoke about the mapping of identities through their dispersion in place and time. Questions about the marks of memory are persistent in postmodernity. What I have written here are further articulations of these questions and perhaps some tentative approaches to answers.

And, as I said earlier, a euro-centrifugal tale.

In 1970, while traveling in Italy, I was literally stopped in my tracks in the church of Santa Croce in Florence. A prone funerary sculpture of a woman arrested my attention. In that uncanny instant I was certain that she bore an unmistakable resemblance to my mother, whose face I only knew from photographs. When my eyes began to scan the scene it became apparent that the inscriptions on the tomb beneath her figure were not in Latin or Italian but in Polish—my mother's native language, but not one I knew, except insofar as its peculiarities had always made my last name difficult to spell in America. Unable to decipher anything but the dates of her stay in Italy, I know I returned to the church another day to copy down what was engraved there. Some other time, somewhere else, I would have it translated.

In the last months of finishing this book, this memory, which had been unretrieved for a decade or two, resurfaced when someone I knew mentioned she was taking a trip to Florence. Because I had been writing about such moments, no doubt—Canetti in Marrakesh, Hurston in Haiti, for example—I asked her to bring back any evidence of this event, whether a copy of the inscription or simply tourist pamphlets about the church. It turned out to be the case that in the days she was there the Uffizi Galleries had been bombed, and visits to the church of Santa Croce were impossible because of security in the surrounding streets.

Quite by coincidence, another friend of mine was going to spend two days in Florence at the end of the summer of 1993. Now that my efforts had been so oddly frustrated by an act of civil terrorism, I was even more eager to see what I could do to better recall the moment in Santa Croce in 1970, for the notes I took then had long since disappeared through repeated discarding of personal effects in peregrinations since that time. It turned out that this friend, too, was stymied in her efforts, for the church was under major repairs, and the side galleries, where I remembered sighting the figure, were emptied.

Notes

Travel as/is

1. One of the earliest works with which I wanted to enter into dialogue when this book began to take shape was Johannes Fabian's *Time and the Other: How Anthropology Makes Its Object*; his insight that the structures of colonialism require the denial of a time in history shared between the colonizers and their subjected peoples is what he names the "denial of coevalness." More specifically sociolinguistic are Fabian's *Language on the Road: Notes on Swahili in Two Nineteenth Century Travelogues* and *Language and Colonial Power: The Appropriation of Swahili in the Former Belgian Congo, 1880–1938*. Moments of dislocation are dislocating precisely because of assumptions untheorized about the discrete boundedness of time and place. These boundaries function, in fact, more like semipermeable membranes. Parts of the postmodern scene could be read as a reaction to those membranes becoming ever thinner, with all that suggests about the anxieties that attend our relations to borders, frontiers, and rebellions against them, as well as the rush to defend them when endangered. Both immunology and anthropology have something to do with investigations of borders coming into being and breaking down and with breakthroughs in such systems; see, for example, Donna Haraway, "The Biopolitics of Postmodern Bodies: Constitutions of Self in Immune System Discourse," in *Simians, Cyborgs and Women: The Reinvention of Nature*; and Cindy Patton's analysis of vectoral as opposed to dispersive economies of disease (paper delivered at the "Queer Rhetorics, Queer Politics" session, Marxism in the New World Order Conference, Amherst, Mass., Nov. 12–14, 1992).

2. Think for just a moment of the massive popular signification granted to cultural variations on the greeting: the "Russian" bear hug, the "Indians" who may still be endowed by schoolteachers in the United States with some "grunt" rendered as "How!"; the African-American high five; the secret handshakes of white male "brotherhoods." Entire histories of national character or stereotypification are written in the spaces between strangers.

3. There are numerous examples of the debates among ethnic minority writers as to who will "be" their voice. To take one specific instance, how does the category of gender inflect the impasse between Asian-American writers Maxine Hong Kingston and Frank Chin (*Los Angeles Times*, June 24, 1990)? Or try to follow the ever fractious splits among feminists, among women, about who shall name them, and to whom: the cultural versus radical feminists of the 1970s as against the antiporn versus prosex feminists of the pre-AIDS 1980s; "feminist" versus "womanist," as yet another kind of naming. Some of these splits represented fault lines of age and political generations; others came to stand for splits along lines of sexual orientation; and still others came to stand for splits between white feminists and women of color. Think elsewhere across the globe of linguistic minorities in Spain, France, India, Canada, and elsewhere who demand their say, or again of named peoples who may no longer exist as such due to geopolitical fractures and reconstitutions: are there still Soviet people, East Germans, Rhodesians, Burmese? If so, what would these designations signify now? Each time I come to update and revise this note, what strikes me is the absolutely unacademic nature of these questions and their lived reality.

4. There are numerous discursive sites of nostalgia and loss that could be illustrative here—from a critic like Roland Barthes, ineffably postmodern and therefore making a tempo-

rary shelter out of language rather than a prisonhouse, to the more politically charged discourses on homelessness as a postmodern condition, whether a matter of life on the streets of contemporary cities large or small, or of the statelessness of groups like the Palestinians or Kurds. We need only browse the front pages around us to recognize the millenial ambience not of the promise and progress of the nineteenth century but of plague and scarcity as they have come to define the *fin* of this *siècle*.

5. A model for my work is the kind of rhetorical study undertaken by Mary Louise Pratt in *Imperial Eyes: Travel Writing and Transculturation*. I will carry on from some of Pratt's work in my further exploration of her figure of the "seeing-man" as traveler, ordinary and exemplary at once. The questions will center on what can and does occur in those sociogeographical spaces Pratt names the "contact zones."

6. See Rosemary Marangoly George, "Traveling Light: Of Immigration, Invisible Suitcases, and Gunny Sacks," on what she terms the immigrant genre.

7. For a further discussion of these issues, see Gayatri Chakravorty Spivak, "In a Word: Interview."

8. Along these lines, two recent works that have spurred me to clarify further my own project are Chris Bongie's *Exotic Memories: Literature, Colonialism and the Fin de siècle* and Dennis Porter's *Haunted Journeys: Desire and Transgression in European Travel Writing*.

9. Polo's text is of interest for countless reasons, among them its status as "prison memoir" ostensibly ghostwritten by a fellow prisoner; it is rather a foolhardy leap in terms of narrative and history, but I want to suggest a connection (which I cannot follow up here) to DeLillo's preoccupation in his novel with Americans abroad and criminality/imperialism as embodied in a secret and perhaps murderous language.

10. It might be said that the sound and fury over "political correctness" that has been stirred up by the forces of reaction is fueled by a terrible anxiety over the destabilizing of pronominal order—that it is no longer so clear who "we" are, and that "they" are *not* "us." Pronouns may no longer be the exclusive currency of those who have felt free to name. One could read the discourses of liberation that have brought us toward an acknowledgment of the fact of multicultures as a series of struggles over pronouns and names, how they do or do not "stand for," and the critical issue of who is in possession of the agency to decide which verbs may be performed by which speakers.

11. Riley's text scripts the shifting ground of identity when it is taken up as object or subject (for another) rather than as effect, or aura, as Walter Benjamin might have said. For a discussion of identities and their dispersive effects that enlarges on Riley's laconic and suggestive text, see Christina Crosby, "Dealing with Differences," in *Feminists Theorize the Political*, ed. Judith Butler and Joan Scott, 130–44.

Time and the Traveler

1. The filiation from Gauguin to Segalen is complex; it is on returning to France from Oceania in 1904 that Segalen first conceives of and begins to take notes for a project to write an essay on exoticism. It is also the case that when he arrives on the island where Gauguin had lived and where he spends time studying Gauguin's work, the visual artist's images haunt him and inspire him to attempt in words what he believes Gauguin was after in his paintings and sketches. Appended to the 1986 publication of the *Essay on Exoticism* are three texts on Gauguin, an "Hommage" written in 1916 and intended to introduce the publication of letters between Gauguin and Georges-Daniel de Monfried; an article, "Gauguin dans son dernier décor," written in and sent from Tahiti in 1904 and published in *Le Mercure de France* in June of that year; and a short fiction, "La Marche du feu," originally intended for a collection of writings called *Les Exotiques* but never published in that context.

2. In Bongie's opening chapter, "An Idea without a Future," he asserts that to understand

the relation between the exotic and memory, or nostalgia—to shift the picture somewhat—we must understand that an elsewhere had "ceased to exist." Moving from Conrad to Pasolini, an itinerary I very much appreciate, I want nevertheless to register my disagreement with Bongie, for an elsewhere may be degraded and even disappeared in some geo- and topographical ways, but psychopolitically, elsewheres seem to keep being born out of experiences with that which is newly encountered in the materials of everyday life. I would cite here in juxtaposition to Pasolini the work of another filmmaker, Jim Jarmusch, who speaks to the elsewheres that will not go away, the ones that are "stranger than paradise," nonutopian but as yet unmapped social spaces.

3. This characterization is Gilles Manceron's; he wrote the opening statement and introductory essay for the 1986 revised and enlarged republication of the *Essai*.

4. The word *équipée* is a cognate for escapade, and also suggests being outfitted or equipped for such an outing or adventure. Translations of passages from Segalen's *Essai sur l'exotisme: Une esthétique du divers* and *Equipée: Voyage au Pays du Réel* are mine.

·   5. It is no surprise that three recent texts that actively engage the status of travel writing do so largely on the ground of that tradition in French letters. I am both implicitly and sometimes explicitly trying to engage with these texts in this book. I have in mind not only Dennis Porter's *Haunted Journeys* and Chris Bongie's *Exotic Memories*, both already cited, but also George Van Den Abbeele's *Travel as Metaphor: From Montaigne to Rousseau*.

6. Bongie notes two things that are crucial to my reading of Segalen and to his own: "the massive influence of Pierre Loti on the spiritual geography of an entire generation; the central role of vision in registering the exotic" (120). We both then proceed to read Segalen, hunting down his displacements of these dominant tropes of exoticism, but our agendas differ.

7. Jean Mambrino in "Segalen ou l'immobile voyageur," 347–52.

8. "What is represented in ideology is therefore not the system of the real relations that govern the existence of individuals, but the imaginary relation of those individuals to the real relations in which they live." Louis Althusser, "Ideology and Ideological State Apparatuses (Notes towards an Investigation)," in *Lenin and Philosophy and Other Essays*, 165.

9. Manceron, Segalen's recent editor, notes that the reason for cutting short his trip to China was news of the outbreak of the First World War in Europe in 1914.

10. The 1983 republication of Lévinas's *Le Temps et l'autre* consists of four transcribed lectures delivered under this title in 1946–47 at the newly established Collège Philosophique in Paris. Translations from this work are mine.

Seeing Is Believing

1. The degree and frequency of surprise is quite manageable, even marketable—the management of the desire for surprise of a geo-cultural kind is what produces the travel industry. Another aspect of critical writing on travel emerges from the more sociological impetus of cultural studies, such as in John Urry, *The Tourist Gaze: Leisure and Travel in Contemporary Societies*; Dean McCannell, *The Tourist: A New Theory of the Leisure Class*; and Maxine Feifer, *Tourism in History: From Imperial Rome to the Present*.

2. Allegret was on assignment to record indigenous dances for the ethnographic film archives of the Musée de l'Homme in Paris.

3. "Indicible langueur. Heures sans contenu ni contour." These phrases without subject or verb in French suggestively draw the reader into the disorientation and dislocation produced by the elsewhere, all the while soothing the potential anxiety such liminality might evoke. The Gide quotations in this chapter are from the English edition of *Travels in the Congo*.

4. Porter notes that Gide "had traveled widely in Europe with his mother's blessing"; this blessing is bound up with Gide's "individual code that is constructed out of a series of interlocking oppositions between, on the one hand, *famille* (family), *foyer* (home), *province* (region), and

patrie (homeland), and, on the other, *voyage* (travel), *vagabondage* (vagabondage), *errance* (wandering), and *déracinement* (uprootedness). And connected to that are the motifs of rebellion against the paternal Law" (235). In Porter's reading of Gide's relation to desire and transgression, the mother is never in clear view; she recedes into the distance as the traveling son flees.

5. For a psychoanalytic contribution to the discussion of the relations to space/place, see Thomas Ogden, whose (unfortunately named) "autistic-contiguous position is understood as a sensory-dominated, presymbolic area of experience in which the most primitive form of meaning is generated on the basis of the organization of sensory impressions, particularly at the skin surface. A unique form of anxiety arises in this psychological realm: terror over the prospect that the boundedness of one's sensory surface might be dissolved." *The Primitive Edge of Experience*. Another psychoanalytic treatment of identity formation through senses other than the visual is Didier Anzieu, *The Skin Ego*.

6. Both the published narrative of the journey and Gide's journals, as well as a long dossier of letters, take up the depredations of one Sergeant Yemba, a functionary of the colonial government, and his mistreatment of the men who worked for him.

7. In a commentary on African-American linguistic practice, Hurston writes in *Dust Tracks on a Road* about her gratitude to the J. B. Lippincott editor who accepted by wire her manuscript of *Jonah's Gourd Vine* for a $200 advance at a time when she was thoroughly broke: "So you see why that editor is *Colonel* to me. When the Negroes in the South name a white man a colonel, it means CLASS. Something like a monarch, only bigger and better. And when the colored population in the South confer a title, the white people recognize it because the Negroes are never wrong. They may flatter an ordinary bossman by calling him 'Cap'n' but when they say 'Colonel,' 'General' and 'Governor' they are recognizing something internal. It is there, and it is accepted because it can be seen" (212).

8. An intertextual note: Roland Barthes's first published article (1942) is on Gide's *Journal*; in it he suggests that Gide used his *Journal* as a place of "perpetual self-correction." Barthes also remarks that Gide works as his own scholiast. I have chosen as stopping points in many instances the footnotes to the *Travels*, for it is in these textual margins that Gide can indulge in the same desire to correct and comment later on the text written and not much reworked during the trip itself. It is these same footnotes and appendices (the longest and most substantial of which are not available in the English translation published by the University of California in 1962) that detail Gide's encounter with the French administrators of these territories and his efforts to find correctives to some of the colonial abuses he hears about from the men he has hired as porters and from villagers along the way.

9. Striking in Barthes's preciousness are the echoes of Marco Polo, simple traveler and businessman in the court of the khan, relying on his senses to make sense of the otherness he had felt compelled to find.

10. This is taken from Barthes's "La Lumière du sud-ouest," one of four posthumously published essays in his *Incidents*.

11. See my "Roland Barthes' Secret Garden" and "A Fearful Fancy: Some Reconsiderations of the Sublime" for a thorough discussion of these ways of reading Barthes's discursive practices.

12. Butor's essay has appeared in more than one form. The version I am citing was first published in French in 1972, and was first translated into English by John Powers and K. Lisker in 1974.

Voodoo and Fetish

1. Sara Mills, *Discourses of Difference: An Analysis of Women's Travel Writing and Colonialism*.

2. Katherine Frank, *A Voyager Out: The Life of Mary Kingsley*.

Among Camels and Women

1. Christina Crosby, "Dealing with Differences," in *Feminists Theorize the Political*, ed. Judith Butler and Joan Scott, 140.

2. Rana Kabbani, in *Europe's Myths of Orient*, has done a critique of Canetti that aligns him with the Orientalist project; I am in agreement with Gareth Stanton's critique of Kabbani that she relies on rather than refining Said's "original formulation" and that she therefore dismisses *Voices of Marrakesh* as remaining "tangled in the myth" of Orientalism itself (Stanton, "The Oriental City: A North African Itinerary," 3–38).

3. Jane Gallop, *Reading Lacan*; see the chapter "Where to Begin?," esp. 80–85.

4. In *Marvelous Possessions: The Wonder of the New World*, Stephen Greenblatt follows a historical trajectory in the European understanding of "medieval wonder as a sign of dispossession to Renaissance wonder as an agent of appropriation" and suggests that a moment like this one in Canetti's voyage embodies "the utopian moment of travel: when you realize that what seems most unattainably marvelous, most desirable, is what you almost already have, what you could have . . . at home" (24–25). For Canetti it seems a matter of finding what had been lost.

Casablanca Revisited

1. It is notable that the Fanon I have in mind here speaks in the introduction to *Black Skin, White Masks* of the black man's "internalization—or better, the epidermalization—of this inferiority" (11); a further theorizing of the interweaving of race and shame has yet to be done. However, I cannot help but think of Toni Morrison's phrase from *Beloved*, describing white men as the "men without skin," as an inversion of the values of difference weighed in racial terms.

2. Kaja Silverman, in *The Acoustic Mirror: The Female Voice in Psychoanalysis and Cinema*, speaks so clearly to the way in which the cinema gives us access to and puts us in thrall to the "skating" mobility of identities that is clear for Phillips in this passage. Silverman notes, "What passes for 'femininity' is actually an inevitable part of all subjectivity. . . . [W]hat is needed here is not so much a 'masculinization' of the female subject as a 'feminization' of the male subject— a much more generalized acknowledgment, in other words, of the necessary terms of cultural identity" (149). My work means to further complicate the terms of cultural identity, at least insofar as race *and* gender are concerned, and that is partly why Phillips occupies a terrain that begins the shift from traveler toward ethnic and immigrant.

3. Gayatri Chakravorty Spivak, "French Feminism Revisited: Ethics and Politics," in *Feminists Theorize the Political*, ed. Butler and Scott, 56.

4. Octave Mannoni, *Prospero and Caliban: The Psychology of Colonization*, was first published simply as *Psychologie de la colonisation*. Fanon's direct response to Mannoni's work is to be found in chapter 4 of *Black Skin, White Masks*, "The So-Called Dependency Complex of Colonized Peoples."

From Snakes to Ice

1. In Homi Bhabha's "Signs Taken for Wonders: Questions of Ambivalence and Authority under a Tree outside Delhi, May 1817," the "fortuitous discovery of the English book" literalizes postcoloniality; in Kpomassie's case, the French book that comes to reinscribe the place of this particular young man in postcolonial life is Robert Gessain's *Les Esquimaux du Groenland à l'Alaska* (Paris: Bourrelier, 1947).

2. Kpomassie deliberately searches out neither books like those read in school nor the religious primers that made up the inventory of the Evangelical Bookshop; he finds a rarer item, with its intriguing cover illustration of a "hunter dressed in clothes made of animal skins and leaning on a spear" (46).

3. Jean Malaurie, a French Arctic anthropologist who writes the preface to the English translation of Kpomassie's book, speaks of how Kpomassie "acts as a two-way mirror" in this cultural confrontation; he also notes that Kpomassie's comfort among the Greenlanders showed how he "enjoyed giving free rein to certain deep-seated tendencies to dominate, to possess—in short, to play the king a little" (xiii, xv).

4. Silvan Tomkins has been a key contributor to the recent provocative psychological and psychoanalytic discussions of theories of shame. His work concentrates on very fine distinctions to be made in the sources and manifestations of affect. Shame is an affect he reads primarily through its facial expressions. In a recent summary and overview of his own earlier multivolume work he notes the opposition between shame and what I want to call wonder in imagining the following scenario: "The child who is burning with excitement to explore the face of the stranger is nonetheless vulnerable to shame just because the other is perceived as strange" (Tomkins, "Shame," in *The Many Faces of Shame*, ed. Donald L. Nathanson, 144). Tomkins's major work is *Affect/Imagery/Consciousness*, vol. 1, *The Positive Affects*, and vol. 2, *The Negative Affects*.

5. "Feminist Politics: What's Home Got to Do with It?" by Biddy Martin and Chandra Talpade Mohanty, in *Feminist Studies/Critical Studies*, ed. Teresa de Lauretis, is a key piece of feminist theory on the politics of location. It raises certain issues that are displaced in Kpomassie's text into a postcolonial context; curiously, the reading these authors do of Minnie Bruce Pratt's autobiographical narrative, "Identity: Skin Blood Heart," circles around Pratt's changing sense of herself in relation to her father, whose "position and vision" she rejects out of a need to change. Martin and Mohanty's reading of a narrative by a Southern white lesbian from the United States resonates with my perspective on Kpomassie in ways that would seem to cut across those differences that we have come to take as definitive and determining, while speaking to the relational aspects of identities that Martin and Mohanty also insist upon and the intersubjective processes that occur between people and places.

6. Kpomassie's meeting with Robert Mattaaq transposes Bhabha's scene between Anund Messeh and the book of God to an encounter between a displaced French postcolonial subject and a resistant but wondrous citizen of a dominated culture. Bhabha's reading of the arrival of the book, here the magazine, rewrites the scene of split subjectivity, hybridity, and what he calls "negative transparency" outside a strict economy of colonialism while retaining some of its specific intersubjective features, as we will see.

7. Rob Shields, in *Places on the Margin: Alternative Geographies of Modernity*, does a thoroughgoing reading of the "space-myth" of "The True North Strong and Free" as it operates in the formation of Canadian identity in relation to its southern American neighbor and its own southern regions.

8. I want to thank Kwessan Satchivi, a Rutgers graduate student from Togo and of the Mina group, for reading this chapter and expanding my understanding of local practices concerning kinship and its promises and constraints.

9. An example here is Barbara Johnson's highly self-consciously framed essay, "Thresholds of Difference: Structures of Address in Zora Neale Hurston," in *"Race," Writing, and Difference*, ed. Henry Louis Gates Jr., whereby, in becoming the addressee of Hurston's texts, Johnson's initial "desire to re-referentialize difference" becomes instead a process in which she finds "difference as a suspension of reference," where "the terms 'black' and 'white,' 'inside' and 'outside,' continue to matter . . . not by erasing these differences but by foregrounding the complex dynamism of their interaction (328).

10. I am thinking especially of the first part of Lévi-Strauss's three-part study of myth, *The Raw and the Cooked*.

From Travelers to Ethnics; or, Looking for America

1. Among the moments in which I forged these thoughts on displacement were weeks where the mass media confronted us with photographs—picture writing, so visceral in its appeal and its effects—of Kurdish refugees desperately fleeing what had been "home" for some safer border crossing. We had seen this group persecuted and in flight before. The phenomenon was not new, only the degree. Refugees in the modern world have tended to be defined as ethnics. These movements between borders were offered by the electronic and print media to let us believe "we" were making "them" and their plight central to our power politics. But it is clear that, airlifts aside, other kinds of concerns predominated in the aftermath of war. Aftermath— the numbers are somehow always staggering; it is part of what, in fact, defines the refugee as opposed to the exile. The words that collect around the phenomena of im- and emigration point to gradations of privilege, opportunity, movements of collectivities, not individuals. Where the expatriate "suffers" the oppressions of "freedom," the exile suffers the oppression of repression; the refugee, however, suffers oppression and possible death at the hands of the oppressors. (The case of Salman Rushdie is one in which, from a choice of a new land to a need to hide from all lands, the traveler/immigrant/refugee has been transformed into a fugitive.)

The ethnopolitics of death reached proportions for which the twentieth century needed to find new words like *genocide*, a post-1945 coinage, although not a new fact of life. After the meager reporting of the six-week Persian Gulf war and its blackout of images associated with the deaths we know war brings, we were instead fed images and fragmentary narratives of lives broken by this war—signed, stunning photos of women, children, families, orphans—shards of lives. I could not help but see in this one of the latest Orientalist productions.

2. The traveler has been so thoroughly conventionalized as male that "women's travel writing" has taken up the space of a feminist "sub"-genre in recent years, spawning the reprinting of old texts and the busy critical production of secondary texts.

3. Judith Butler's book, *Gender Trouble: Feminism and the Subversion of Identity*, lays bare the archaeology of one particular site of identity construction and formation. Other current critical work on identities lets us know that gender is only one of the inevitably troubled sites. See, for example, the putting in quotes of "race" in much of Henry Louis Gates Jr.'s anthology *"Race," Writing, and Difference*, or the complication of the question of nationality throughout the essays collected in Homi Bhabha's *Nation and Narration*, to cite just two other recent works that deal with trouble with identities of many kinds.

4. It is through the ongoing debates within and across feminist theories that we have come to appreciate the complexity and signification of these politics. Among the texts that shore up my work here are those by Adrienne Rich, "Notes toward a Politics of Location (1984)," in *Blood, Bread, and Poetry: Selected Prose, 1979–1985*, 210–33; Donna Haraway, "A Manifesto for Cyborgs: Science, Technology and Socialist Feminism in the 1980's," 65–105; Biddy Martin and Chandra Talpade Mohanty, "Feminist Politics: What's Home Got to Do with It?" in *Feminist Studies/Critical Studies*, ed. de Laurentis, 191–212; and Diana Fuss, "Reading Like a Feminist," especially her intervention in terms of the need for "interrogating not only the place of essentialism but the essentialism of place," a discussion that I hope this work augments.

5. In the ongoing debates surrounding postcolonialism we can read some of the most provocative renderings of the simultaneous urges to claim and refuse namings. To offer a few of these sites, see Lila Abu-Lughod for her discussion of "'halfies'—people between cultures," a term that she attributes to a personal communication with Kirin Narayan, in her article, "Can There Be a Feminist Ethnography?" See also Homi K. Bhabha's further working through of his horti-cultural problematic of hybridity in "Signs Taken for Wonders," in *"Race," Writing, and Difference*, ed. Gates, where he meditates on the formulation of the "less than one and double" aspects of identities constructed and imposed under colonialism.

6. In *Beyond Ethnicity: Consent and Descent in American Culture*, Werner Sollors does the

very careful and needed work to move past the category of ethnicity while also rethinking its uses and histories. I am in agreement with his "broadly conceived" notion of ethnicity in which race becomes an aspect of the larger category, all the while recognizing that the reclamation and performance of ethnicity in contemporary life in the United States "was directly influenced by the black civil rights movement and strengthened by its radicalization" (36).

7. Consider the case that the balance of the power in naming was meant to shift at the moment when "American Indians" renamed and reclaimed themselves as native Americans; a populist response to this emerged in the appearance of bumper stickers (always telling political ephemera) proclaiming "native" next to a map of whatever state of the union was pictured. The "we were here first" childish standoff this exemplifies may speak to the fact that "native" is not a category that takes well to revitalization or takes in fact too well. The currently preferred term, "indigenous peoples," and its sometimes offered alternative of "tribal peoples" represent the problematic currency that is language in post- and neocolonial times and places. The restlessness and rootlessness of these renamings is legible as well in the troublesome areas of race and sexuality: American Negroes reclaiming "black" and more recently "African-American" as their own preferred designations, or gays and lesbians working together under the current reappropriation of "queer."

8. Within the critical literature on male travelers, Porter's text is a welcome addition because it recognizes a complex set of issues along the axis of power and knowledge sought and gained by travelers. Porter's book also gives further evidence of how this literary genre contributes richly to the cluster of issues dominating the discursive and disciplinary formation of what goes by the name of cultural studies.

9. Silvan S. Tomkins, "Shame," in *The Many Faces of Shame*, ed. Nathanson, 133–61. This collection brings together some of the work presented at a symposium held in Los Angeles in 1984 as part of the 137th Annual Meeting of the American Psychiatric Association.

Going North

1. Nellie McKay, "Crayon Enlargements of Life: Zora Neale Hurston's *Their Eyes Were Watching God* as Autobiography," in *New Essays on Their Eyes Were Watching God*, ed. Michael Awkward, 51–70.

2. Nellie McKay, "Race, Gender, and Cultural Context in Zora Neale Hurston's *Dust Tracks on a Road*," in *Life/Lines: Theorizing Women's Autobiography*, ed. Bella Brodzki and Celeste Schenck, 175–88.

3. Rosemary George, in "Traveling Light: Of Immigration, Invisible Suitcases, and Gunny Sacks," notes the flexible identities of the immigrant genre, in which making oneself at home may be a project that is never complete; certainly this is the case in Hurston's wanderings.

4. The issue of *Critical Inquiry* that became the collection *"Race," Writing, and Difference*, edited by Henry Louis Gates Jr., did some of the much-needed work to approach recognizing how race as a category must necessarily be one under erasure. In a more recent aphoristic mode, one that speaks to the nominative shift from "black" to "African-American," Gates pronounced, "We're all ethnics" (*New York Times*, May 4, 1991).

5. See, for example, Mary Helen Washington, "Zora Neale Hurston: A Woman Half in Shadow," her introduction to *I Love Myself When I Am Laughing . . . : A Zora Neale Hurston Reader*, ed. Alice Walker (Old Westbury, N.Y.: Feminist Press, 1979), 7–25; Alice Walker, *In Search of Our Mothers' Gardens* (San Diego: Harcourt Brace Jovanovich, 1983); Elizabeth Fox-Genovese on Hurston in "My Statue, My Self: Autobiographical Writings of Afro-American Women," in *The Private Self: Theory and Practice of Women's Autobiographical Writings*, ed. Shari Benstock; and Claudine Raynaud's two articles, "Autobiography as 'Lying' Session: Zora Neale Hurston's *Dust Tracks on a Road*," in *Studies in Black American Literature*, vol. 3, *Black Feminist Criticism and Critical Theory*, ed. Joe Weixlmann and Houston A. Baker Jr., and "Rub-

bing a Paragraph with a Soft Cloth: Muted Voices and Editorial Constraints in *Dust Tracks on a Road*," in *De/Colonizing the Subject: The Politics of Gender in Women's Autobiography*, ed. Sidonie Smith and Julia Watson, 34–64. Robert Hemenway's introduction to *Dust Tracks* set the tone for reading this text as failed autobiography; I would hope that my reframing the text as immigrant discourse on displacement and shame might shed light on some of its failures and render them successes in other ways.

6. Franz Boas, her teacher and mentor at Columbia University, where she was a graduate student in anthropology, became another surrogate white father.

"Where Do You Live?"

1. In "Sandra Cisneros' *The House on Mango Street* and the Poetics of Space," Julian Olivares does a Bachelardian reading of *House* that deals with the interior space that is maternal and sanctions daydreaming, in *Chicana Creativity and Criticism: Charting New Frontiers in American Literature*, ed. María Herrera-Sobek and Helena María Viramontes, 160–70.

2. Gloria Anzaldúa's *Borderlands/La Frontera: The New Mestiza* tends to concentrate on Chicano identity and its location in the region of the Texas-Mexico border; Cisneros brings the borders north and into the urban Midwest. In *Woman Hollering Creek*, many of the stories move back to the mestiza South, and like Anzaldúa's text, Cisneros works much more frequently back and forth in Spanish and English, making an implicitly strong case that the reader unable to negotiate Spanish is less than adequately literate in contemporary America.

3. Ellen McCracken, who calls *House* "a modified autobiographical novel, or *Bildungsroman*," makes a similar point when she notes that Esperanza "conceives of a house as communal rather than private property," even as the dream house of her own "alleviates the ethnic anguish" and "becomes a symbol of the writer's attainment of her identity through artistic creation." McCracken, "Sandra Cisneros' *The House on Mango Street*: Community-Oriented Introspection and the Demystification of Patriarchal Violence," in *Breaking Boundaries: Latina Writing and Critical Readings*, ed. Asunción Horno-Delgado et al., 62–71.

4. I would agree with María Herrera-Sobek in "The Politics of Rape: Sexual Transgression in Chicana Fiction" that Esperanza "discovers a conspiracy of two forms of silence: silence in not *denouncing* the 'real' facts of life about sex and its negative aspects in violent sexual encounters, and *complicity* in embroidering a fairy-tale-like mist around sex," while I would nevertheless want to distinguish rape as motif and metaphor from this scene in "Red Clowns" *as* a rape scene; that remains ambiguous.

Careless Baptisms

1. Nancy K. Miller's "The French Mistake," in *Getting Personal: Feminist Occasions and Other Autobiographical Acts*, 48–55, follows through the emotional phenomenology of such moments of mis-speaking.

2. I am thinking in particular of the work Judith Butler does with categories of gender and performance and Naomi Schor's reading of Irigaray on femininity and mimesis; however I also mean to allude here to the earlier tradition within psychoanalytic and film theory that takes up femininity as, following the landmark essay by Joan Rivière, masquerade.

3. Among the conjunctural identities Clifford investigates are two other earlier "polyglot refugees, Joseph Conrad and Bronislaw Malinowski, Poles shipwrecked in England and English," in James Clifford, *The Predicament of Culture: Twentieth-Century Ethnography, Literature and Art*, 10.

Survival Elsewhere

1. Walter Benjamin, *Illuminations*, 83–110.

2. Michel de Certeau, *L'Invention du quotidien, 1. Arts de faire*.

3. Dominick LaCapra, *Representing the Holocaust: History, Theory, Trauma.*

4. Let me cite one among numerous cautionary critical receptions of the Washington, D.C., museum, Philip Gourevitch's article, "Behold Now Behemoth, the Holocaust Memorial Museum: One More American Theme Park," in which he notes "that exposure to barbarism is *not* an antidote against it."

Speaking Memory

1. The writings that deal specifically with Delbo's experiences during the war years include *Le Convoi du 24 janvier*, recalling her deportation to Auschwitz in January 1943; *Qui rapportera ces paroles?*, written in 1966, but not published until 1974, translated by Cynthia Haft as *Who Will Carry the Word?* in *The Theater of the Holocaust: Four Plays*, ed. Robert Skloot; and *Aucun de nous ne reviendra*, translated by John Githens as *None of Us Will Return.*

2. Nomberg-Przytyk's text is organized as a collection of interconnected tales that generally follow a chronology of events leading from internment to the liberation of Auschwitz and a brief period thereafter.

3. The two tapes I viewed were half-hour edited versions of histories taken in a style best described as psychoanalytic. I thank Sandra Rosenstock, the archivist on the project at that time, for her assistance in leading me to materials I felt were most appropriate for my interests in making links to Delbo's works.

4. Jean Améry, "In the Waiting Room of Death: Reflections on the Warsaw Ghetto," in *Radical Humanism: Selected Essays*, ed. Sidney Rosenfeld and Stella P. Rosenfeld, 21–36. Améry was the son of a Catholic mother and Jewish father and was imprisoned for being a Jew, an identity that he had not lived until then. The philosophical grounding of my use of the dystopian-utopian framework for discussing Holocaust narratives is based on my understanding of Adorno's "Meditations on Metaphysics" section in *Negative Dialectics* and Ernst Bloch's *Principle of Hope*. Both men fled Nazi Germany along with other members of the Frankfurt School's Institute for Social Research and came to the United States in the 1930s. From the privileged, if uprooted, vantage point of having escaped, they each had to come to grips with what popular psychology has taught us to call the guilt of the survivor, and each of them offers models of understanding that at moments seem mirror-image reversals. Even their titles indicate the divergence in perspectives to be found here. In Adorno's work the section called "After Auschwitz" begins with the words, "We cannot say any more," enacting negation by negation, the "thinking against itself" his system advances. Bloch's three-volume work, *The Principle of Hope*, defines the utopian moment as thinking that which is "not yet"—that which has not appeared in history and which is desired and, therefore, is to be produced and recognized wherever it occurs, from the phenomena of everyday life to sustained political resistance to systems of oppression. Bloch was alone in offering a Marxist rewriting of utopia, a concept left bankrupt since the early distinction made by Marx and Engels between scientific and utopian socialism.

5. See also my *Feminist Utopias*, where the texts I discuss present scenes of recognition among women as they might be transformed or coded in systems in which oppression and repression, domination and exploitation are provisionally undone through a nonhierarchical marking of gender.

6. Let me suggest that the mix of verbal tenses in such statements may be more than the lapses of a nonnative speaker. They are naked representations of the mix of memory, history, past, and future quite insistently lodged in the present of the speaking subject. I am repeatedly reminded of Toni Morrison's *Beloved*, which, from its dedication "To the Sixty Million and more" to its closing chant, "This is not a story to pass on," resonates with the tropes of mid-twentieth-century forgetting and remembering of this more recent chapter of enslavement.

7. Primo Levi, *Survival in Auschwitz: The Nazi Assault on Humanity.*

8. I imagined I heard this agonized whisper as I read, on August 2, 1993, of the "low

moans" that were heard among the Holocaust survivors in the Jerusalem courtroom where John Demjanjuk had just been acquitted of the crimes of "Ivan the Terrible," who committed atrocities in Treblinka, a camp devoted exclusively to extermination.

9. Irena Klepfisz, *Keeper of Accounts.*

10. Eric Santner, *Stranded Objects: Mourning, Memory, and Film in Postwar Germany.* Santner's first chapter underscores my earlier alignment of the postmodern and the post-Holocaust and LaCapra's instrumentalization of their intertwining.

11. Rosette Lamont, who has situated Delbo's play in the mode of Aeschylean tragedy, reads *Who Will Carry the Word?* as a postwar rewriting of the myth of Demeter and Kore in her article, "Charlotte Delbo's Frozen Friezes."

12. In Levi's account of the night when there was an explosion that destroyed one of the crematoria at Auschwitz, he reflects with wonder at men who are "helpless and exhausted slaves" being responsible for this stunning act. He seems to have been unaware of the fact that four women were hanged for this. In Nomberg-Przytyk's account it is an event that calls forth another spontaneous round of the "International."

13. In feminist utopian texts of the 1970s a repeated projection is an abundance of mothers or parents, which also speaks to the construction of femininity through not-good-enough mothering.

14. The echo in Levi's account reads: "We say *hunger, tiredness, fear, pain,* we say *winter* and they are different things. They are free words. . . . If the Lagers had lasted longer a new harsh language would have been born" (112). Levi offers examples of what this language had already invented.

15. Seweryna Szmaglewska, *Smoke over Birkenau,* trans. Jadwiga Rynas; and Liana Millu, *Smoke over Birkenau,* trans. Lynne Sharon Schwartz. The latter will be discussed in the following chapter.

16. In an essay published in the April 14, 1985, *New York Times Book Review,* Elie Wiesel, speaking about why he writes, says, "Not to transmit an experience is to betray it." Almost a decade later we might well question just how the experience of the Shoah has been and is being "transmitted." There is a terrible transparency to the monumentalizing and memorializing efforts that insist on concretization to constitute the abstraction of taking in such histories, ones that even those who lived them cannot always bear.

17. Jacques Derrida, "feu la cendre" (translation mine).

18. This observation was made in conversation by Geoffrey Hartman, adviser to the Video Archive Project, as he spoke about his contacts with many second-generation groups gathering testimonies.

Time and the Other Laid Bare

1. The name "mussulmen" suggested emaciated "Oriental" holy men who could only be conceptualized somewhere outside the European Judeo-Christian universe. Although women survivors knew this term, it is not clear to me that it was as frequently used by them as it was among the men who survived to tell.

2. This is the kind of knowledge and reality Langer attempts to articulate in his notion of living on/dying on, surmortality as opposed to survival.

3. Cited in Gershen Kaufman, *The Psychology of Shame: Theory and Treatment of Shame-based Syndromes.*

4. Millu notes "that atrocious, despairing lager phrase they would repeat day in and day out," which translates, depending on the circumstances, as "Who gives a shit?" and "the same old shit!" (175).

5. Jonathan Boyarin, *Storm from Paradise.*

6. Isaac Deutscher, "Who Is a Jew?" in *The Non-Jewish Jew and Other Essays.*

Bibliography

Abu-Lughod, Lila. "Can There Be a Feminist Ethnography?" *Women & Performance: A Journal of Feminist Theory* 5, no. 1 (1990): 7–27.

———. *Writing Women's Worlds: Bedouin Stories*. Berkeley: University of California Press, 1993.

Adorno, Theodor. *Negative Dialectics*. Translated by E. B. Ashton. New York: Continuum, 1973.

Althusser, Louis. *Lenin and Philosophy and Other Essays*. Translated by Ben Brewster. New York: Monthly Review Press, 1971.

Améry, Jean. *Radical Humanism: Selected Essays*. Translated and edited by Sidney Rosenfeld and Stella P. Rosenfeld. Bloomington: Indiana University Press, 1984.

Anderson, Benedict. *Imagined Communities: Reflections on the Origin and Spread of Nationalism*. Revised edition. London: Verso, 1991.

Anzaldúa, Gloria. *Borderlands/La Frontera: The New Mestiza*. San Francisco: Spinsters/Aunt Lute, 1987.

Anzieu, Didier. *The Skin Ego*. Translated by Chris Turner. New Haven, Conn.: Yale University Press, 1989.

Augé, Marc. *Non-Lieux: Introduction à une anthropologie de la surmodernité*. Paris: Seuil, 1992.

Awkward, Michael, ed. *New Essays on Their Eyes Were Watching God*. Cambridge: Cambridge University Press, 1990.

al-'Azm, Sadik Jalal. "Orientalism and Orientalism in Reverse." *Khamsin* 8 (1981): 5–26.

Barthes, Roland. *L'empire des signes*. Geneva and Paris: Skira and Flammarion, 1980. Translated by Richard Howard, under the title *Empire of Signs*. New York: Hill and Wang, 1982.

———. *Incidents*. Paris: Seuil, 1987. Translated by Richard Howard, under the title *Incidents*. Berkeley: University of California Press, 1992.

———. *Mythologies*. Translated by Annette Lavers. New York: Hill and Wang, 1972.

Bartkowski, Frances. "A Fearful Fancy: Some Reconsiderations of the Sublime." *Boundary 2*, Fall 1986/Winter 1987, 23–32.

———. *Feminist Utopias*. Lincoln: University of Nebraska Press, 1989.

———. "Roland Barthes' Secret Garden." *Studies in Twentieth Century Literature* 5, no. 2 (Spring 1981): 133–46.

Baudrillard, Jean. *Amérique*. Paris: Grasset, 1986. Translated by Chris Turner, under the title *America*. London: Verso, 1988.

Benjamin, Walter. *Illuminations*. Translated by Harry Zohn. New York: Schocken, 1969.

Benstock, Shari, ed. *The Private Self: Theory and Practice of Women's Autobiographical Writings*. Chapel Hill: University of North Carolina Press, 1988.

Bergmann, Martin S., and Milton E. Jucovy, eds. *Generations of the Holocaust*. New York: Columbia University Press, 1982.

Bhabha, Homi K. "Signs Taken for Wonders: Questions of Ambivalence and Authority under a Tree outside Delhi, May 1817." In *"Race," Writing, and Difference*, edited by Henry Louis Gates Jr., 163–84. Chicago: University of Chicago Press, 1985.

———, ed. *Nation and Narration*. London: Routledge, 1990.

Bloch, Ernst. *Principle of Hope*. Translated by Neville Plaice, Stephen Plaice, and Paul Knight. Cambridge, Mass.: MIT Press, 1986.

Bongie, Chris. *Exotic Memories: Literature, Colonialism and the Fin de siècle*. Stanford, Calif.: Stanford University Press, 1991.

Boyarin, Jonathan. *Storm from Paradise*. Minneapolis: University of Minnesota Press, 1992.

Brodzki, Bella, and Celeste Schenck, eds. *Life/Lines: Theorizing Women's Autobiography*. Ithaca, N.Y.: Cornell University Press, 1988.

Broucek, Francis. *Shame and the Self*. New York: Guilford Press, 1991.

Bulhan, Hussein Abdilahi. *Frantz Fanon and the Psychology of Oppression*. New York: Plenum Press, 1985.

Burroway, Janet. "Slaves to Fate." Review of *Crossing the River*, by Caryl Phillips. *New York Times Book Review*, January 30, 1994, 10.

Butler, Judith. *Gender Trouble: Feminism and the Subversion of Identity*. New York: Routledge, 1990.

Butler, Judith, and Joan W. Scott, eds. *Feminists Theorize the Political*. New York: Routledge, 1992.

Butor, Michel. *Mobile*. Paris: Gallimard, 1962. Translated by Richard Howard, under the title *Mobile: Study for a Representation of the United States*. New York: Simon and Schuster, 1963.

———. *Répertoire IV*. Paris: Minuit, 1974.

———. *Répertoire V*. Paris: Minuit, 1982.

———. "Le Voyage et l'écriture." *Romantisme* 4 (1972): 4–19; first translated into English by John Powers and K. Lisker, under the title "Travel and Writing," *Mosaic* 8, pt. 1 (Fall 1974): 1–16.

Canetti, Elias. *Earwitness: Fifty Characters*. Translated by Joachim Neugroschel. New York: Seabury Press, 1979.

———. *The Tongue Set Free: Remembrance of a European Childhood*. Translated by Joachim Neugroschel. New York: Seabury Press, 1979.

———. *The Voices of Marrakesh: A Record of a Visit*. Translated by J. A. Underwood. New York: Seabury Press, 1978.

Cary, Lorene. *Black Ice*. New York: Knopf, 1991.

Caute, David. *Frantz Fanon*. New York: Viking Press, 1970.

Celan, Paul. *Collected Prose*. Translated by Rosmarie Waldrop. Manchester: Carcanet Press, 1986.

Cisneros, Sandra. "Ghosts and Voices: Writing from Obsession." *Americas Review* 15, no. 1 (Spring 1987): 69–73.

———. *The House on Mango Street*. Houston: Arte Publico, 1984.

———. *Woman Hollering Creek*. New York: Vintage. 1992.

Clifford, James. *The Predicament of Culture: Twentieth-Century Ethnography, Literature, and Art*. Cambridge, Mass.: Harvard University Press, 1988.

Clifford, James, and George E. Marcus, eds. *Writing Culture: The Poetics and Politics of Ethnography*. Berkeley: University of California Press, 1986.

Cohen, Yaier. "Elias Canetti: Exile and the German Language." *German Life and Letters* 42, no. 1 (October 1988): 32–45.

Crosby, Christina. "Dealing with Differences." In *Feminists Theorize the Political*, edited by Judith Butler and Joan Scott, 130–44. New York: Routledge, 1992.

Dale, Peter N. *The Myth of Japanese Uniqueness*. New York: St. Martin's Press, 1986.

Darras, Jacques. "Le Voyage en Afrique." *Esprit* 128 (July 1987): 1–12.

De Certeau, Michel. *L'Invention du quotidien, 1. Arts de faire*. Paris: Gallimard, 1990.

Deck, Alice A. "Autoethnography: Zora Neale Hurston, Noni Jabavu, and Cross-Disciplinary Discourse." *Black American Literature Forum* 24, no. 2 (Summer 1990): 237–56.

Delbo, Charlotte. *Aucun de nous ne reviendra.* Paris: Minuit, 1970. Translated by John Githens, under the title *None of Us Will Return.* Boston: Beacon, 1968.

———. *Le Convoi du 24 janvier.* Paris: Minuit, 1965.

———. *Maria Lusitania.* Paris: P. J. Oswald, 1975.

———. *Qui rapportera ces paroles?* Paris: P. J. Oswald, 1974. Translated by Cynthia Haft, under the title *Who Will Carry the Word?* In *The Theater of the Holocaust: Four Plays,* edited by Robert Skloot. Madison: University of Wisconsin Press, 1982.

———. *Spectres, mes compagnons.* Lausanne: Maurice Bridel, 1977.

DeLillo, Don. *The Names.* New York: Vintage, 1983.

Derrida, Jacques. "feu la cendre." *Anima* 5 (1983): 48–99.

Des Pres, Terrence. *The Survivor: An Anatomy of Life in the Death Camps.* New York: Oxford University Press, 1976.

Deutscher, Isaac. *The Non-Jewish Jew and Other Essays.* New York: Hill and Wang, 1968.

Durosay, Daniel. "Les Images du *Voyage au Congo*: L'oeil d'Allegret." *Bulletin des amis d'André Gide* 15 (January 1987): 57–79.

———. "Images et Imaginaire dans le *Voyage au Congo*: Un film et deux 'auteurs.'" *Bulletin des amis d'André Gide* 16 (October 1988): 9–30.

Eagleton, Terry, Fredric Jameson, and Edward W. Said. *Nationalism, Colonialism and Literature.* Introduction by Seamus Deane. Minneapolis: University of Minnesota Press, 1990.

Eisen, George. *Children and Play in the Holocaust: Games among the Shadows.* Amherst: University of Massachusetts Press, 1988.

El Saadawi, Nawal. *My Travels around the World.* Translated by Shirley Eber. London: Minerva, 1991.

Fabian, Johannes. *Language and Colonial Power: The Appropriation of Swahili in the Former Belgian Congo, 1880–1938.* Cambridge: Cambridge University Press 1986.

———. *Language on the Road: Notes on Swahili in Two Nineteenth Century Travelogues.* Hamburg: H. Buske, 1985.

———. *Time and the Other: How Anthropology Makes Its Object.* New York: Columbia University Press, 1983.

Fanon, Frantz. *Black Skin, White Masks.* Translated by Charles Lam Markmann. New York: Grove Press, 1967.

———. *A Dying Colonialism.* Translated by Haakon Chevalier. New York: Grove Press, 1965.

———. *The Wretched of the Earth.* Translated by Constance Farrington. New York: Grove Press, 1968.

Feifer, Maxine. *Tourism in History: From Imperial Rome to the Present.* New York: Stein and Day, 1986; previously published in Great Britain under the title *Going Places.*

Ferguson, Russell, Martha Gever, Trinh T. Minh-ha, and Cornel West, eds. *Out There: Marginalization and Contemporary Cultures.* New York: New Museum of Contemporary Art; Cambridge, Mass.: MIT Press, 1990.

Fox-Genovese, Elizabeth. "My Statue, My Self: Autobiographical Writings of Afro-American Women." In *The Private Self: Theory and Practice of Women's Autobiographical Writings,* edited by Shari Benstock, 63–89. Chapel Hill: University of North Carolina Press, 1988.

Frank, Katherine. *A Voyager Out: The Life of Mary Kingsley.* Boston: Houghton Mifflin, 1986.

Frassica, Pietro, ed. *Primo Levi as Witness.* Proceedings of a symposium held at Princeton University, April 30-May 2, 1989. Fiesole: Casalini Libri, 1990.

Fuss, Diana. "Reading Like a Feminist." *differences* 1, no. 2 (1989): 77–92.

Fussell, Paul. *Abroad: British Literary Traveling between the Wars.* Oxford: Oxford University Press, 1980.

Gallop, Jane. *Reading Lacan.* Ithaca, N.Y., and London: Cornell University Press, 1985.

Garrett, George. "Separate Prisons." Review of *Cambridge,* by Caryl Phillips. *New York Times Book Review,* February 16, 1992, 1, 24–25.

Gates, Henry Louis, Jr. "The Master's Pieces: On Canon Formation and the African-American Tradition." *South Atlantic Quarterly* 89, no. 1 (Winter 1990): 89–111.

———. ed. *"Race," Writing, and Difference.* Chicago: University of Chicago Press, 1985.

Geismar, Peter. *Fanon.* New York: Dial Press, 1971.

Gendzier, Irene L. *Frantz Fanon: A Critical Study.* New York: Pantheon Books, 1973.

George, Rosemary Marangoly. "Traveling Light: Of Immigration, Invisible Suitcases, and Gunny Sacks." *differences* 4, no. 2 (1992): 72–99.

Germain, Gabriel. *Victor Segalen: Le Voyageur des deux routes.* Mézières-sur-Issoire: Rougerie, 1982.

Gesenway, Deborah, and Mindy Rosenbaum. *Beyond Words: Images from America's Concentration Camps.* Ithaca, N.Y.: Cornell University Press, 1987.

Gide, André. *Voyage au Congo, suivi de Le retour du Tchad: Carnets de route.* Paris: Gallimard, 1927. Translated by Dorothy Bussy, under the title *Travels in the Congo.* New York: Penguin Books, 1986.

Gourevitch, Philip. "Behold Now Behemoth, the Holocaust Memorial Museum: One More American Theme Park." *Harper's,* July 1993, 55–62.

Greenblatt, Stephen. *Marvelous Possessions: The Wonder of the New World.* Chicago: University of Chicago Press, 1991.

Han, Françoise. "L'Autre espace." *Europe: Revue Littéraire Mensuelle* 696 (April 1987): 88–92.

Haraway, Donna. "A Manifesto for Cyborgs: Science, Technology and Socialist Feminism in the 1980's." *Socialist Review* 80, no. 15, part 2 (March-April 1985): 65–105.

———. *Simians, Cyborgs and Women: The Reinvention of Nature.* New York: Routledge, 1991.

Harris, Eddy L. *Native Stranger: A Black American's Journey into the Heart of Africa.* New York: Vintage, 1993.

Heinemann, Marlene E. *Gender and Destiny: Women Writers and the Holocaust.* New York: Greenwood Press, 1986.

Hemenway, Robert E. *Zora Neale Hurston: A Literary Biography.* Urbana: University of Illinois Press, 1977.

Herrera-Sobek, María. "The Politics of Rape: Sexual Transgression in Chicana Fiction." In *Chicana Creativity and Criticism: Charting New Frontiers in American Literature,* edited by María Herrera-Sobek and Helena María Viramontes, 171–81. Houston: Arte Publico, 1988.

Hirsch, Marianne. "Pictures of a Displaced Girlhood." In *Displacements: Cultural Identities in Question,* edited by Angelika Bammer. Forthcoming.

Hiss, Tony. *The Experience of Place.* New York: Knopf, 1990.

Hoffman, Eva. *Lost in Translation: A Life in a New Language.* New York: Penguin, 1989.

Horno-Delgado, Asunción, Eliana Ortega, Nina M. Scott, and Nancy Saporta Sternbach, eds. *Breaking Boundaries: Latina Writing and Critical Readings.* Amherst: University of Massachusetts Press, 1989.

Hsieh, Yvonne. "Les Femmes historiques et légendaires de la Chine chez Victor Segalen." *Europe: Revue Littéraire Mensuelle* 696 (April 1987): 54–62.

———. *Victor Segalen's Literary Encounter with China: Chinese Moulds, Western Thoughts.* Toronto: University of Toronto Press, 1988.

Hurston, Zora Neale. *Dust Tracks on a Road.* Urbana: University of Illinois Press, 1984.

———. *Tell My Horse.* Berkeley, Calif.: Turtle Island, 1983.

Irigaray, Luce. *Ethique de la différence sexuelle.* Paris: Minuit, 1984.

————. *Parler n'est jamais neutre*. Paris: Minuit, 1985.

Janeway, Elizabeth. *Powers of the Weak*. New York: Morrow Quill, 1980.

Johnson, Barbara. "Thresholds of Difference: Structures of Address in Zora Neale Hurston." In *"Race," Writing, and Difference*, edited by Henry Louis Gates Jr., 317–28. Chicago: University of Chicago Press, 1985.

Kabbani, Rana. *Europe's Myths of Orient*. London: Pandora, 1986.

Karen, Robert. "Shame." *Atlantic Monthly*, February 1992, 40–70.

Kaufman, Gershen. *The Psychology of Shame: Theory and Treatment of Shame-based Syndromes*. New York: Springer, 1989.

Klepfisz, Irena. *Keeper of Accounts*. Watertown, Mass.: Persephone Press, 1982.

Kpomassie, Tété-Michel. *An African in Greenland*. Translated by James Kirkup. New York: Harcourt Brace Jovanovich, 1983.

Krupat, Arnold. *The Voice in the Margin: Native American Literature and the Canon*. Berkeley: University of California Press, 1989.

LaCapra, Dominick. *Representing the Holocaust: History, Theory, Trauma*. Ithaca, N.Y.: Cornell University Press, 1994.

Lamont, Rosette. "Charlotte Delbo's Frozen Friezes." *L'Esprit créateur* 19, no. 2 (Summer 1979): 65–74.

Lang, Berel, ed. *Writing and the Holocaust*. New York: Holmes and Meier, 1988.

Langer, Lawrence L. *Holocaust Testimonies: The Ruins of Memory*. New Haven, Conn.: Yale University Press, 1991.

————. *Versions of Survival: The Holocaust and the Human Spirit*. Albany: State University of New York Press, 1982.

Ledbetter, James. "Victorian's Secret." Review of *Cambridge*, by Caryl Phillips. *Village Voice*, April 28, 1992, 67.

Levi, Primo. *The Drowned and the Saved*. Translated by Raymond Rosenthal. New York: Vintage, 1989.

————. *If Not Now, When?* Translated by William Weaver. New York: Summit Books, 1985.

————. *The Mirror Maker*. Translated by Raymond Rosenthal. New York: Schocken Books, 1989.

————. *The Monkey's Wrench*. Translated by William Weaver. New York: Summit Books, 1986.

————. *Other People's Trades*. Translated by Raymond Rosenthal. New York: Summit Books, 1989.

————. *The Periodic Table*. Translated by Raymond Rosenthal. New York: Schocken Books, 1984.

————. *The Reawakening*. Translated by Stuart Woolf. New York: Collier Books, 1993.

————. *The Sixth Day and Other Tales*. Translated by Raymond Rosenthal. New York: Summit Books, 1990.

————. *Survival in Auschwitz: The Nazi Assault on Humanity*. Translated by Stuart Woolf. New York: Collier, 1961.

Lévi-Strauss, Claude. *The Raw and the Cooked*. Translated by John and Doreen Weightman. New York: Harper Torchbooks, 1969.

Lévinas, Emmanuel. *Le Temps et l'autre*. Paris: Quadrige/PUF, 1983.

McCannell, Dean. *The Tourist: A New Theory of the Leisure Class*. New York: Schocken, 1976.

McCracken, Ellen. "Sandra Cisneros' *The House on Mango Street*: Community-Oriented Introspection and the Demystification of Patriarchal Violence." In *Breaking Boundaries: Latina Writing and Critical Readings*, edited by Asunción Horno-Delgado, Eliana Ortega, Nina M. Scott, and Nancy Saporta Sternbach, 62–71. Amherst: University of Massachusetts Press, 1989.

McCulloch, Jock. *Black Soul White Artifact: Fanon's Clinical Psychology and Social Theory.* Cambridge: Cambridge University Press, 1983.

McKay, Nellie. "Crayon Enlargements of Life: Zora Neale Hurston's *Their Eyes Were Watching God* as Autobiography." In *New Essays on Their Eyes Were Watching God*, edited by Michael Awkward, 51–70. Cambridge: Cambridge University Press, 1990.

———. "Race, Gender, and Cultural Context in Zora Neale Hurston's *Dust Tracks on a Road*." In *Life/Lines: Theorizing Women's Autobiography*, edited by Bella Brodzki and Celeste Schenck, 175–88. Ithaca, N.Y.: Cornell University Press, 1988.

Madou, Jean-Pol. "Segalen: Un exotisme nietzschéen." *French Literature Series* 13 (1986): 89–101.

Mambrino, Jean. "Segalen ou l'immobile voyageur." *Etudes*, October 1982, 347–52.

Mani, Lata, and Ruth Frankenberg. "The Challenge of *Orientalism*." *Economy and Society* 14, no. 2 (May 1985): 175–91.

Mannoni, Octave. *Ça n'empêche pas d'exister.* Paris: Seuil, 1982.

———. *Psychologie de la colonisation.* Paris: Seuil, 1950. Translated by Pamela Powesland, under the title *Prospero and Caliban: The Psychology of Colonization.* Ann Arbor: University of Michigan Press, 1990.

Martin, Biddy, and Chandra Talpade Mohanty. "Feminist Politics: What's Home Got to Do with It?" In *Feminist Studies/Critical Studies*, edited by Teresa de Lauretis, 191–212. Bloomington: Indiana University Press, 1986.

Mikell, Gwendolyn. "When Horses Talk: Reflections on Zora Neale Hurston's Haitian Anthropology." *Phylon* 43 (September 1982): 218–30.

Miller, Nancy K. *Getting Personal: Feminist Occasions and Other Autobiographical Acts.* New York: Routledge, 1991.

Mills, Sara. *Discourses of Difference: An Analysis of Women's Travel Writing and Colonialism.* London: Routledge, 1991.

Millu, Liana. *Smoke over Birkenau.* Translated by Lynne Sharon Schwartz. Philadelphia: Jewish Publication Society, 1991.

Minh-ha, Trinh T. *Woman, Native, Other: Writing Postcoloniality and Feminism.* Bloomington: Indiana University Press, 1989.

Morrison, Toni. *Beloved.* New York: Knopf, 1987.

Nathanson, Donald L., ed. *The Many Faces of Shame.* New York: Guilford Press, 1987.

Naylor, Carolyn A. "Cross-Gender Significance of the Journey Motif in Selected Afro-American Fiction." *Colby Library Quarterly* 18, no. 1 (March 1982): 26–38.

Nomberg-Przytyk, Sara. *Auschwitz: True Tales from a Grotesque Land.* Translated by Roslyn Hirsch and edited by Eli Pfefferkorn and David H. Hirsch. Chapel Hill: University of North Carolina Press, 1985.

Ogden, Thomas. *The Primitive Edge of Experience.* Northvale, N.J., and London: Jason Aronson, 1989.

Olivares, Julian. "Sandra Cisneros' *The House on Mango Street* and the Poetics of Space." In *Chicana Creativity and Criticism: Charting New Frontiers in American Literature*, edited by María Herrera-Sobek and Helena María Viramontes, 160–69. Houston: Arte Publico, 1988.

Osherson, Samuel, and Steven Krugman. "Men, Shame, and Psychotherapy." *Psychotherapy* 27, no. 3 (Fall 1990): 327–38.

Parry, Benita. "Problems in Current Theories of Colonial Discourse." *Oxford Literary Review* 9, nos. 1–2 (1987): 27–58.

Patton, Cindy. "Queer Rhetorics, Queer Politics" session, Marxism in the New World Order Conference, Amherst, Mass., November 12–14, 1992.

Perinbaum, B. Marie. *Holy Violence: The Revolutionary Thought of Frantz Fanon.* Washington, D.C.: Three Continents Press, 1982.

Phillips, Caryl. *Cambridge*. New York: Knopf, 1992.

———. *The European Tribe*. New York: Farrar, Straus, Giroux, 1987.

———. *The Final Passage*. London: Faber and Faber, 1985.

———. "Living and Writing in the Caribbean: An Experiment." *Kunapipi* 11, no. 2 (1989): 44–50.

———. *A State of Independence*. New York: Collier, 1986.

Pinckney, Darryl. *High Cotton*. New York: Penguin Books, 1992.

Polo, Marco. *The Travels of Marco Polo*. Translated by Ronald Latham. New York: Penguin, 1958.

Porter, Dennis. *Haunted Journeys: Desire and Transgression in European Travel Writing*. Princeton, N.J.: Princeton University Press, 1991.

Pratt, Mary Louise. *Imperial Eyes: Travel Writing and Transculturation*. New York: Routledge, 1992.

Pratt, Minnie Bruce. "Identity: Skin, Blood, Heart." In *Yours in Struggle: Three Feminist Perspectives on Anti-Semitism and Racism*, edited by Elly Bulkin, Minnie Bruce Pratt, and Barbara Smith. Ithaca, N.Y.: Firebrand, 1988.

Raynaud, Claudine. "Autobiography as 'Lying' Session: Zora Neale Hurston's *Dust Tracks on a Road*." In *Studies in Black American Literature*. Vol. 3, *Black Feminist Criticism and Critical Theory*, edited by Joe Weixlmann and Houston A. Baker Jr., 111–38. Greenwood, Fla.: Penkevill, 1988.

———. "Rubbing a Paragraph with a Soft Cloth: Muted Voices and Editorial Constraints in *Dust Tracks on a Road*." In *De/Colonizing the Subject: The Politics of Gender in Women's Autobiography*, edited by Sidonie Smith and Julia Watson, 34–64. Minneapolis: University of Minnesota Press, 1992.

Relph, E. *Place and Placelessness*. London: Pion, 1976.

Retamar, Roberto Fernandez. *Caliban and Other Essays*. Translated by Edward Baker. Minneapolis: University of Minnesota Press, 1989.

Rich, Adrienne. *Blood, Bread, and Poetry: Selected Prose 1979–1985*. London: Virago, 1987.

Riley, Denise. *"Am I That Name?": Feminism and the Category of "Women" in History*. Minneapolis: University of Minnesota Press, 1988.

Rosenberg, Alan, and Gerald E. Myers, eds. *Echoes from the Holocaust: Philosophical Reflections on a Dark Time*. Philadelphia: Temple University Press, 1988.

Said, Edward W. *After the Last Sky: Palestinian Lives*. Photographs by Jean Mohr. New York: Pantheon, 1986.

———. *Culture and Imperialism*. New York: Knopf, 1993.

———. "Identity, Authority, and Freedom: The Potentate and the Traveler." *Transition* 54 (1991): 4–19.

———. *Orientalism*. New York: Random House, 1978.

———. *The Question of Palestine*. New York: Vintage, 1979.

Sangari, Kumkum. "The Politics of the Possible." *Cultural Critique* 7 (1987): 157–86.

Santner, Eric. *Stranded Objects: Mourning, Memory, and Film in Postwar Germany*. Ithaca, N.Y.: Cornell University Press, 1990.

Sarvan, Charles P., and Hasan Marhama. "The Fictional Works of Caryl Phillips: An Introduction." *World Literature Today* 65 (Winter 1991): 35–40.

Saunders, Kay. "Caryl Phillips: Interview." *Kunapipi* 9, no. 1 (1987): 44–52.

Scemla, Jean. "La Dégradation du divers: Le cas tahitien." *Europe: Revue Littéraire Mensuelle* 696 (April 1987): 20–26.

Schor, Naomi. "This Essentialism Which Is Not One: Coming to Grips with Irigaray." *differences* 1, no. 2 (1989): 38–58.

Segalen, Martine, ed. *L'Autre et le semblable: Regards sur l'ethnologie des sociétés contemporaines.* Paris: Presses du Centre National de Recherche Scientifique, 1989.

Segalen, Victor. *Equipée: Voyage au Pays du Réel.* Paris: Gallimard, 1983.

———. *Essai sur l'exotisme: Une esthétique du divers.* Paris: Fata Morgana, 1978.

Shields, Rob. *Places on the Margin: Alternative Geographies of Modernity.* London: Routledge, 1991.

Silverman, Kaja. *The Acoustic Mirror: The Female Voice in Psychoanalysis and Cinema.* Bloomington: Indiana University Press, 1988.

Smith, Sidonie, and Julia Watson, eds. *De/Colonizing the Subject: The Politics of Gender in Women's Autobiography.* Minneapolis: University of Minnesota Press, 1992.

Sollors, Werner. *Beyond Ethnicity: Consent and Descent in American Culture.* New York: Oxford University Press, 1986.

Soyinka, Wole. *Isarà: A Voyage around "Essay."* New York: Vintage Books, 1989.

Spivak, Gayatri Chakravorty. "French Feminism Revisited: Ethics and Politics." In *Feminists Theorize the Political,* edited by Judith Butler and Joan W. Scott, 54–85. New York: Routledge, 1992.

———. "In a Word. Interview." With Ellen Rooney. *differences* 1, no. 2 (1989): 124–56.

———. "Naming. Interview." With Maria Koundoura. *Stanford Humanities Review* 1, no. 1 (1989): 84–97.

Stanton, Gareth. "The Oriental City: A North African Itinerary." *Third Text* 3–4 (Spring 1988): 3–38.

Suleri, Sara. *Meatless Days.* Chicago: University of Chicago Press, 1989.

Swift, Graham. "Caryl Phillips. Interview." *Kunapipi* 13, no. 3 (1991): 96–103.

Szmaglewska, Seweryna. *Smoke over Birkenau.* Translated by Jadwiga Rynas. New York: Holt, 1947.

Tanner, Tony. *The Reign of Wonder: Naivety and Reality in American Literature.* Cambridge: Cambridge University Press, 1965.

Taussig, Michael. *Shamanism, Colonialism and the Wild Man.* Chicago: University of Chicago Press, 1987.

Taylor, Charles. *Sources of the Self: The Making of the Modern Identity.* Cambridge, Mass.: Harvard University Press, 1989.

Todorov, Tzvetan. *The Conquest of America: The Question of the Other.* Translated by Richard Howard. New York: Harper and Row, 1984.

Tomkins, Silvan. *Affect/Imagery/Consciousness.* Vol. 1, *The Positive Affects,* and Vol. 2, *The Negative Affects.* New York: Springer, 1962 and 1963.

Torgovnick, Marianna. *Gone Primitive: Savage Intellects, Modern Lives.* Chicago: University of Chicago Press, 1990.

Urry, John. *The Tourist Gaze: Leisure and Travel in Contemporary Societies.* London: Sage, 1990.

Van Den Abbeele, George. *Travel as Metaphor: From Montaigne to Rousseau.* Minneapolis: University of Minnesota Press, 1992.

Virilio, Paul. *L'Espace critique.* Paris: Christian Bourgois, 1984.

Wald, Priscilla. "Becoming 'Colored': The Self-Authorized Language of Difference in Zora Neale Hurston." *American Literary History* 2, no. 1 (Spring 1990): 79–100.

Weixlmann, Joe, and Houston A. Baker Jr., eds. *Studies in Black American Literature.* Vol. 3, *Black Feminist Criticism and Critical Theory.* Greenwood, Fla.: Penkevill, 1988.

Williams, Patricia J. *The Alchemy of Race and Rights.* Cambridge, Mass.: Harvard University Press, 1991.

Wilson, Emmett, Jr. "Shame and the Other: Reflections on the Theme of Shame in French Psychoanalysis." In *The Many Faces of Shame,* edited by Donald L. Nathanson. New York: Guilford, 1987.

Wülfing, Wulf. "On Travel Literature by Women in the Nineteenth Century: Malwida Von Meysenbug." In *German Women in the Eighteenth and Nineteenth Centuries: A Social and Literary History,* edited by Ruth-Ellen B. Joeres and Mary Jo Maynes, 289–304. Bloomington: Indiana University Press, 1986.

Young, James E. *Writing and Rewriting the Holocaust: Narrative and the Consequences of Interpretation.* Bloomington: Indiana University Press, 1988.

Zahar, Renate. *Frantz Fanon: Colonialism and Alienation.* Translated by Willfried F. Feuser. New York: Monthly Review Press, 1974.

Zorach, Cecile. "The Outsider Abroad: Canetti in Marrakesh." *Modern Austrian Literature* 16, no. 3–4 (1983): 47–64.

Index

Segalen, Victor, 3, 5-17, 19-20, 23
self. *See* identification
senses, 10-11, 14, 79
shame, xix-xx, xxvi, 35, 55, 60-61, 75, 85-86,
    102, 125, 132-33; and the body, 87, 99,
    105, 124; and the concentration camps,
    141, 146; and gender, 134-35; and race,
    99; theory of, 87, 94, 133, 142, 144
slavery, 88, 142
solitude, 14, 21, 68
Spivak, Gayatri Chakravorty, 70
subjectivity, xvii-xviii, xxi-xxii, xxv-xxvi, 11,
    13, 18, 20, 116, 121, 144
survival, xxvi, 3, 8, 121, 123, 131-32, 146
survivor, 109, 123, 129

Taylor, Charles, 122-23
temporality, 8-9, 13, 17
Togo, 51, 72-81
Tomkins, Silvan, 87-88, 99, 125, 133, 144, 164
    n. 4

transgression, xxvi, 3, 8, 72
translation, xxii, xxv, 85-86
travel, xxiii, 51, 72; and gender, 35-36, 38, 85,
    94, 165 n. 2; and narrative, xix, xxi, 20,
    22, 30, 77, 81; travel writing, xvii, xxi,
    xxvi, 3, 8, 19-20, 39, 72, 85, 89; and
    voyeurism, 21, 34
traveler, xxvi, 8; as child, 62, 65, 73, 76; and
    the sublime, xx, xxvi, 20, 35, 54, 80, 87,
    88, 94, 143
trust, 135-36

United States, xx-xxi, 3, 30-31, 34, 39, 42, 47,
    65, 68, 92, 113

voice. *See* language

West Africa, 3, 43
West Indies. *See* Caribbean
wonder, xix-xx, xxvi, 20, 35, 57, 60-61, 66-67,
    75, 81, 86-88, 100, 125, 147-48

Frances Bartkowski has been director of the women's studies program at Rutgers University since 1989. She is author of *Feminist Utopias* (1989) and has published numerous articles on feminist and literary theory in journals such as *Discourse, Boundary 2,* and *SubStance.*